P9-DMF-558

THE WORLD OF FISHING

Original title: Découverte & Passions de la Pêche

Translation from French: John Williams and Richard Wright in association with First Edition Translation
Editing: Lin Thomas in association with First Edition Translation
Typesetting: The Write Idea in association with First Edition Translation
Project Management: First Edition Translation Ltd., Cambridge, UK
Production: Ursula Schümer

Printing and Binding: Mladinska knjiga tiskarna d. d.

Printed in Ljubljana, Slovenia

ISBN 3-8290-5534-x

10 9 8 7 6 5 4 3 2 1

THE WORLD OF FISHING

Pascal DURANTEL

KÖNEMANN

Contents

Preface

How do you set about becoming a fisherman nowadays, in different kinds of water, seeking the most highly prized species, using the most tried and tested methods as well as newer more sophisticated ones? What equipment do you choose, what lures, what baits, what tackle? Many questions, to which the keen and even the passionate angler will find answers in this magnificent book, written and compiled by my good friend Pascal Durantel.

More than just a writer describing what he sees, reporting what he hears or what people want to tell him, Pascal shares with us his passion, his knowledge and the marvellous experiences he has gained in Europe and throughout the world, in pursuit of this passion. More than a mere practitioner or observer, this modern-day crusader knows what he is talking about. His training in biology is complemented by a lively child-like curiosity, continually discovering the marvellous forces of nature, from tiny plankton to the enormous predators. With his wide knowledge in this field, he describes in a practical and sensitive way everything one needs to know to be a successful angler, whether fishing for predators like pike, or for the various members of the salmon family, or for the cyprinids. He also tells us all about regional variations and about the species themselves, some of which we have gone in search of together: the Atlantic salmon of Quebec at Tadoussac, or the enormous silurids of the Ebro at Mequinenza in Spain which have fired the imagination of many an angler and reader of fishing magazines. We share the same passion, the same love of nature, the same approach to fishing which, for those who experience it as we do, makes it a veritable art of living, which has as much to do with a knowledge of nature as with the simple act of fishing. Catching a fish is not the goal in itself but a kind of culmination which leads us to discover more about nature, about the forces of life and about the wild places that are still untouched by man. These are the experiences we wish to share with others.

Daniel Sabatini.

Fishing in the wild

If you like challenges and solitude, if you like long walks through wild countryside, this is the kind of fishing for you. You will rediscover nature intact and preserved, foaming streams where real excitement awaits you – and wonderful fish!

The Brow

n Trout

The European Brown Trout, with its superb speckled body, is one of the most sought-after fish in France. It offers a good day's sport.

A much-prized lady

Latin name: *Salmo trutta fario*
Family: Salmonidés

The techniques needed for fishing in a ravine, like a classic recipe, need no special comment, unless we mention the limitations connected with the situation, notably that one is fishing downstream. Even if the trout are not used to being fished, and less suspicious than elsewhere, one nevertheless has to observe a degree of caution which is at times difficult: when the water is very clear, or when one has had to scramble noisily down a steep slope or even had to take to the water. Any technique can be used: bait-casting, spinning or fly-fishing. Some are easier to handle than others; spinning, for example, because you do not need to carry so much equipment. When practicable, fly-fishing is very effective. In this sort of closed environment, with its own microclimate, hatchings and rises may occur at any time of day, even when the heat is most intense. As to tackle, it must above all be tough. Using sophisticated expensive equipment will result in disaster if you have a fall, which is only to be expected in this kind of activity.

■ ***Chalk stream trout may have distinctive stripes.***

FLY-FISHING

Once confined to a few privileged initiates, fly-fishing is nowadays open to anyone. Modern equipment, available to match every pocket, and the proliferation of fishing schools, have made things a lot easier for the beginner to take his first steps.

There is much to learn about the art of fly-fishing, most of which can be gained through observation and experience.

Fly-fishing is a lot more than just another leisure activity. For the aficionado it is first and foremost an art, involving respect for a principle which places greater emphasis on elegance, seeking out the difficult catch, and protecting the fish and their environment, than simply on the number of fish caught. (It should be noted that fly-fishing has come under strong Anglo-Saxon influence: catch and release is, if not obligatory, at least warmly encouraged.) Even if a certain snobbery among fly-fishing purists may be criticized, it should be recognized that, just like their confreres, the hunters of woodcock, they are first of all lovers of nature and not simply mechanical killers.

This method of fishing, considered one of the most sophisticated, enables you to catch most types of fish, from the tiny bleak to the mighty tarpon.

The evening rise – here near the North coast of Quebec- is an especially good time for catching trout with a fly.

The tackle

There is an amazing number of fly rods, divided according to model into three broad categories:

- Rods with parabolic action, the most up-to-date and best adapted to dry-fly fishing on French rivers, which flex along their entire length.
- Tip-action rods, which use only the tip when casting, and flex along all or part of their length.
- Traditional English rods, which operate primarily from the butt, and are more suitable for wet-fly fishing.

The appropriate length of rod, expressed in feet and inches, depends on the fish and on the prevailing conditions. Single-handed rods measure between 6 and 11 feet (2–3.6 m), the shorter ones better suited for rocky streams, the bigger ones for longer casts in reservoirs, for example. For river fishing the best rods are between 8 and 9 feet. The materials used are roughly of two kinds:

- carbon fibre (lighter but more expensive).
- split cane (for those who prefer traditional materials).

For each rod there is a corresponding line of a particular weight, usually indicated on the rod. The numbers range from 3 to 12, and fly-lines for trout rods do not generally exceed AFTM No. 5 or No. 6. Other line weights exist for salmon, or big predators, or for fishing in salt-water.

There are four types of line on the market:

- double-taper lines, the most commonly used.
- parallel lines, for slow-action rods.
- forward taper lines, which allow for longer casting.
- shooting tapers, short 30 feet (9 m) lines, attached to a nylon backing line, designed for distance casting.

Some floating lines (the cheapest and most popular) need little care or maintenance. Lines made from natural materials need more care. They need to be regularly greased and carefully dried when wet. Lines made from mixed material also need a preliminary greasing to ensure that they float.

Hooking a trout feeding near the bank.

The fly reel plays a much less important role than in fishing with a bait-casting reel and serves simply to store spare line. Manual reels, which are lighter, are better suited for wet-fly fishing or for big fish. Automatic reels, which are heavier, allow you to reel in quickly by pressing a lever.

Whether fly-fishing or spinning, some specially-equipped anglers think nothing of venturing into the deepest ravines! Take care; use a wading stick.

In dry- or wet-fly fishing the leader is very important for the correct positioning of the fly. The diameter decreases steadily from the line to the bait, accounting for the name rat's tail. Everyone has their own secret method for making a balanced cast. The leader is made up using lengths of monofilament of varying diameter. There are also knotless and braided casts, which are very supple and elastic.

Casting technique

The marvellous arabesque patterns made by the line flicking gracefully above the surface of the water make fly-fishing the most elegant and aesthetic of piscatorial activities. Although it looks so spectacular, casting a fly can be learnt in only a few sessions with the aid of a good instructor. This is advisable, and will allow the beginner to start catching fish without acquiring bad habits which would otherwise be difficult to lose later.

The cast is a slow action performed at a rhythm dependent on the length of line required. It consists of four steps: grasping the line, making the back cast, making the forward cast and placing the fly. A series of backward and forward casts (false casting) serves to dry the fly and lengthen the line.

A much-courted lady

Mistakes often made when casting

Three mistakes commonly made by beginners are:

– Too short a pause: the rod is brought forward while the line is still in the casting loop, not having reached its backmost limit.

– The rod, when performing the back cast, slips too far behind the vertical position: the line, instead of staying high, hits the ground behind the caster.

– If the fisherman makes no pause, or handles the rod poorly, the rod no longer acts like a spring, responding to the beginner's movements. The fisherman makes uncoordinated movements, which cause a poor, sometimes disastrous placing of the fly. He must learn to lengthen his casting distance by pulling out a length of line with his left hand. At each forward cast, at the moment when the line is released, he lets out about 15 inches (40cm) of line.

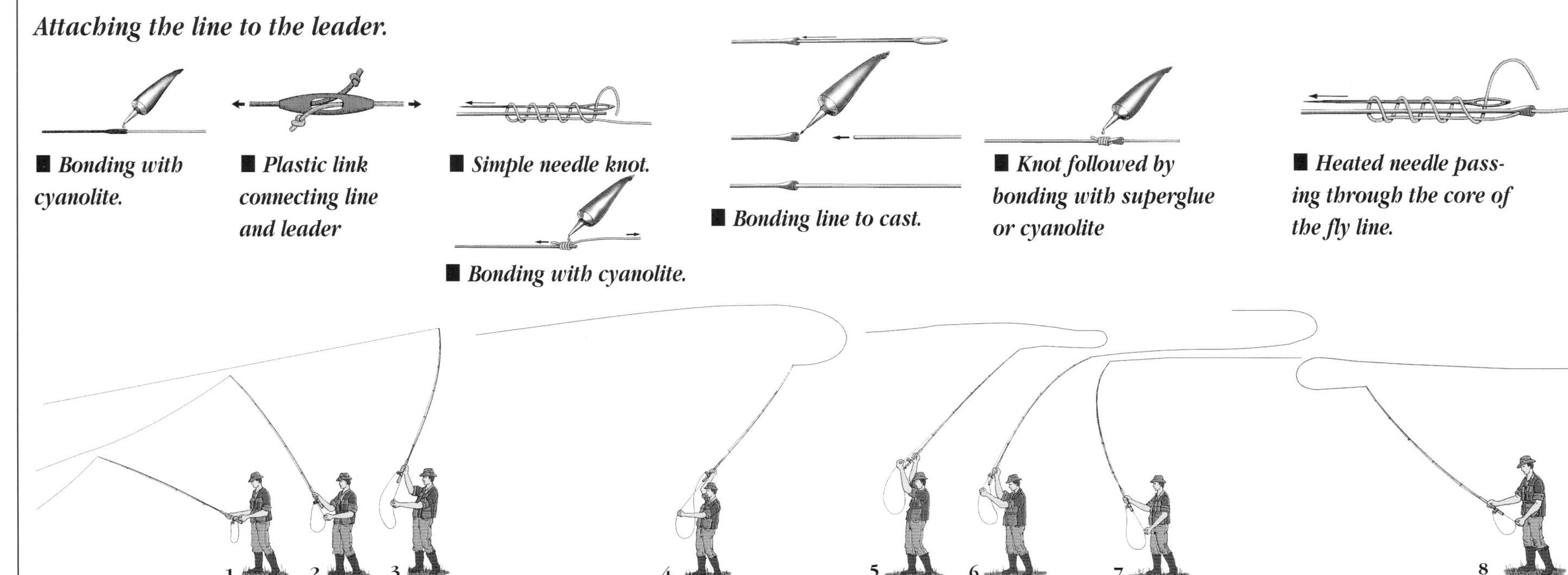

Attaching the line to the leader.

■ *Bonding with cyanolite.*

■ *Plastic link connecting line and leader*

■ *Simple needle knot.*

■ *Bonding with cyanolite.*

■ *Bonding line to cast.*

■ *Knot followed by bonding with superglue or cyanolite*

■ *Heated needle passing through the core of the fly line.*

■ *Taking the line (1, 2, 3) and start of the back cast (4), completing the back cast (5, 6, 7), and start of the forward cast (8). This is the most all-purpose type of casting. It is usually the first one to be taught to beginners.*

Hauling the line

1 – Taking the line.

2-3 – Back cast: the fisherman hauls on the line to accelerate it.

4 – Pause: the line unfurls behind the caster

5 – The fisherman turns to check that the line is fully extended.

6-7-8 – Forward cast : the fisherman casts forward while pulling on the line with the left hand to accelerate it.

9 – The fisherman allows the line to shoot, releasing the spare line coiled at his feet.

■ *Fishing on the Sioule, Puy-de-Dome, France.*

The overhead cast: The beginner should first learn this cast, which is the most widely used. All the other casts derive from it. First of all the fisherman pulls out several yards of line at his feet, and then, holding the line firmly against the rod with his index finger, grasps the line with a rapid movement, his elbow pressed to his side (only the wrist and forearm are used). This movement brings the rod up to the 1 o'clock position. The line, having travelled upwards, shoots backwards. The rod is held still. This pause allows the line to be fully extended behind the caster, before he makes the forward cast. Its weight loads the rod, which is then pulled forward by a movement of the wrist to the 10 o'clock position. The rod should be moved slightly to the right to prevent the line from hitting it. The line is extended in front of the caster, who can then begin a second back cast. To place the fly it is enough to let the line travel forwards, with the rod held at 10 o'clock, then to move the tip of the rod to drop the line straight down.

Shooting the line: This allows you to lengthen the cast considerably. The left hand holds 12 to 16 feet (4-5 m) of coiled line in reserve. At the end of the forward cast the fisherman lets go this spare line, which runs out through the rings. The placing will be accurate if you aim for a point two to three feet above the target area.

Hauling the line: This involves increasing the casting length by giving the line greater speed. You begin while the line is still extended forwards, just as you are about to start the back cast. The left hand then pulls firmly on the line (the left arm moving out further as the line travels backwards), until the rod is at 1 o'clock. The back cast is made normally, and, at the moment when the line begins to extend behind (the loop has almost straightened out), the left hand releases the length of slack line, which is taken up as the line shoots forward again. This technique lengthens the casting distance considerably.

The reverse overhead cast: This is a variation of the overhead cast, enabling casting where there are obstructions, or where the surrounding vegetation prevents normal casting.
Constant practise of all these techniques builds up the considerable skill needed to become a "natural" caster.

The great expert Piam with one of his catches.

■ *Trout caught with a mayfly nymph.*

The side cast: This is identical to the overhead cast, except for the position of the rod which can be held in all positions to the horizontal to allow you to fish under overhanging vegetation.

The roll cast: This type of cast facilitates fly-fishing when there is an obstacle behind the fisherman, preventing the use of other techniques. You cannot cast very far, and it only works if the line floats well. The line, extended at the fisherman's feet, hangs from the tip of the rod. The fisherman holds the rod in the side position and draws in the line to the side of his position. The rod is then cast forward and, angled to the right, it stops at an angle of 45 degrees. The acceleration causes a loop which travels along the line, lifts the leader and places the fly.

Fly-fishing for trout demands excellent powers of observation and great skill, especially when the fisherman makes his own materials. That's the supreme art! To deceive a fish with an imitation you have made yourself, using all your imagination and artistic skill, and all the experience garnered from long observation on the riverbank: that's the exquisite pleasure of fly-fishing...

Dry-fly fishing

The tackle

A medium-action parabolic rod measuring 8ft 6in to 9ft made of split cane or carbon fibre, depending on your preference and your pocket.

A double-tapered No. 3 or No. 5 line according to the strength of the rod.

A nylon rat's tail leader or a woven cast with a 0.12 or 0.18 mm. tip.

The flies

An encyclopaedia would not be enough to describe all the different types of fly on the market, not to mention personal, regional and even international specialities.

Each river, each fisherman, and probably each local family of trout has their own particular flies. There are those who insist on the "perfect fly", who try to imitate nature exactly and produce a fly which accurately resembles a hatching insect, and there are those who stick faithfully to one model throughout the season. From the observations of countless anglers, it seems that size is more important than colour or exact shape. This is not the place to enter into the debate, which will rage for many years to come, but we will give some general guidelines about a range of all-purpose flies. These are ones which work well in most waters, bearing in mind of course that even the finest collection of artificial flies is no substitute for the single fly which works on the day the fish are sulking.

First of all, the ubiquitous sedges, which hatch in great quantities at dusk from May to September and whose neutral colouring ranges between grey and brown (mounted on a No. 12, 14 or 16 hook). Then there are the no less indispensable palmers, real winners! They imitate everything and nothing, and you can choose from a variety of colours (beige, brown, black, grey) mounted on a range of hooks (Nos. 12 to 18). Among these there is Bresson's famous three-colour "French".

The ephemerids, among them the famous mayfly mounted on a No. 10 hook, include all the little spider-flies which imitate most of the families in the great order of ephemeroptera. Keen fly-tiers will know better than anyone the flies which work on their river and on their trout!

The keen traveller must have a few basic flies of different sizes and colours: sombre olives with yellow bodies on No. 14 or No.16 hooks, little reddish, greenish or brownish ones on Nos. 14 to 18 hooks and big ones on No. 12 hooks for the start of the season. The fisherman can also use tiny midges and ants mounted on Nos. 10 to 18 hooks.

A much-courted lady

Cul-de-canard sedge

Peute

Hackled Medium Olive

Three-coloured palmer

March Brown variant

A fine rise is met with an instant strike!

Fishing method

The fisherman usually operates when the fish are rising, that is, when they are close to the surface because the insects are hatching. The hatches occur where there is a steady current or over swift-flowing water where the fish lie in wait and rise according to a precise rhythm and in a well-defined area. The fisherman's skill lies in minute observation of the conditions: of the insects, so as to present a suitable imitation, and of the behavior of the fish. When he decides that the moment has come, he casts the line where it cannot be seen by the fish. He has carefully chosen a spot about ten yards away. This is the ideal distance in order to remain unobserved, and at the same time not to have to use too long a line, which might spoil the strike. The rise is approached from three-quarters upstream, and the line, delivered accurately, will allow a gentle presentation of the fly at a very short distance from the rise (the trout, near the surface, has a very narrow window of vision). On the other hand, a cunning fish lying deeper will need a cast which delivers the fly about one yard upstream of the rise. His wider window of vision will allow him to perceive the imitation fly, which he can observe at leisure before rising to take it. The delicacy of the placing is just as important as its accuracy, and most refusals are due to faulty presentation. That's why the line, unless one is fishing downstream or immediately across the rise (in which case the drift is very short), should land on the water in a gentle zigzag motion to avoid drag.

As the current takes the line the fisherman draws it in with his left hand, in order to avoid having too much slack when he strikes. The strike must be firm and instantaneous, without being too violent, which can cause damage. More mistakes are made by striking too early than by striking too late.

Sometimes the trout will cause the surface to bulge in a manner similar to a rise when he approaches the fly to investigate it. Before reacting too quickly the fisherman must make sure that the fly has been properly taken by the fish.

When the fish are not rising, the fisherman has to "fish the water", keeping to the classic lies (near the bank, downstream from obstacles, etc.). While it is easy to spot a fish rising in smooth water, it is more difficult to see them when the water is rougher (though rises are just as frequent in rough water in summer as at other times).

Trout on the River Allier in France, taken on visible nymph.

A superb trout caught with a nymph on the River Loue.

Wet-fly fishing

Unfairly looked down on by dry-fly purists, this very subtle technique is just as difficult to master. The fact that you cannot see the fish calls for a perfect knowledge of the water, the best locations and the habits of the trout. It is a pity to limit wet-fly fishing to those periods when the fish are not rising, or to fast-moving or muddy waters. It is a very effective technique and allows you to search for fish at any depth.

The tackle

The 9 foot (2.7 m) rod used for dry-fly fishing can work well. Sometimes however it is better to use a 10-foot (3m) tip-action rod to achieve better control over the drift. A double-taper line with a sinking tip or a natural silk line which has been left ungreased over the last few yards both perform well, fitted with a leader tapering to a 0.16 or 0.18 mm tippet, identical to that used for dry flies. A dropper situated about two feet (60 cm) from the point-fly carries a bob-fly at its tip. A manual reel should be used to give more control.

The flies

Pallaretas, with big swollen bodies mounted on No. 10 or No.12 hooks are perfect for point-flies.

The bob-fly is often one of the spiders, mounted on a No.12 or a No. 14 hook.

Spanish dressings are very good too. Colours vary according to region and type of river: the faster and muddier the river, the brighter the fly.

Fishing method

This consists in letting the team of flies drift downstream. It thus explores the water at different depths with the aid of the sinking point and the arrangement of the two flies. Casting is reduced to a minimum (avoid unnecessary casting, which dries out the flies and prevents them from sinking); cast the team of flies from a position three-quarters downstream.

Do not try to fish from too far away: the ideal distance is about 9–11 yards (8–10 m). More than that and failure is frequent, because it is difficult to feel the takes and because the strike is often made too late. You must also avoid raising the sunk line too vigorously when lifting off, as this can strain the rod. The line should not be too taut as it drifts downstream. If it is, the trout, which does not take strongly, will become unhooked at the strike.

Explore carefully all the places likely to shelter a fish (runs between patches of weed, downstream from obstacles and currents where the bottom is rocky), using this dead-drift technique, with the tip of the rod pointing towards the water. You will often get a take just as the fly has alighted or at the end of the drift. The fish often hooks itself, from the effect of the tension of the line. Do not hold the line too high, or a break is inevitable.

Fishing with a nymph

This very visual technique requires very rapid reactions and can really only be used in the summer, when the water is low and very clear. It consists in presenting the fish with imitations of larvae which are familiar to them, at every stage of their development including the final stage, which takes place just under the thin film on the surface of the water and which immediately precedes their flight.

The tackle

The recommended equipment is more or less the same as that used with a dry fly.

Use a longish slow-action rod about 9 feet (2.7m) long: when using heavy deep-water nymphs, casting with ordinary tackle can be difficult, if not impossible. In this case, consider using a rod capable of carrying a No. 6 or No. 7 line.

A delicate line which floats perfectly is essential. A reel with a high quality adjustable drag is recommended.

■ *A team of traditional wet flies.*

■ *The difficult choice of nymph.*

Nymph NY3

The Nymphs

There are three types of nymph, all with common characteristics: swollen thorax and subdued colours. They are mounted on No. 12 to No. 18 hooks.

Unweighted nymphs fished close to the surface imitate insects in the last stage of development, when they lose their last shreds of skin a few millimetres from the surface before taking wing.

Medium nymphs are those beginning to make their move up to the surface.

Bottom nymphs are heavier and imitate all the larvae which move about on the river-bed.

■ ***Big jurassic trout taken with a nymph.***

Fishing method

The fishing action is much the same as with a dry fly, in that you fish upstream of rising fish, without letting the fly drift below you as with a wet fly. The same care has to be taken when placing the fly. Take great care to avoid making splashy casts or allowing the line to furrow the water. The deeper the fish, the further away you cast, upstream from the rise. As soon as it hits the surface of the water the nymph must sink. Strike at the first telltale sign on the leader at the surface or as soon as the line tightens. If the nymph is ignored the first time, you can move it a bit the next time by gently lifting the rod, as it passes gradually through the fish's window.

Bringing the nymph to life is more important when you are using heavier nymphs for deeper fishing. The need for a very quick strike at the slightest signal (e.g. tightening of the line, or movement of the fish towards the nymph) means that you must retrieve the line as it drifts to take up the slack.

Crystal clear water often requires the use of fine tippets (down to 0.08 mm) which call for a quick but gentle strike to prevent a break.

Spinning for trout at dusk in the Laurentides, Quebec. A change from fly-casting.

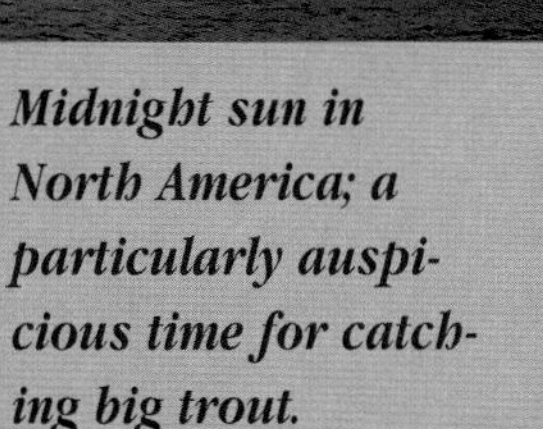

Midnight sun in North America; a particularly auspicious time for catching big trout.

SPINNING FOR TROUT

Spinning, or bait-casting, is in fact suitable for all predator fish including salmon. For this reason we usually divide the type of cast into four categories, according to the thickness of the line and the weight of the lures used: heavy spinning, medium spinning, light spinning and ultra-light spinning. The first two are for salmon and predators like pike or zander, the other two for most of the other salmonids. Spinning with rod and reel has increased greatly in popularity in France since the 1950s, with the appearance of fixed-spool reels, which have greatly facilitated casting techniques. The result has been the destruction of an incalculable number of trout and pike, irresistibly attracted by the vast range of unfamiliar lures. Most of these fish are now more educated, and the fisherman has to show some ingenuity to overcome their suspicion.

Spinning techniques

First of all attach the reel to the handle of the rod. It must be fixed at the point of balance, which you can easily test by supporting the handle on one finger, so that the rod stays level.

Filling the spool: very carefully load the line so that it fills the spool to the lip. If the spool is too full, it causes a lot of problems, above all when the line gets inextricably tangled at the moment of casting. If there is not enough line, the line brushes against the spool lip, affecting the accuracy of the cast.

Most spools have too much line capacity – up to 300 yards (275 m), although 100 yards (90 m) is enough. You should pad the spool first with old cotton or nylon. It is a good idea to have someone to help you wind on the new line. One person holds the spool of monofilament on a pencil placed through the hole in the middle, allowing it to revolve, while the other winds it on to the reel, pinching it slightly between his or her fingers so that it remains taut and coils smoothly.

Regulating the drag is an important procedure, carried out by drawing on the line passing through the rings. It must be set neither too tight, so that it causes a break when striking, nor too loose, for a fish once hooked will simply make off and hide himself in difficult water. A soft drag can also cause the fish to shed the hook.

The casts

The straight or horizontal cast:
While this is probably the easiest cast to learn, you need space on either side and it is therefore impracticable on rivers or streams where there are a lot of obstacles. Take out about 10 inches of leading-line (equivalent to the length of line between the rod-tip and the lure) and hold it a few inches above the pick-up with the tip of the index finger. Open the pick-up: you will feel the line pulling on your finger, preventing the spool from releasing line under the weight of the lure. Give the rod a sharp flick with the wrist, keeping the lure horizontal. The flex of the rod will cast the lure. Let go the line just at the moment the rod-tip begins to return to its normal position, which will have the effect of propelling the lure towards its target. Keep the tip of the rod pointing towards the target until the lure touches the water.

Common mistakes: first and easiest to avoid is to forget to open the pick-up. If this happens, of course, the lure goes nowhere, unless it shoots up into the unsuspecting fisherman's face! Another common error is to let go of the line too soon or too late, which means that the lure lands smartly at your feet or shoots up in a magnificent arc into the branches of the surrounding poplars. Again, the wrist movement can sometimes be too weak, causing too short a cast, or too strong, in which case the spoon gets hooked in the tree-roots of the far bank.

■ *Horizontal cast.*

The backhand cast:
Harder to master, this can also be a casting style to use with ultra-light tackle in difficult water, when too much vegetation to the angler's righ prevents the use of the previous technique. The technique is similar to that used with the horizontal lure, except that the fisherman must take care not to swing the rod too wide or too high, which will simply land the lure among the branches of the trees. A little flick of the wrist is enough for this short cast.

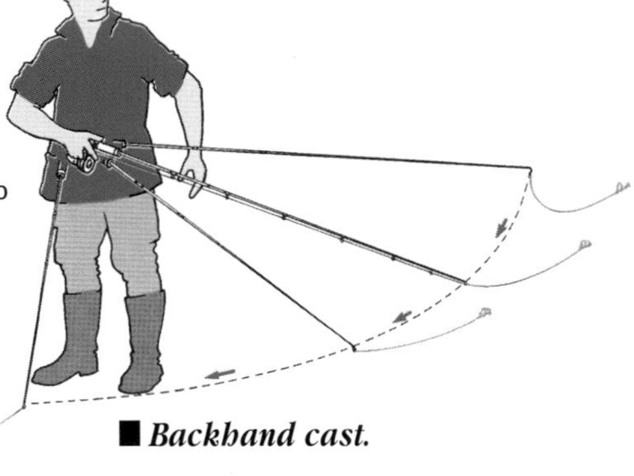

■ *Backhand cast.*

The underarm cast:
This is an all-purpose cast which allows you to work in any conditions. If you can master it, it is the main technique used in ultra-light casting, permitting extremely accurate casts in the most difficult conditions, such as in narrow and congested streams. The length of line between rod-tip and lure, longer than for the horizontal cast, should be slightly shorter than the distance between the rod-tip and the reel. Swing the lure in a gradually accelerating pendulum movement, which has the effect of tautening the rod. At the right moment, flick the wrist, and the lure swinging forwards is at full stretch. Let go the line at the same moment, the rod-tip pointing at your target. This is a difficult cast and mistakes are common, connected essentially with releasing the lure either too soon or too late.

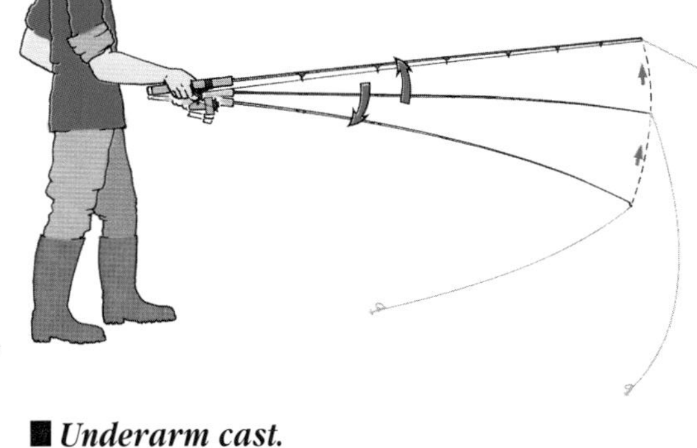

■ *Underarm cast.*

■ ***This trout succumbed to a small-blade spinner in a high mountain lake.***

Spoon-fishing

This type of fishing is disdained by many practised fishermen, who regard it as a blind and systematic combing of the river, carried out by a bunch of fishmongers, killing young trout and pike indiscriminately. Nevertheless, fishing with spoons requires skill and accuracy , and is in fact a subtle technique if you are willing to take the trouble to seek out fish in more inaccessible places, and do not just want to fish the water, mechanically waiting for a take. It is furthermore a sport for those who love adventure, enabling you to fish in difficult situations which would be impossible using other techniques.

The tackle

A rod about 5–7 feet (1.5–2.1 m) long is best. A lightweight fixed-spool reel with a wide spool is recommended. It must be of good quality, robust and with a reliable bail-arm (pick-up), with quick recovery and smooth action. The reel is at least as important as the rod, the slightest defect having disastrous consequences for precise casting and recovery of the lure. A pick-up arm which closes too slowly, for example, will mean that the spoon becomes completely embedded in the bottom of the river. About 100 yards (90 m) of 0.16 or 0.18 mm line is enough.

Equipment

A pair of thigh-length boots or waders is essential in order to negotiate the bigger rivers and get within casting distance of the furthest lies. To complete the outfit you will also need a fishing vest, a wicker creel and a racket-head or telescopic landing-net.

The lures

Finding the right spoon remains an insoluble and controversial problem.

A good all-purpose spoon is a No. 1 with a gold or silver blade. In general the size of the spoon depends on the depth of the water. The shallower the water, the smaller the lure. A box of lures must contain several different models to cover every eventuality: spinners with wide and narrow blades of different designs, wobbling spoons, spinners attached to little fish, and all in various sizes, patterns and colours.

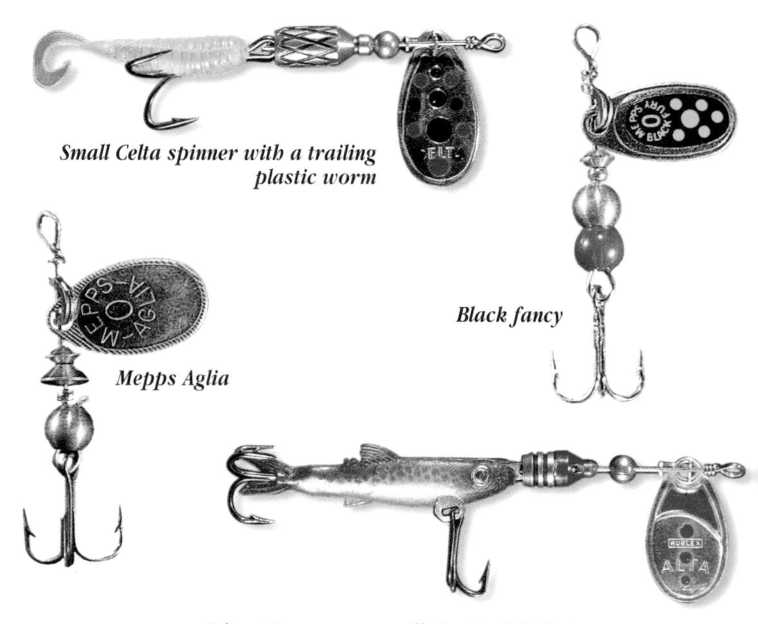

Small Celta spinner with a trailing plastic worm

Black fancy

Mepps Aglia

Celta spinner on a small plastic fish flight

Like the fly-fisherman, the man who spins with an artificial lure won't hesitate to get himself wet to find the best lies.

Fishing method

Although trout have been made wiser by the thousands of lures that they see during the course of their existence in our overfished rivers, it is still worth fishing with spoons if one observes a few elementary rules. No-one knows why fish go for lures, but the element of surprise and the aggressive instincts of the fish are certainly important factors. The careful angler, who has managed not to betray his presence, and who casts accurately so that the bait falls within range of the fish, will have every chance of success. Speed of retrieval is also very important. You must turn the reel-handle just quickly enough for the spoon to spin. If it does not work immediately it enters the water, you must discard it, for it is useless.

As a general principle, which applies to all fish, you should vary your speed of retrieval if you do not achieve the desired effect the first time, and work the lure at different depths. In certain cases, especially with fly-spoons, a touch will only occur if you quickly raise the rod so as to work the lure on the surface. You can also trigger a take if you work the lure like a dead fish, alternately releasing and retrieving it, sink-and-draw style.

Reading the conditions in small rivers and streams usually presents no problems. The fish generally stick to the same lies: downstream of obstacles such as tree-stumps or boulders, under overhanging banks, in pool-tails and in smooth glides.

In bigger rivers it is often much less easy to find the best lies, as the water can be difficult to "read", so the angler should take time to walk the beat and observe.

There is no problem in rocky stretches with a fast current or in smooth water with plentiful weed-beds. But you have to be much more astute in deeper pools and in wide, smooth water devoid of obstacles. It is in these conditions that the spoon-fisher will show his true skill. In fact the current is never uniform and is continually breaking into little ripples and eddies which indicate turbulence beneath the surface. The fisherman has to guess the position of rocks and likely resting lies under the water. The best way to test the water in these conditions is to cast with a revolving spinner from three-quarters upstream, then slowly retrieve the line, letting the lure cover all the likely lies. The technique is identical in wide smooth stretches, where it is a good idea to stand in the middle and cast in an arc while advancing steadily towards the head of the pool.

The fisherman must react instantly to a touch, striking with the rod held high, lowering the angle if the fish is further away. It is useless to go on trying to tempt a fish after a number of failed strikes. With a spoon, and especially if you are using barbless hooks, you must play out the fish as swiftly as possible, taking care not to put the line under undue strain.

Finally, prospecting a stretch of water is generally done upstream. In big rivers strewn with boulders remember one important point: every rock impeding the water-flow causes turbulence downstream of it, creating a reverse current. Trout, which always lie "nose into the current" will therefore be facing the fisher as he moves upriver. He must therefore be doubly watchful and tackle

Landing a brown trout on the upper Allier, in France.

■ *The spinner is a good bet when fishing for trout.*

such locations from a distance so as not to betray his presence. Moreover, always remember that a fish may be anywhere, even directly under your feet! There is no point therefore in casting systematically from a distance: concentrate on accurate casting, taking account of every possible lie, even those quite close to you on the same bank, which one often tends to overlook.

■ *Testing a fast current on the upper stretches of the Allier in France.*

■ *Spinning for trout on one of the Cezallier lakes in the Auvergne.*

Fishing for trout with a dead minnow

This is an exciting and difficult technique. In the hands of an expert it can secure the finest trout, cunning fish which have hitherto disdained all other lures and baits.

The tackle

A bait-casting rod of about 6 to 8 feet (1.8–2.4 m) is long enough. Split cane rods are better for this task. It's a pity that they are so expensive!

A light fixed-spool reel, with 100 yards (90 m) of 0.18 or 0.22 mm line.

Select the simplest mounts you can find.

Fishing method

If you are using a wobbling mount, you should usually cast from three-quarters upstream or indeed straight across, so as to let the bait drift in an arc. Each time you cover a likely lie, try to make the bait more attractive by fishing it with sink-and-draw movements, while it works

■ *Ariel minnow mount.*

for a few moments within range of the fish. It sometimes happens that a fish attracted by the erratic movements of the minnow only bites at the end of the cast, when the minnow is close to the bank. With a dead minnow on a "helmet" mount it is wiser to fish in fairly precise spots. The technique consists in casting from three-quarters upstream in the direction of the lie, so that the minnow falls beyond. When it has reached the right depth and is directly beneath the spot you should give the bait a series of irregular tugs and then bring it to the surface, holding the rod high.

This manoeuvre, which is intended to imitate a fry darting off in alarm, usually provokes an attack. You must react immediately to a touch, which is usually quite evident and feels like a series of barely perceptible nudges, just like those that are felt when fishing with a worm. Let the fish bite for a few second before striking firmly. It sometimes happens that after a few touches the fish does not take, contenting himself with "knocking" the minnow in order to kill it, with his mouth shut.

The mounts

If you are not making your own models there are three kinds worth considering. The wobbling mount combines a vertical action (it has a weighted head) with the wriggling movements of a minnow, caused by the action of the disc when it is retrieved. This light mount is good for shallow water and stretches with a fast current, where you can use it like a Devon minnow. The "helmet" or Bohemian mount is equipped with a heavy head, which gives the minnow a very alluring wobbling movement. The Duborgel mount, which presents the minnow in a slightly curved form, gives it a very appetizing and enticing undulating movement.

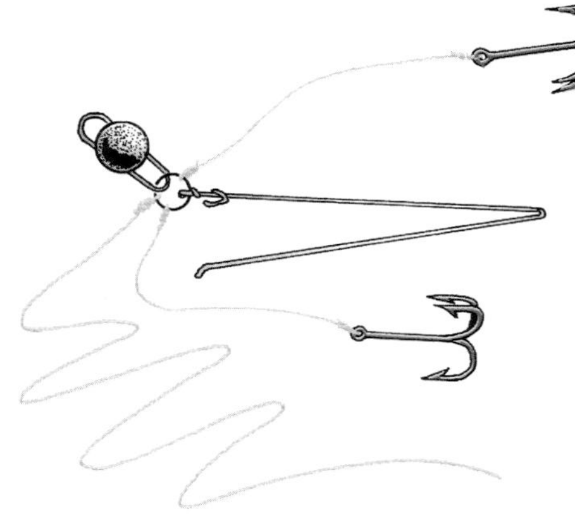

■ *Drabkovich mount.*

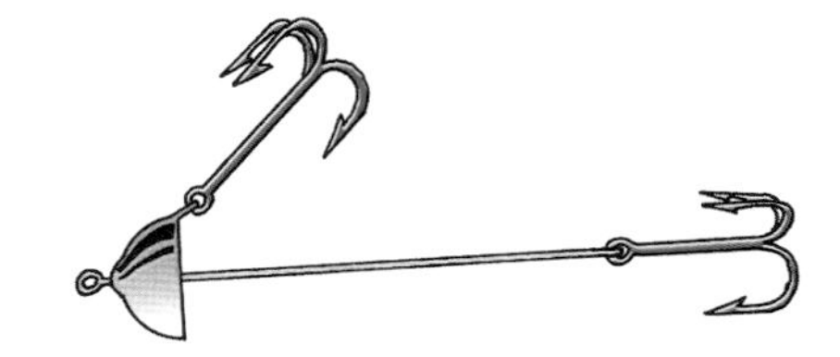

■ *Minnow on a "helmet" mount.*

■ *Dead minnow mount equipped with two No. 16 triple hooks.*

■ *Attaching a minnow to a wobbling mount with the aid of a baiting needle.*

■ *Simple Duborgel mount.*

The ultra-light cast

Just like fly-fishing, ultra-light bait-casting is truly an art, reserved for those keen practitioners who have mastered light casting techniques. A roving pursuit, this exciting technique calls for qualities which make those who practise it into more than just anglers in the true sense of the term: they are subtle and silent hunters, perfectly at one with their natural surroundings, with a profound knowledge of the fishes' habits as well as a very developed understanding of the water and complete accuracy when casting. The real ultra-light caster, though he does not need to cast very far, is able to place his cast exactly where he wants it, to within half an inch, even beneath branches that are touching the water, or close to a rise.

The delicate nature of the tackle you need, especially for bigger fish, greatly enhances the pleasure of this kind of fishing and often makes it more exciting than all the others. Because of the lightness of the tackle, ultra-light casting is the technique favoured by all those who like to seek out the most difficult conditions.

Unfairly disregarded and even looked down on by fly-fishing purists, it has its fervent devotees who pursue it with passion. In any case, there's no-one to disturb or criticize them in the places where they prefer to operate, deep down in hidden ravines or in the secret places beside overgrown streams.

■ ***This trout was ambushed behind a boulder, a classic spot in a rapid river.***

The tackle

Ultra-light bait-casting is usually defined by the weight of the lures, between 0.5 and 3 grams, and by the diameter of the line, which is no more than 0.14 mm. Above that and we are talking about light bait-casting.

Contrary to popular belief (this is a personal opinion), the rod does not have to be very short. The length usually recommended, between 5 and 6 feet (1.5–1.8 m), seems inappropriate, especially in streams. That may appear contra dictory, but it is sometimes the case that a river is so hemmed in that it is impossible to cast. A longer rod (up to 7 feet/2.1 m) can then allow you to reach some of the most inaccessible spots (they are always the best!) in the style of a touch-legering angler. On big rivers with a wide strong current these rods allow longer casts which enable you to reach the opposite bank and above all that special feeding-lie where the most inaccessible trout is rising.

It is difficult to find rods on the market with the right specifications and manufacturers appear unaware of them. If you can find them, they are usually very expensive.

A longer rod provides extra interest when you are fighting a big fish that is using the current to its advantage. The rod's through-action compensates for the fineness of the line. The frequent and rapid casting and the fact that equipment is often dropped in this kind of terrain require a reel of irreproachable quality; it must have an excellent drag, be completely robust and quite light, with rapid retrieval and a wide spool.

As for the line, 330 feet (100 m) of 0.10 to 0.14 mm is enough. See that you use top-quality line that does not get twisted. It is absolutely vital for accurate casting that the spool is filled to the lip.

The lures and baits

All kinds of lures and especially natural baits can be used, even the lightest. It is one of the reasons why ultra-light bait-casting is so effective, because you can happily present to the fish a whole range of lures and baits acquired when using other techniques.

Well-presented No. 0 or No. 00 spinners are very effective. Equipped with single or treble hooks, with or without hackles, which give them the name fly-spoons, they usually require 0.12 or 0.14 mm line. They have the additional advantage of being able to work quite deep, an essential quality in a wide river, when the fish are lurking among the pebbles and under the banks. Use a variety of colours, especially when fishing in very clear water, where the darker models seem to work better.

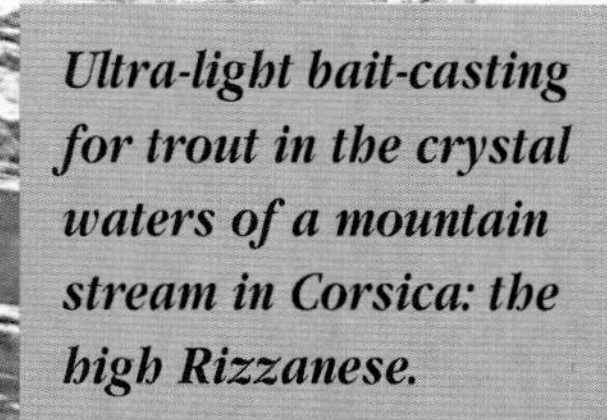

Ultra-light bait-casting for trout in the crystal waters of a mountain stream in Corsica: the high Rizzanese.

■ ***Fishing for trout will often take you to wild, magnificent, steep-sided gorges.***

There are certain tiny revolving spinners which work extremely well in fast water, where they enable you to explore with a Devon minnow lies that are inaccessible to the usual equipment. You can make for yourself little spiralling flies or nymphs, which are difficult to find in shops. They can give excellent results, especially in summer, if you are trying out shady stretches under trees in the heat of the day, and in waters that have been overfished with spoons.

Remember that streamers can also catch fine trout in places where spiral nymphs, which are noisy and less manoeuvrable, do not yield results.

Most natural baits (worms and insects) can be used, but ultra-light bait-casting is essentially a summer technique, and it is better to use crickets or grasshoppers, with or without a weight. The weight can be attached directly to the hook, thus replacing the insect's head.

The may-fly can yield excellent results at dusk. You can increase the weight of the insect by carefully attaching to the hook a little balsa-wood head, which will help it to float on the current for a while.

■ *Fine trout taken on a blade-spoon.*

Casting

Cast with a clean flick of the wrist. The best technique is the underarm cast, which enables you to propel the lure into the most snaggy spots, while maintaining precision.

The bow-and-arrow cast is also useful where you only have a little gap in the vegetation, as are backhand casts on narrow streams.

Fishing method

The lightness of the lures does not generally allow casting at any distance. So the fisherman has to use the utmost discretion in approaching potential lies. He must merge with his surroundings and stay in the shade, avoiding sudden movements. This is real stalking of the quarry, which makes it so exciting and in which accurate casting is more than half the battle.

The lure must be placed gently (to do that, lower the rod towards the water when the bait is in position), so as not to arouse the trout's suspicion. As soon as the bait is in the water, start working it (unless it is in a gully or a deep pool), cranking it in just fast enough to let it work normally.

An attack is often immediate, occurring as soon as the lure enters the water, although some fish pursue the spoon or the spiral nymph right up to the fisherman's boots. If you see a trout following without biting, it is sometimes enough to vary the speed of retrieval in order to provoke the desired reaction. The lure must always be retrieved right up to the rod-tip, as some fish decide to attack only at the last moment.

A gentle strike avoids damage when you are using such fine lines. The fish, especially if it is a fine specimen, must never be bullied. But that's no reason to let him do as he pleases by playing him for too long, for the more time he has to recover his strength the greater the risk of the fish slipping the hook.

Explore all the places where a fish might be sheltering, even the unlikely ones. The key to success lies in this perseverance, which is sometimes rewarded quite quickly, when one discovers the spot where the fish are biting. Just to give an example: one day we were fishing on the upper Allier in France, testing every pebble and every run, and we realized after two hours searching in vain that the fish were hunting along the banks in a few

■ *Two combination lures, with a spinner blade and a plastic fish.*

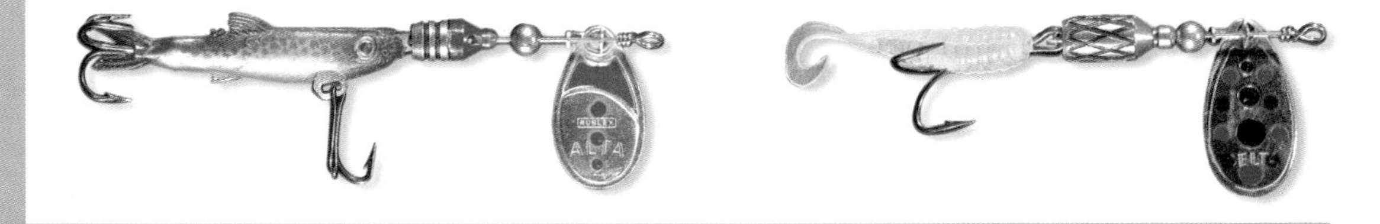

inches of water (and not just the smaller ones either!). Knowing this river and its marvellous locations we could not have imagined that the fish would be hunting just there!

■ *Wading allows you to stand in the river and to cover rising trout with more precision.*

■ *Exploring a small pool on a tributary of the Rizzanese in Southern Corsica.*

"Trotting" specialist Laurent Jauffrey in action on the Pavin, in Puy-de-Dôme, France.

FISHING FOR TROUT WITH NATURAL BAITS

The most rustic of techniques are no less effective, in narrow streams just as anywhere else. Dapping for trout with natural baits calls for a thorough knowledge of the water and the habits of the fish. It is a subtle technique and you need a cautious approach to successfully deceive a particularly wary fish.

Trotting with a worm

This is often the preferred fishing method at the beginning of the season when the rivers are full. It is most effective in cold, coloured water, but remains a killing method throughout the seasons, especially in streams.

■ *Two classic trotting rigs for low clear water.*

■ *Some experts in the high plateaux of the Auvergne in France have attached a grasshopper to a blade spinner.*

The tackle

In order to operate with discretion you need a very long telescopic rod (15 to 20 feet in length). Depending on the size of the stream, you can use a simple bait-casting reel. "In-line" rods, where the line runs through the hollow centre of the rod, will help you to avoid getting caught up in the branches of trees.

The line, if you are using a rod without a reel, must be kept very short (2 or 3 yards/1.8–2.7 m). The diameter will usually be 0.16 or 0.18 mm, or 0.14 or 0.12 mm in clear, still water.

The weights will be arranged differently depending on the current and the size of the river. You need heavy solid weights in fast or deep water, lighter ones in small rivers. This is of course the theory: in practice good fishermen think nothing of changing their weights several times in the course of a single day, depending on the state of the water. Some anglers prefer not to use any weights, so as to present the bait in as natural a manner as possible. Depending on the size of worm, use No. 6 to No. 10 hooks.

Bait

The worms most often used are brandlings, small red earthworms and blue-head lobworms. You can make them firmer and easier to attach to a hook by leaving them in coffee grounds for two or three days. Thread the worm head first on to the hook with the point of the hook just protruding, leaving the worm free to twist and turn, which will make it more enticing to the fish.

■ *Baiting a worm.*

Fishing method

Trout lies vary according to the water and the season. At the start of the season it is better to try the calmer water, places where there are wide eddies or directly under overhanging banks. As the season advances and the water gets warmer, try the swifter pools and those little pockets of fast water that create well-oxygenated lies for the trout. You must proceed with the utmost caution; do not wear bright clothing and approach quietly. You will usually feel a number of perceptible nudges with the tip of the rod. Bigger fish tend to be much more cautious. Do not delay the strike. If you do you will only catch a small fish, condemned to die with a hook stuck in its throat.

A variation of trotting consists in fishing with a heavily weighted worm cast three-quarters upstream. Drifting under perfect control the worm can slowly explore all the trout's likely hiding-places. You must respond immediately to a touch, often barely perceptible, because of the length of the line being used. This is a very effective method in wide fast rivers and enables you to reach locations inaccessible with traditional methods. We recommend a light "Avon" style of rod for this method, fitted with an ultra-light fixed-spool reel.

Fishing with grasshoppers

Fishing with a grasshopper is certainly one of the most effective techniques in the summer, when the hay has been cut. It works particularly well where a stream flows through pasture and on waterways with grassy banks. Grasshoppers are a prime bait for trout, especially in the heat of the day.

The tackle

You need a long 15-20 foot (4.5–6 m) rod to approach trout lies without giving your presence away.

Two to three feet of line is quite enough for fishing in streams, enabling you to control the bait more easily between the branches. Attach the 0.16 mm line to a 0.14 or 0.12 mm leader with a No. 8 or a No. 10 hook, according to the size of the bait. In bigger rivers it is better to use a telescopic rod with rings, fitted with a simple spinning reel.

■ ***When the fish are lying on the bottom, the grasshopper can be weighted with a small split-shot.***

A bubbling stream in the Correze in France. Trout lurk in large numbers under the overhanging banks

The bait

Of the various crickets and grasshoppers that flourish in France, the green grasshopper gives the best results. Alas, he is often rather difficult to catch. What fisherman has not seen a crouching figure in some meadow by a stream trying desperately to capture one of these devilish orthoptera, which leaps off in one bound just as the deadly hand is about to close over it? When at last the unhappy fisher has succeeded in collecting a sufficient number of the creatures, and is just opening his little box to deposit his latest catch, they all leap from their prison in a bunch. The fishing expedition ends in disaster...no bait, and no tackle either, because during the desperate grasshopper hunt, the rod, left lying in the grass a few yards away, has been trampled on by a herd of curious and malicious cows.

To avoid these trials it is better to catch the insects in the early morning, when the dew has just lifted: still bloated after their nocturnal feasting, their senses are somewhat dulled.

Small containers in the shape of a bottle with a narrow neck are good for storing the creatures in and make it easy for you to get hold of them when you want to attach them to the hook.

Other insects can also be used: crickets, for example, or house-flies or cockchafers. To make the grasshopper more enticing, thread the hook through the thorax and bring it out near the end of the tail.

Fishing method

With a long rod you can approach the best locations unobserved, these being often situated close to the bank. The grasshopper must land on the water as naturally as possible. The bait is often taken the instant it settles on the water. If it is not, let it drift for a few moments. When a slight movement of the line or a noisy rise announces the fish's approach, do not strike immediately. In fact the trout will often play with the insect for a few seconds before swallowing it. You can often arouse the fish's interest by making the grasshopper wriggle a bit.

You should not forget to test those inaccessible places under overhanging branches where the finest fish are often hiding in the shade.

■ ***Skilled practitioner, Pierre Sempe, watched attentively by a pupil.***

Fishing with natural larvae

This is a very subtle form of fishing, which makes use of the various kinds of larvae that live in our waters, and is certainly one of the most deadly, since it presents to the fish bait which they consume regularly throughout the year. As well as trout, larvae are also good for catching grayling, which are therefore massacred in great numbers by less scrupulous anglers.

The tackle

It is identical to that described for legering, that is to say a very long rod with a small spinning reel. Only the line diameter and the size of hook are different, because the baits we use are small and easily damaged. The tiny larvae of ephemerids and plecoptera require the use of 0.12 or 0.10 mm. line, with a No. 14 or No. 16 hook. Moth or caddis-fly larvae, which are bigger, can be fixed to No. 12 hooks. Use weights to maintain good line tension in the water.

The bait

The larvae most often used are the moth-grub (it is really a false moth: the wax moth, which flourishes in badly maintained bee-hives), caddis-larva (all the sedges work well, including the forms of the genus *Rhyacophilla* or *Hydropsychae*) and ephemerids (these are flat larvae living under stones in fast, well-oxygenated water, more usually called agile darters, and essentially comprising three genera: *Heptagenia*, *Epeorus* and *Ecdyonorus* belonging to the family of the heptagenids.

Collecting these aquatic larvae is not difficult. Simply lift some stones on the river-bed where there is a current. Hold them from upstream and slightly at an angle to prevent little eddies from forming and making the larvae cling to the undersides. The little creatures are carried along by the water and can be collected in a fine-mesh sieve or a muslin landing-net.

Another method is to turn over the river-bed with a spade, and collect the larvae downstream with a sieve. You can keep the fragile larvae for some time in a well-aerated box filled with damp moss.

Fishing method

Among the baits described above the agile darter is certainly one of the most effective. Trout will rarely refuse such bait, one of the only ones that will work during hot summer days. When using larvae as bait, and particularly the agile darter, remember that the classic lies are behind boulders in turbulent water where there are alternate falls and glides. The strike must be very quick, because the fragile insects soon become detached from the hook.

Jean-Paul Goutte-Quillet, a well-known fisherman from the Correze, in South-Western France, enjoying opening-day on one of his favourite rivers, the Diege.

Fishing with small live bait

Fishing with small live bait allows you above all to target those big trout which obstinately turn up their noses at all other bait and lures, but will allow themselves to be tempted by a minnow, a little gudgeon or perhaps a tiny wriggling bleak!

The tackle

The tackle is similar to that used in legering, but more powerful. A telescopic or sectional ringed rod with a fairly stiff tip is recommended.

You will need a light fixed-spool casting reel. Be sure to set the drag correctly. Fill the spool with about 100 yards (90 m) of 0.20 mm line which is attached to a 0.16 or 0.18 mm. hook-length fitted with a No. 6 or a No. 8 hook. The weight can be simply a 1/8 or 1/4 oz olivette positioned about one foot from the bait. An optional addition is a small sliding float, especially useful if fishing in deep water or lakes.

An English mount for small live bait.

The bait

Minnows, which are the best bait, can be substituted with gudgeon, or small bleak. Small bait-fish are generally attached by lip-hooking.

Fishing method

This technique being especially designed to catch big fish, you must test all their likely lies: beneath the banks, where the water has carved out deep holes, downstream from obstacles such as dead trees, stumps and boulders, wide eddies at the head of a pool and below a waterfall.

Little enticing movements can provoke an attack after the bait has been allowed to sink to the river-bed.

Big trout may be in any of the tributaries feeding a natural lake or a reservoir. A sliding float helps greatly in these locations.

Trotting in a mountain brook.

Grayling

His dorsal fin, which he displays proudly, has given him the name Standard-bearer.

The grayling is making a strong comeback in French rivers for reasons which are not always easy to discern: possibly the result of good water management over a number of years or quite simply a change in the quality of the water. Whatever the answer, the grayling offers the fly-fisher the opportunity to fight it out with a fine secondary species during the trout's close season.

FISHING FOR GRAYLING WITH A FLY

The grayling is a magnificent sporting fish, a determined and spectacular fighter. Some fishermen seek him with natural baits such as an agile darter or mayfly nymph, lethal lures unworthy of so noble an adversary!

These predatory anglers have blindly laid waste to a large number of our rivers and streams. They think nothing of committing their sinister misdeeds at the height of the spawning season, pretending that they are looking for gudgeon. These are not fishermen but fishmongers.

Sporting etiquette demands that a fly be used when fishing for grayling, and there are many passionate devotees of the art.

Dry-fly fishing

The tackle

The good grayling rod must fulfil several criteria: it must be able to cast a long way, possess a smooth action and enable the fisherman to be able to control the drift of the fly perfectly.

When you are fishing on very wide rivers with big flat smooth stretches you should use a 10 or 11 foot (3–3.3 m) rod with a long cast. Choose a parabolic-action rod which is both strong and supple, capable of placing the fly very gently. A carbon rod is recommended, its lightness enabling you to fish for hours at a time without tiring.

In a smaller river an 8ft 6in. or 9ft (2.6–2.7 m) rod is long enough. Use a classic fly-reel, manual or automatic. Given the fact that the grayling fisher does not move very far, he might do better without an automatic reel as its weight is cumbersome when making frequent casts.

A capricious gentleman

Latin Name: *Thymallus thymallus*
Family: Thymallidae

The fly-line should be a delicate one: AFTM No. 3 or No. 4. Ones woven from fine nylon strands (0.08 to 0.10 mm), similar to those used in making leaders, are very suitable as they enable you to place the fly very carefully, essential in view of the grayling's customary wariness.

The leader is a crucial element in the grayling fisher's tackle. Generally very long (10 to 18 feet/3–5 m), it has a tip of not more than 0.12 mm, depending on the size of the flies being used. Some fishermen even use 0.065 mm. Such specialists cannot operate everywhere, because struggling to bring under control a big grayling straining at the line in a fast current is taking a great risk if you are using such very fine monofilament!

When fishing with nymphs, the imitation should sink on contact with the surface. To ensure this, degreasing the line with a detergent such as washing-up liquid sometimes helps.

The flies

The grayling will take surface food until very late in the season, as late as December or January. At this period only tiny insects are hatching (chironomids and ephemerids such as *Caenis*), and many anglers maintain that this fish, with its small mouth, will only take artificial flies mounted on No. 18 or No. 20 hooks. In fact this is not the case, and, depending on the season, grayling may very well rise for sedges or mayfly on a No. 10 hook. Grayling flies are often not the most aesthetic specimens and confound the purists who prefer exact imitations. They are often wet featherless patterns, hanging just underneath the surface. Cul-de-canard styles of fly are very effective, especially when offered as sedge imitations.

Ant

Cul-de-canard palmer

Cul-de-canard sedge

Cul-de-canard

Many anglers use small, wool-tailed palmer patterns with a vivid tag, such as the Red Tag. It is well-known that the grayling has a lively imagination and that

■ *The grayling can be fished with a fly late in the season.*

■ *Presentation is a vital element in success.*

he will rise for an imitation bearing no resemblance to any aquatic invertebrate, so that some fly-tiers produce colourful models in blue, red, violet or green, sometimes even fluorescent ones. He likes colours that shine too so that people add tinsel to their flies. But sometimes the grayling will refuse all these patterns, and will only rise for grey models with yellowish, bluish or grey bodies. In all these cases and as with all other fish that rise, the presentation and quality of the drift are more important to success than the fly itself.

Fishing method

The grayling usually takes up a very precise position on the bed of the river, where he calmly waits for his prey, gently moving in the current. When an insect passes within his cone of vision, he leaves his position with a characteristic swinging movement. Having seized his prey on the surface, he returns to his look-out post.

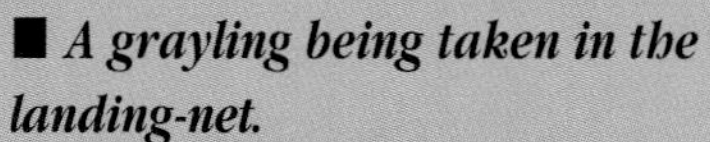

■ *A grayling being taken in the landing-net.*

This behaviour leads one to certain conclusions:

- The grayling can clearly see his prey while it is still upstream. He can react promptly and seize it when it is directly above his resting-place.

- When he sees the insect immediately above him, if he sees anything unusual about it, he will let it drift on downstream for a moment before seizing it.

In general, it is estimated that a grayling situated at a depth of 2 feet can see his prey when it is 2 feet upstream, and will sometimes seize it when it is 2 feet downstream. This means that the angler will have to allow his fly to drift perfectly for 4 to 5 feet, sometimes difficult if there are a lot of obstacles, such as weed for example, or if there are eddies or shifts in the current, and bearing in mind that the grayling never moves sideways.

Strike at the first touch. After a number of failed strikes, delay your response and let the fish suck the fly in for a fraction of a second. The grayling defends himself fiercely and spectacularly. Very powerful, and used to battling against the strongest currents, he sometimes sticks obstinately to the river-bed. He can also perform a series of violent somersaults, which can severely test a 0.08 mm leader!

He has the reputation of being a delicate creature. When practising catch-and-release, you must unhook the fish with great care, keeping it in the water.

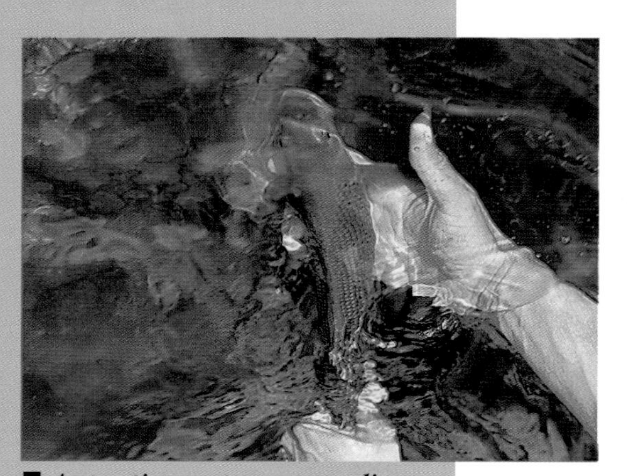

■ *A sporting gesture: a grayling is returned to the water.*

The fisherman who wants to keep some of his catch for the table must be careful to put his fish into an aerated basket filled with damp greenery (nettles are very good), as the grayling's flesh deteriorates very quickly. To appreciate this exquisite fish at its best, it should be eaten as soon as possible after being caught, perhaps over a camp fire on the river bank.

Wet-fly fishing

The tackle

The tackle is identical to that used for trout-fishing, that is to say a 9 foot (2.7 m) rod with a manual reel and a fine parallel or medium line. The point-fly must be heavy enough to work near the bottom. The dropper-fly is replaced by a fly placed in an intermediate position, designed to work just below the surface.

The flies should be made of materials which absorb water and sink quickly (boar's hair, for example).

The technique

This consists in casting three-quarters downstream: take care to cast a straight line out and then let it drift. Bring the team of flies to life by releasing and retrieving the line and by gently shaking the tip of the rod.

Some fishers simply follow the current, keeping the rod-tip at water level parallel with the line, letting the current work the flies. The line must not be too taut or the fish can easily slip the hook. Strike at the first touch. As you feel a slight drag or pause lift the rod with a quick deft movement, avoiding damage to the leader.

FISHING WITH A NYMPH

Fishing for grayling with a nymph is a subtle and exciting sport calling for lightning reflexes and keen eyesight. The technique is used both on the river-bed and at or close to the surface, and, depending on the depth, requires a range of equipment. Those who only occasionally fish with a nymph use no special tackle but content themselves with a classic 8ft 6in. or 9ft (2.6–2.7 m) trout rod. The real experts however use a shorter rod (7ft 6in./2.3 m) and leaders between 5'2 and 7'2 yards (5-7 m) long, which allow the nymph to be placed very gently and to enter the water immediately.

Nymph-fishing for grayling on the surface is similar to fishing for trout, but on the river-bed it is fundamentally different. Here you have to cast the line upstream of the rise, then let it drift until it is level with the fish.

At the precise moment you activate the nymph with little movements, making it appear to be swimming to the surface. The fly is often weighted, especially if the river is deep or there is a strong current.

You need to have very sharp eyesight: a pair of anti-glare polaroid glasses will help.

A good haul from the River Alagnon in France.

Wet-fly fishing at dawn on the Allier.

Fishing for grayling: two rules

Fish the correct "line":
The fly must pass precisely through the fish's window

Present the fly with utmost care:
As far as the first rule is concerned, one of the great difficulties is to observe and pinpoint the exact position of the rise, a task made even harder by the fact that it is difficult to judge distances accurately when you are wading in water up to your chest.

A rise in slow-moving or smooth water is easy to spot (likewise the effects of a bad drift!), although it is possible to confuse it with that of a trout or a dace. The grayling has a characteristic "surging" rise.

It is not the same in fast turbulent water. The ripples from the rise disappear at once, and often all you will see is a slightly ruffled surface. On the other hand, the grayling will not want to lose any prey passing within reach, and is often less wary and less sensitive to a bad drift.

Once the rise has been accurately pinpointed, the fly must be made to pass near to it so that it drifts into the fish's cone of vision (place the fly at a distance which is twice the depth of the river).

The second difficulty is good presentation of the fly, that is to say avoiding a poor drift and excessive drag, which might awaken the grayling's suspicion. Cast from a quarter downstream or straight across, so as to present the tackle fly-first, with the monofil out of sight.

It can happen that such casts are impossible because of the presence of obstacles. In that case one casts straight out at right angles to the current or at roughly 25 degrees downstream, always taking care to position oneself well to the side of the fish: rises are then easier to mark down, and the grayling find it harder to detect the presence of the angler. The fly-line should never be delivered in a straight line, or you will risk an immediate drag on the fly.

Delivering the fly-line and leader with a "wiggle" will delay the onset of drag. When one casts straight across the stream, it is almost obligatory to "mend" the line a number of times to counter drag.

All these unsightly casting techniques, which result in a seemingly untidy heap of line, will give the beginner the impression that the seasoned angler he is observing cannot in fact control his line. He must however be aware that these variations on the basic technique are part of the grayling specialist's repertoire.

There are times when a grayling will refuse a succession of well-presented flies. It is important to stress that in such situations a fish will sometimes rise to an artificial on its twentieth drift past. If this does not happen, do not hesitate to change patterns several times, even presenting the most extravagant models.

■ A fine grayling from the Allier, about to return to his element.

The Rainbow Trout

Queen of the reservoirs

Latin name: *Oncorhyncus mykiss*
Family: Salmonidae

■ *The backdrop to La Landie, one of the most beautiful reservoirs in Europe.*

■ *A beautiful rainbow belonging to the Kamloops strain.*

Introduced comparatively recently in France, the techniques of reservoir fishing have come to us from England, where they are highly popular.

These techniques are designed for catching rainbow trout, a fish specially adapted to these enclosed environments, and they offer new opportunities to fly-fishers!

Fishing with streamers

The tackle

The long casts you have to make require a 9 or 10 foot (2.7 or 3 m) progressive or tip-action rod.

You will need a No. 7 or No. 8 sinking line if the water is deep. In England, where they cast up to 50 yards (46 m), they use a special very short (10 yards/9 m) high density line, called a shooting head. It is attached to a 50 yard backing line, or "running line". Use a large capacity manual reel.

When you are fishing with a streamer, the leader is very short (between 18 ins and 3 ft/45 cm and 1 m), so as to be able to deliver the lure to the desired depth quickly. The diameter varies between 0.16 and 0.26 mm, depending on the size of the fish and the difficulty of the position.

The streamers

Apart from the ones which look vaguely like a fry, most streamers have nothing in common with any aquatic animal. With their bright colours and bizarre shapes, they serve mainly to provoke the fish's aggression.

Fishing method

This consists to begin with in casting as far as possible towards the open water, delivering the streamer deep down from the beginning of the retrieve: you must be very good at the double haul cast. The streamer is then retrieved, the left hand hand-lining in slow irregular movements, giving it a little shake from time to time: you proceed to " fish the water" either at random or methodically, in a fan.

Other imitations

Wet flies are used above all in cloudy or rainy weather, when a stiff westerly breeze ruffles the surface with little lapping sounds or when the insects are not hatching. This is the time to play on the fish's aggressive instincts by presenting the so-called attractors: brightly coloured flies with shining features. Among the ones most commonly used are: Alexandra, Butcher, Peter Ross, Zulu, Wickham's Fancy, Coachman and March Brown.

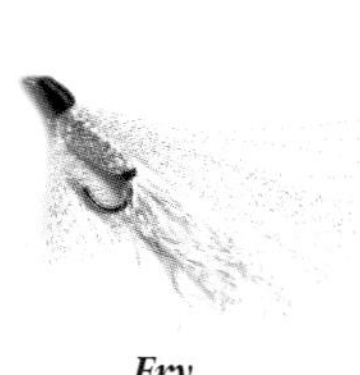

Fry

Dog nobbler

Exact imitations

Skilfully crafted by expert tiers, these are designed to imitate all the invertebrate that live in reservoirs, at different stages of their evolution. The chironomids are the most often used, because they form the most significant biomass. There are imitations of all their stages: larva, or bloodworm, for fishing on the bottom; the pupa, for fishing below the surface; and adult or imago. We should also mention the ephemerids (notably the famous *Ephemera danica* or mayfly) and the larvae of dragon-flies, coleoptera, hemiptera and trichoptera at all the stages of their development.

Shrimp imitation

Shrimp nymph

Fry streamer

Fry streamer

Sedge

The Shad

A ferocious fighter

Latin name: *Alosa alosa*
Family: Clupeidae

It is chiefly on the River Dordogne, from the dam at Bergerac down to Agen, that the shad is fished in France. They defend themselves with ferocious tenacity and for the angler who loves excitement they will provide some unforgettable experiences.

■ *The large shad is making a strong comeback in European rivers.*

Spoon-fishing

This is the most usual method.

The tackle

It must be tough enough to deal with this powerful fish. You will need a spinning rod, from 8 to 12 feet (2.4–3.6 m) long, fitted with a light fixed-spool reel containing 150 yards (137 m) of 0.26 or 0.28 nylon.

The lures

These are chiefly small shiny silver blade spoons (No. 1 or No. 2), attached to a single hook (Nos. 2-4), which ensures penetration of the fish's thick buccal membranes. The lure is weighted above with a coffin lead or a bored bullet, weighing 5 to 10 grams, depending on the depth of the water and the strength of the current.

■ *Spoons for shad are always fitted with a single hook.*

Fishing method

Having found a good position (at the head of a pool, downstream from rapids) the fisherman casts as far as possible straight across towards the opposite bank, then reels in the lure in an arc across the bottom. A touch will be felt as a sharp drag, followed by a steady pull and a series of rapid somersaults. The fish must be brought in quickly, because he is frequently only lightly hooked.

Fly-fishing

The tackle

A light one-handed salmon rod is enough, fitted with a large capacity manual reel containing an AFTM 9 sinking line attached to 50 yards (46 m) of backing line. The leader, which is no longer than 6 feet (1.8 m), should have a diameter of 0.26 or 0.28 mm. Some anglers use 12 to 14 foot (3.6–4.2 m) salmon rods with a line weight of AFTM 10-12.

Currently the flies most often used are large orange nymphs mounted on simple No. 7 or No. 8 hooks or on small double hooks. A brightly colored streamer will also work.

■ *Francois Grebot, an expert fly-fisher for shad.*

Fishing method

Start at the head of the pool and work your way down it. The shad will make himself known by rising, rolling in the water like a porpoise and breaking the surface with little snatching movements. Cast straight across, letting the line out in an arc pointing downstream, your rod at 45 degrees. Control the drift of the fly along the bottom with the left hand on the line.

The touch will be a sudden tug, followed by a violent attempt to escape. Just as when using a spoon, you should bring the fish under control and get him into the landing-net as quickly as possible.

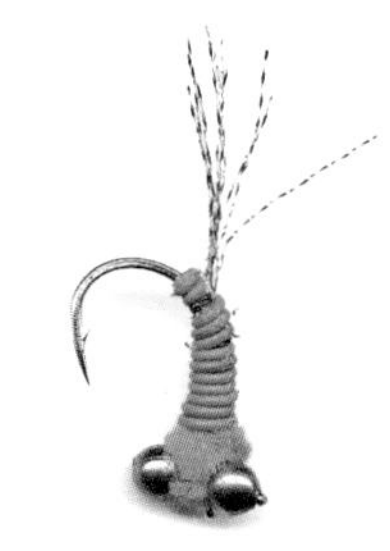

■ *Nymph weighted with beads from a wash-basin chain.*

■ *Nymphs for shad often look like small crustacea.*

Shrimp

The chars

The cristivomer

Latin name: *Salvelinus namaycush*
Family: Salmonidae

A native of the northern United States and central Canada, the lake trout, or Canadian char was introduced into some lakes in the Alps (the lac de Tignes, for example) and the Pyrenees from 1954 onwards. Formerly abundant in the Great Lakes in North America, it has suffered severe depredations from a parasitic species, the sea lamprey. The latter has invaded these regions using recently constructed canals which connect with the sea, steadily adapting themselves to freshwater conditions. A spawning migrant, it has settled in freshwater and brought disaster to the salmon farmers. In France the lake trout has chiefly been introduced into lakes at high altitudes, and this has sometimes necessitated the use of helicopters. This activity is now being restricted because of the ferocious appetite of the lake trout, who has the annoying tendency to feed himself at the expense of the indigenous trout. For this reason, the lakes situated within the Pyrenees National Park are no longer being stocked with fry. These activities are now confined to the lac d'Ardiden and the lac du Cap de Long.

■ ***The alarming appearance of the Northern Lake Trout with its powerful body and leopard spots and capacious jaws.***

FISHING FROM THE BANK

Fishing with a live minnow

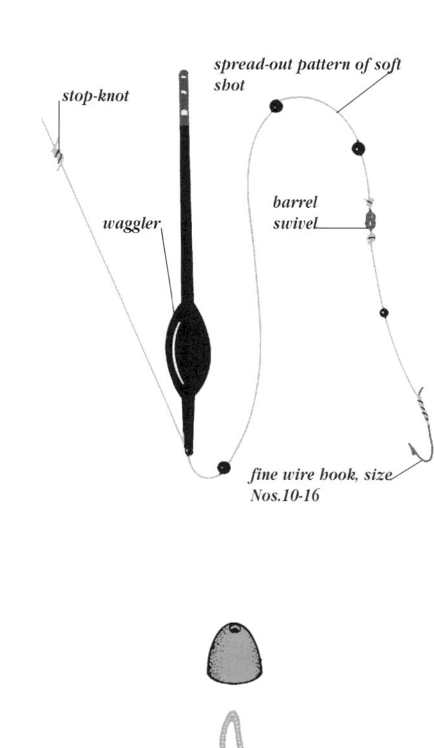

■ ***Classic European dead-bait mount.***

The minnow is certainly the "ultimate weapon" in high altitude lakes, but the problem is how to get them there when there are several hours' walking ahead of you. However, you can keep them alive for some time in a very cool thermos flask. The minnow, hooked by a single No. 6 hook through the top lip is cast gently into open water. With the aid of an olivette weight and a sliding float you can keep it at the required depth. The minnow can also be presented close to the bottom with the aid of a weight or a paternoster rig.

You can also let the minnow "roam". In this case it is better to use a long (20 to 25 ft./6–7.6 m) telescopic ringed rod. The live minnow, weighted at the head, is immersed and allowed to explore the slopes and the crevices in the rocks just below the bank. Skilfully handled it will undoubtedly be successful in enticing a lake trout.

These techniques can also be used with earthworms or a bunch of brandlings.

■ ***Lake trout caught with a wobbled minnow.***

SPINNING

Fishing with dead bait

This technique is also effective, because it allows you to fish at any depth, beginning with the shady areas near the bank, where there may be rocky overhangs, before exploring the open water by fan-casting. Using a dead minnow fixed to a helmet mount, this method is rather similar to that used with zander: retrieve the line slowly, pausing, and releasing and jogging it from to time. In deep lakes a bigger weight (8 to 10 grams) will be needed. The take, which is sometimes violent, will need a very well-controlled drag. The minnows can be kept in an ice-bag or thermos flask.

Fishing with spoons

There is a wide variety of spoons to choose from. You will need to use designs that sink and work near the bottom, with wide blades in the willow-leaf style, heavily weighted. No. 1 and No. 2 spoons (No. 3 for bigger fish) with wide blades or little wob-

■ *Flexible lures (two Vitalas on the left, a Shad with a lead-shad on the right) are very good for exploring deep water.*

blers can also work wonders at certain times of the day. Do not hesitate to choose models in different colours, and remember that sombre tints often produce better results in very clear water. Just as when fishing with dead bait, search the water meticulously at every depth.

Fishing with plug-baits

This is a very effective method at certain times of day, especially at dawn. Choose a big sinker (a Rappala Shad Rap, for example) to explore the water at all levels, alternately retrieving and releasing.

Fishing with flexible lures

This is similar to fishing with dead bait. React instantly to the take, which is usually quite gentle, because a lake trout will immediately let go of the lure. Again retrieve slowly, pausing and releasing.

Fishing with a bubble float

Less appealing than fishing with a short pole or whip, it nevertheless enables you to reach otherwise inaccessible fish and above all to offer the lake trout live insects (grasshoppers and crickets, for example) which he enjoys on summer evenings (especially those little crickets that live in high Alpine meadows or among the scree. The bubble float also allows you to use a live minnow at the surface, a deadly method when the fish leave the deep water in the middle of the season. Cast out into the open water, then, if you do not feel a touch, retrieve slowly, paying particular attention to the likely lies.

FLY-FISHING

Fly-fishing for lake trout is a wonderful experience, confined to the rare occasions when they come to the surface to rise for airborne insects, usually at dusk. In fact, this deep-water denizen is extremely spirited and pugnacious and puts up a remarkable fight. He will lose himself in the depths only to dart up suddenly to the surface to perform a spectacular somersault, an unforgettable sight in the fading light of the setting sun against a backdrop of magnificent mountain scenery. The basic tackle is much the same as that used when fishing for trout in reservoirs. Distance casting requires long rods (10ft., 10ft.6in., 11ft.). The fish's determined defense calls for a strong line, and a leader with a 0.18mm. tippet.

As for flies, see that you have some big sedges in neutral colours like gray or brown mounted on No.10 or No.12 hooks. In twilight there is a special technique which consists in making the flies drag while hauling in the line. Some fishers use big dressings that imitate the crickets that live at high altitudes. Whatever method you use, the lake trout's violent reaction means that your reel must have a very well-regulated drag. It is very important to avoid bullying the fish. It will fight to the last breath, often becoming unhooked as it lashes about desperately. The fisher will never forget the delicious taste of lake trout eaten under the stars...

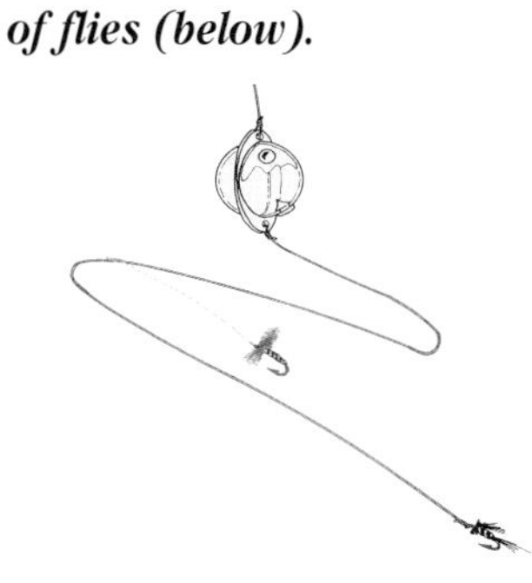

■ *Two ways of mounting a bubble-float: at the tip of the dropper (above), or above the team of flies (below).*

■ *Preparing the fish after a successful day.*

■ *A lake trout will sometimes come to the surface to snatch an insect. The fly-fisher must approach gently.*

Fishing for trout in high mountain lakes

■ ***You have to walk for many hours to reach the high mountain lakes of the Mercantour, but the trout and char will reward you.***

Fishing for lake trout often takes place in magnificent surroundings, and sometimes necessitates a long walk. They can reach quite a respectable size and are ferocious fighters. They are also very capricious and their behaviour is highly unpredictable, which usually means that you have to spend the night out, in a mountain refuge or under the stars.

Moreover camping in the mountains seems somehow the appropriate way to tackle this fish, whose unique nature, rarity and combativeness deserve such a sacrifice... if it really is a sacrifice for the true sporting fisherman!

The fishing methods are similar to those used when lake-fishing for brown trout, with one important exception: the lake trout keeps away from the light and will make his appearance at different depths during the course of the day, even during the course of a single hour, depending on the intensity of the light passing through the water. If a big cloud passes overhead, for example, the fish will swim towards the surface. Apart from those special moments at dawn and dusk, therefore, the fish must be sought in shaded areas.

This does not mean however that he avoids the light by staying in the deep water. Boulders and hollows affording dark hiding-places near the bank are excellent lies. Similarly, at any point where a stony gully or stream enters the lake there is a veritable aquatic labyrinth, a likely haunt of the lake trout.

If a search of these locations proves fruitless, look for the fish in the open water, and under rocky overhangs in the lake margins. It is very important to keep in mind the depth where the first take occurred, which will indicate the level at which the fish appear to be active.

The Canadian lake trout is on the whole less wary than other salmonids, because of his ravenous appetite, which leads him into committing all kinds of follies and indiscriminately attacking any lure or live prey passing within his reach.

Nevertheless the fisherman must display the greatest discretion when prospecting the edges of a lake that has steep banks. His silhouette will be perfectly visible to any trout lurking at a depth of 20 feet (6 m) in crystal-clear water.

The basic tackle should be as simple as possible, to avoid being overburdened. It should consist of a 9 to 11 foot (2.7–3.3 m) fly rod and light bait-casting tackle on a reel filled with strong line (0.18 to 0.20 mm), for catching big fish. Take plenty of warm woolly garments, a sleeping-bag and perhaps even a tent so that you can spend the night on the spot and enjoy those very special moments at dawn and dusk. And, a tasty meal of freshly caught fish cooked over a camp fire.

Another inhabitant of mountain lakes, but one which has also been introduced into many rivers in France, the brook trout behaves in very similar ways to the brown trout. He is however less suspicious, and, more important, has a voracious appetite. From observations in an aquarium we have seen that, like the black bass, he is a fish of rare intelligence, which quickly adapted to the new environment, and which in a few days had become one of the family, demanding his food by nudging the glass with his nose and performing somersaults above the surface. His appetite was insatiable: he was capable of swallowing such huge quantities of food (fry, worms and other titbits) that his distended stomach prevented him from making any movement and immobilized him at the bottom of the tank!

Fishing methods are similar to those used for the brown trout or for the lake trout. Ultra-light techniques are better for this determined defender, in lakes as well as in rivers, using small lures and natural baits. You can also use streamers, especially in shallow lakes.

Fishing with dry fly, streamer or nymph

The tackle

A strong 9 to 10 foot (2.7–3 m) progressive action rod is recommended.

An AFTM 7 or 8 weight line with a sinking tip. In big lakes you can use short 10 yard (9 m) shooting heads attached to 50 yards (45m) of fine light running line. This kind of tackle considerably increases your casting distance. The line is attached to a 0.18 mm monofilament leader, not more than about 3 feet (1 m) long. Use a manual reel.

Flies

Several different dressings can be used:

– heavily weighted Pallareta or pheasant-tail nymphs;

– brightly-colored wet flies, such as Alexandra;

– streamers and fly-lures, such as Marabou, Muddler Minnow or any of the other standard lures according to choice, the imagination of fly-tiers being limitless in this field!

Alexandra

Streamer

Palaretta

The Brook Trout

Latin name: *Salvelinus fontinalis*
Family: Salmonidae

Like the char, the front edge of the brook trout's pectoral, pelvic and anal fins are white.

Fishing method

The fish lie at different depths according to the prevailing conditions: sunshine, wind, waves, temperature. The fisher will therefore have to cast as far as possible in order to be able to explore different depths, beginning with the bottom. When using a streamer, give it a little jerking movement, by pulling the line slowly and then releasing it, making it appear like an injured fish. The touch may occur as the bait descends, in which case it will take the form of a gentle movement of the line, or as it rises, when it will be much sharper. The angler must strike at once.

Distance-casting for brook trout

In mountain lakes fishing with natural or live baits is certainly one of the most effective ways to catch brook trout. First of all the performance of the equipment used makes possible long-distance casts – not by any means a negligible factor when the fish are patrolling in the open water – beyond the reach of conventional casting. The fish may be found at any depth, most usually between 20 and 40 feet (6–12 m). The tackle consists of a traditional English rod of about 12 feet (3.6 m), fitted with a fixed-spool reel containing 150 yards (137 m) of 0.15 mm line.

An English float – the waggler – is designed to present the bait at a predetermined depth. The flexible flat weights are made from soft metal and narrow in diameter towards the hook-end of the rig to prevent tangles during casting. As the fish move continually at different depths depending on their mood and above all on the intensity of the light, you need to vary the levels at which you are fishing, until you find the right one... the one where the fish are!

A superb brook trout. Note the powerful jaws and capacious mouth of this lively and voracious salmonid.

The Arctic Char

Latin Name: *Salvelinus alpinus*
Family: Salmonidae

Lord of the depths, the arctic char is a native of large Alpine lakes, where he became marooned when the glaciers retreated. He has been introduced into a number of mountain lakes in the Alps, the Pyrenees and the Massif Central in France, where he is prized for the delicacy of his flesh. In Scandinavia he is a spawning migrant.

■ ***An arctic char caught in Lake Pavin in France with a dead minnow.***

FISHING WITH LURES

Fishing for arctic char using the traditional rod-and-line methods described in the section on the lake trout is only possible in some small mountain lakes. In bigger lakes the species is almost exclusively fished with a dragnet.

Fishing with a downrigger

■ ***An arctic char caught by the well-known fishing journalist Georges Cortay in Lake Victor, near the North coast of Quebec.***

The line consists of a thin steel line, 150 to 200 yards (137–182 m) long, attached to a 1 lb or 2 lb (0.5-1kg) weight and wound round a downrigger. A touch is detected by a steel rod with a little bell. A series of nylon leaders, from 5 to 10 yards (4.5–9 m) long are attached along the line. They are 0.30 mm in diameter and attached to the end are spinning and wobbling spoons, quite large and shiny. The line is slowly wound in, at a speed of not more than 2 m.p.h. The lures are sunk to a great depth, between 55 and 75 yards (50–68 m). When he catches a fish, the angler makes the rig pass through a series of concentric circles in an effort to catch further specimens, as the arctic char live in shoals.

OTHER KINDS OF FISHING

In small mountain lakes – the term is used to distinguish this kind of water from the big natural Alpine lakes, like Lake Geneva, where the use of a downrigger is not feasible – there are many other ways of catching the arctic char. The floating line described above works wonders, or fishing with a dead minnow can also be very effective if small mounts are used (taking into account the fish's narrow mouth) with No.16 to No.18 treble hooks. The minnow is retrieved very slowly along the lake bottom and then finally worked enticingly in the water directly beneath the boat.

It's often at this moment that the char decides to strike. Another method, a new introduction, is the tirette. The rig consists of an 8 to 10 gram sliding olivette on the main line, which has at the end a soft weight to protect the swivel, to which is attached a 16 in. (40 cm) long 0.12 mm hook-length carrying a No.10 to No.12 iron Sempe hook, with a long shank. The bait traditionally used is the tinea/clothes moth. In order to make the bait more visible to the fish in places where there are a lot of obstructions on the river-bed you can attach a little ball of polystyrene above the bait to keep it off the bottom. The fishing method consists in gently drawing the bait along the river-bed, holding it still from time to time.

The take, which may be quite gentle and easily mistaken for a snag, calls for an immediate strike.

These two arctic char experts prepare to fish with a downrigger, a traditional technique in high Alpine lakes, to catch these fish, which swim in shoals.

There is another innovation: the bombette. It is a kind of spindle-shaped weight, capable of being cast considerable distances and produced in various densities: there are floating ones, sinking ones and, perhaps most interesting, ones with a density close to that of water. These sink very slowly, which is an advantage when you are fishing for char, since they shun the light and are always on the move to lies where they feel more at ease. This variety of bombette will quickly reveal the level at which the fish are lying.

■ *In the breeding season, the arctic char displays a very fine reddish-orange livery.*

■ *All the salmonids taste delicious, cooked "en papillotte" over a wood fire.*

Cooking your fish over the camp fire

Preparing your fish for your supper according to a country recipe and then enjoying it under the stars must be one of the supreme pleasures of fishing. Cooking trout and char in the open needs very few ingredients. A Corsican recipe consists in taking a flat stone from the river-bed and heating it in a wood fire. When the stone is piping hot simply

rub some fat on it and lay the fish on top. The fish should not be very big: the little Corsican stream trout are excellent cooked like this. Five minutes' cooking on each side will release all the subtle flavours of a fish taken straight out of the water.

Another method is to cook the fish "en papillotte" in the ashes of a wood fire.

For this you use aluminium foil, which when folded takes up very little room in your pack. You can add herbs gathered on the spot, such as thyme or mint, which are sure to enhance the flavours of the freshly caught fish. Thus you do not have to take frying-pans, saucepans and other cooking paraphernalia, which take up a lot of room in your backpacks, and whose weight would begin to tell cruelly after a few days' walk.

The Great Migrants

Let us enter this magic world that haunts our wildest dreams: the world of big fish! This is the realm of the majestic salmon, the object of a real cult for some anglers, and of the mysterious sea trout.

Atlantic

A spectacular run of big Atlantic salmon on the river Vormo, Norway.

Salmon

The ocean athlete

Latin name: *Salmo salar*
Family: Salmonidae

Of all types of fishing, it is the pursuit of salmon that creates the most devoted followers; they are said to suffer from the strange malady "acute salmonitis". Stubborn and steadfast, they regard their sport as a way of life. Devoted to running water, to the surrounding splendours of nature and to this mysterious fish, this cult has something about it akin to the quest for the Grail, so rarely is one caught. However, owners of private estates and river beats in the UK and Ireland are presently running breeding and stocking programmes, in an endeavour to keep salmon in their rivers.

■ ***Dam operations expose some of the river bed and are partly responsible for the death of eggs and fry.***

SOME SPECIFICS OF SALMON FISHING

Salmon fishing is often likened to a lottery in which the outcome – the capture of one of these splendid migrants – owes much more to luck than good management. Although it is true a beginner may hook a salmon on his first cast, it must be noted that some 80 to 90 per cent of the fish caught in our waters are taken by a mere 10 per cent of the fishermen. Luck, which in fishing is anything but dependable, may occasionally favour some fortunate person a few times, but can never account for constant, repeated success. After all, a fisherman who takes fish is better than the others. He owes his superiority to a multitude of small details acquired through experience: in-depth knowledge of the terrain and the fish's haunts and behaviour; an ability to observe, to blend with the environment, and be unobtrusive. Nobody can

■ ***A rare sight: a pair of salmon over their spawning bed, on the upper river Allier, France.***

A settled salmon: the huchen

The huchen (*Hucho hucho*) is a magnificent salmon originating in central Europe (the Danube basin and its neighbourhood). Its introduction in France is currently under study, because it possesses some very interesting characteristics. First, its interest to anglers: the huchen reaches a respectable size (6 to 7 feet/1.80–2.20 m with a weight of up to 44 lb/20 kg); this fact, combined with its unusual combativeness make it a choice adversary for the game fisherman. Next, its role in controlling fish populations. This big predator lives in the upper and middle reaches of large rivers and eats good numbers of white fish, with the hotu forming the basis of its diet. Finally, its behaviour bears no resemblance to that of the anadromous Atlantic salmon. The huchen is a "sedentary" fish: it only undertakes short migrations upstream to breed. This makes its management and supervision easier. Some "wild" introductions have already taken place. Unfortunately, because of the small size and numbers involved, the local fishermen took the fish for "funny grey trout". And because the introduction of this fish is still forbidden in France, the release could scarcely have been accompanied by a fanfare of publicity and recommendations for careful treatment. Some attempts have been made to introduce it in Spain and Morocco. Like the Atlantic Salmon and other wild fish it is in great danger of decimation by pollution and lack of river management.

catch salmon regularly without knowing or "sensing" (the decided "feel" for the water that some anglers have) the precise outline of the river bed, the position of obstructions and the location of stopping and resting pools. Nor is this enough because, depending on the force and volume of the current, this or that stretch will be occupied or vacant, since the level of the river is the most important factor influencing the positioning and movement of the fish. Even a submerged stone can shelter a salmon immediately upstream, downstream, at its side, or not at all, depending on the level of the water. Only the experience of local anglers who know these places and how to exploit them can help the beginner or someone new to the water. Without a guide, the "stranger" can always put his trust in riverside car parks. When these are full of cars, it's a good spot. Even though two anglers may be fishing with great concentration in the same pool, fortune will smile on the one who fishes his lure at the right depth, exactly where he knows a fish is lying.

The behaviour of salmon towards lures or baits is so unpredictable and inexplicable that whole bibles have been written on the subject. We can only make some general remarks based on the experience and observation of various anglers, which may serve instead of comparative or statistical results or hard and fast rules.

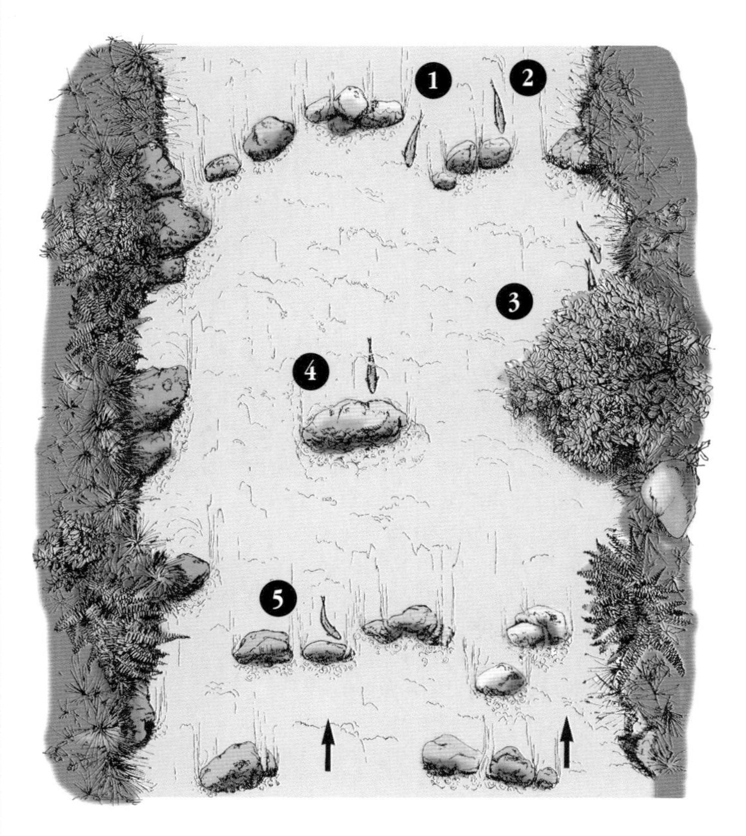

■ ***Salmon lies.***
1-2 - Entering the pool: bites often.
3 - Resting close to the bank: bites possible.
4 - Resting in mid-pool: bites unlikely.
5 - Leaving pool: bites.

■ *A superb Norwegian salmon caught on a spinner.*

Spinning with lures

Spinning, the method used by many salmon fishermen, is most effective at the start of the season when the water is high and cold and the fish, lacking strength, are unwilling to leave their resting places.

The tackle

In powerful rivers a rod of the type used on the Allier or in the Pyrenees is recommended, 10 to 12 feet (3–3.50 m) long and capable of casting up to about 80 g. In practice a pike or zander rod seems to perform perfectly well, especially when fishing rivers in Brittany, Normandy or Ireland. About 8 feet (2.50 m) long, it should be able to cast lures weighing from 8 to 12 g.

The fixed-spool spinning reel, heavy, medium or light according to the size of the river, is loaded with 500–650 feet (150–200 m) of 0.30 to 0.50 mm nylon line.

A relic leaps: a salmon in the Alagnon, a tributary of the river Allier, in Auvergne, France.

Lures

In many rivers the devon comes ahead of other lures at the start of the season. Some importance should be given to its size and colour. The most "fetching" colours are gold, silver, red, brown and blue. Fishermen in the Pyrenees and on the Allier often dress their devons with a skirt cut from a piece of red and black striped gas tubing. In Great Britain, small wooden devons work so well that they account for 80 per cent of the catch at the beginning of the season. The advantage of devons is that they can be fished deep, efficiently exploring the lowest levels of the water. Their disadvantage is that they twist the line. This can be lessened by putting a barrel swivel 20 inches (50 cm) above the lure and using a cast slightly thicker than the line itself.

Spinners make excellent lures. The shape of the blade is chosen according to the strength of the current, long blades being preferable in a strong current, and oval (fluttering) blades in slow, deep waters. Spinners are normally weighted at the head with a boat-shaped lead of about 8–30 g. Choose from size 2 to 4.

Wobbling spoons, self-weighted (excellent) or with a weight on the line 2 feet (60 cm) above, usually have a very long, dull, blade (some anglers put them in vinegar to remove the shine). A weight of 10–30 gm is chosen according to the height of the water and the strength of the current. These lures have the advantage of offering low resistance to the current, and they work well in deep water.

Despite their effectiveness plug baits are little used (the reason is the cost; the beds of most large rivers are real lure traps). A size in the range from 3 to 6 inches (8–15 cm) is chosen according to the height of the water, the smallest being reserved for when it is low and clear.

Many anglers persist in using very heavy tackle (a big rod, thick line and large lures). In fact it so happens, especially in the summer, that the finer the line and the smaller the lure, the greater the success.

In Ireland, for example, we saw that fishing with 0.22 to 0.26 mm nylon line and size 1 or 2 spoons weighted with a swan shot significantly increased the number of bites – and this was no accident. Just as with a fly, the lure is more mobile and works better when not being winched along on a cable. Casting can be quieter and more accurate, and the lies can be fished more efficiently. One precaution: change to a heavy wire hook.

■ ***A fine Scottish double taken on the Spey.***

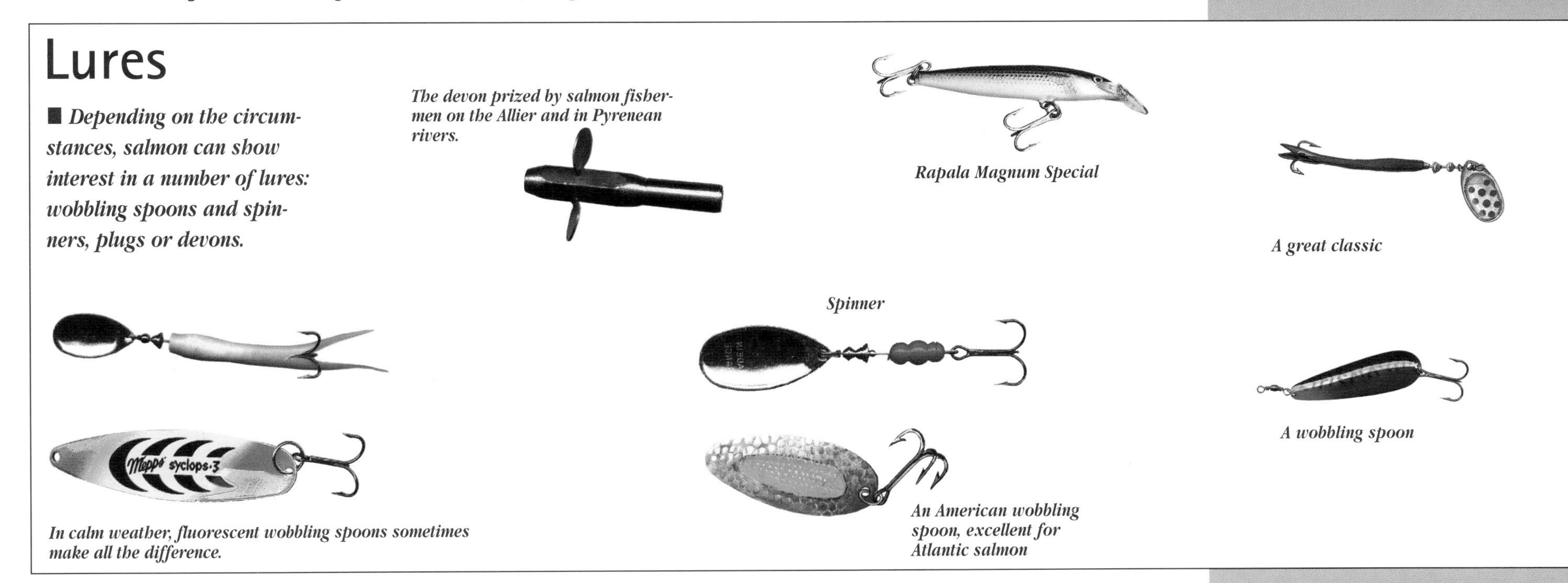

Lures

■ ***Depending on the circumstances, salmon can show interest in a number of lures: wobbling spoons and spinners, plugs or devons.***

The devon prized by salmon fishermen on the Allier and in Pyrenean rivers.

Rapala Magnum Special

A great classic

Spinner

A wobbling spoon

In calm weather, fluorescent wobbling spoons sometimes make all the difference.

An American wobbling spoon, excellent for Atlantic salmon

Fishing method

Highly distinctive, fishing takes place downstream. The angler stands at the head of the pool and casts directly across to the opposite bank or three-quarters downstream. He may sometimes have to cast slightly upstream to make sure the lure attains the right height above where the salmon is thought to be. He then lets the lure sweep round in an arc to his own side, using the reel to control the drift, and avoiding turning the handle as much as possible, since this causes the lure to accelerate and rise in the water. The lure should just brush the bottom; retrieval should be made only at the end of the swing or when winding in the amount of line necessary for proper control of the lure. When the lure approaches the presumed lie, it can be held back and let go a few times, changing the way it swims to provoke the salmon's aggression or arouse its curiosity. This is a very suspicious fish, so it is essential to avoid the dull sound of the spoon or devon hitting the water. When casting, lightly brake the line coming off the reel with the index finger, and lower the rod at the same time. This also helps to avoid catching the spoon on the lead above it. This downstream technique should be carried out with great care, progressing slowly down the pool.

Though from time to time the bite of the salmon can be unbelievably violent, it may also be quite unobtrusive and betrayed only by a slight stoppage. If in the least doubt, strike vigorously. Because this is a fish with such a spectacular defence, the drag needs to be correctly adjusted (not so heavy as to break the line, but firm enough to set the hook properly). The hook points are continuously making contact with pebbles, so they should be inspected and sharpened regularly.

■ ***Grilse come up the rivers in fine weather. This one took a plug bait.***

The salmon

Description

■ ***A male breeding salmon.***

The adult salmon is a magnificent fish with a long spindle-shaped body covered in small silver scales The broad stemmed tail fin is slightly indented, and the greyish adipose fin has no red spots. The long, pointed head has a mouth reaching back to below the eye. Only the rear part of the vomer bears teeth. Young salmon can be mistaken for trout; they are distinguished from them by the indented tail and the fact that the jaws join just forward of the level of the eye. There are six or seven highly visible bluish markings on the sides.

Colouring

The adult has a grey back, and is lighter on the sides, turning to silver with irregular black spots. During spawning, the male acquires striking colours: yellow sides with red spots on the gill covers.

How to distinguish salmon from trout?

Look for three features:

- The salmon has a smaller mouth. The end of the jaw does not pass the level of the eye, which it does in the trout.
- The tail fin is deeply indented in the salmon, slightly in the trout.
- The adipose fin, bluish in the salmon, has an obvious orange-red border in the trout.

If it is difficult to tell, the best thing is to return the fish to the water: most often a "funny trout" is a salmon

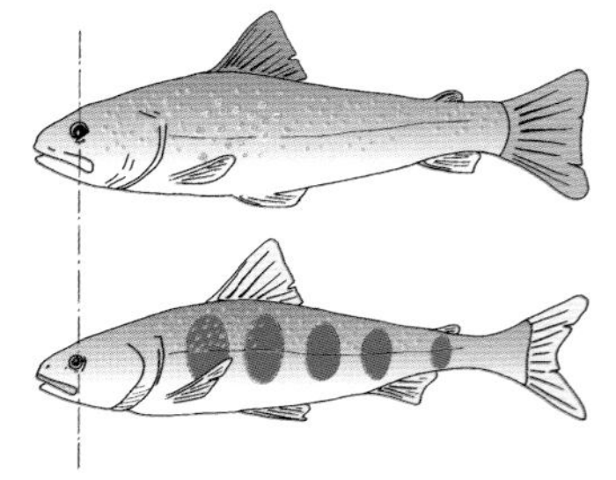

■ ***A trout (above) and a salmon (below).***

The ocean athlete

■ *The slender silver shape of an adult salmon.*

Size
From 20 inches (50 cm) up to 4 feet (1.20 m) for the largest specimens, at a summer weight for grilse of 4–6 lb (2–3 kg), 11–17 lb, (5–8 kg) for spring salmon, and between 20 and (exceptionally) 50 lb (9–23 kg) for winter salmon.

■ *A silvery little salmon: a smolt just before its descent to the sea.*

Habitat

During the first two years of its life the salmon lives in fresh water, in the upper reaches of specific rivers.
It then enters the ocean for a period of from one to four years, before migrating to the spawning grounds to reproduce.

Biology

Diet
The diet of young salmon is identical to that of young trout. The adults feed mainly on crustaceans and fish taken out at sea (prawns and herrings). They do not generally feed during their passage upriver.

Reproduction
The salmon lays its eggs in fresh water between November and December in the upper reaches of particular rivers. Each female prepares one or more redds in the gravel in shallow, richly oxygenated water. To make these depressions, she lies on her side and strikes the riverbed with her tail, removing the sand from a roughly circular area some 2 feet (60 cm) in diameter. The male then joins the female and stays at her side. As soon as the eggs, numbering some 2,000 to 3,000 per kilogram, are laid, they are fertilized by the milt from the male. The eggs incubate for about 90 days. During this period the male defends the redd from predators, but as the weeks pass its aggressiveness lessens. About two months after the eggs are laid, the exhausted parents attempt a downstream journey from which many of them will not return.
The alevins remain in the redd for a few days after they hatch, then disperse in the current to occupy the same habitat as trout. After two years they become smolt, miniature silver-coloured salmon, and descend to the sea to feed and grow.

Behaviour

To touch on the behaviour of the salmon brings up the story of an extraordinary traveller, but above all it makes us wonder about the mysterious instinct,
the fantastic sense of direction that unfailingly guides it in a 3,000 mile (5,000 km) journey to its native river, some years after its descent. The salmon is an anadromous migrant, that is, it reproduces in fresh water but passes the whole of its period of growth and fattening in the sea. Though as a salmon parr it shares a world of rapid currents and waterfalls with the trout, after two years, at a length of about 8 inches (20 cm), it undergoes strange physiological and morphological changes. Its colouring, which until this time could often be confused with that of a trout, takes on the splendid silver hue and fine iridescence of the adult. The transformation to a smolt is induced by hormonal changes. However, the transformation does not account for the psychological "trauma" that unleashes in the smolt an imperative need to migrate downstream, nor for the fact that it already possesses the necessary information enabling it to orientate itself in the vast expenses of the sea. During its voyage to the sea the smolt conserves its energy by taking to the swiftest currents. Then, travelling as far as 30 miles (50 km) per day it reaches the food rich zones of the north Atlantic, off the coast of Iceland and the Faeroe Islands and towards the Davis Strait.
It should be noted that some smolt (mainly in Iceland, Ireland, and Scotland) stay close to the estuaries and never make this journey. The salmon remain in the fattening zones for one to four years; thanks to an abundance of prawn, herring, smelt and sardines they grow very rapidly, then return to the river of their birth to reproduce. Many questions about the mysterious sense of direction remain unanswered, and many hypotheses have been advanced to explain it. The salmon may orientate itself by the position of the sun. This is not a sufficient explanation, because the frequently bad weather conditions in the north Atlantic would not allow continuous guidance. Other hypotheses have been advanced, such as the influence of the earth's magnetism, to which the salmon does not seem very sensitive, or variations in the force of gravity (weaker at the equator than at the poles), or the effect of electromagnetic fields; none is satisfactory. Recent studies carried out in Norway claim the possibility that descending smolt mark their river of origin with bile salts. Some years after the descent, thanks to an extremely well-developed sense of taste and smell, the adult salmon would then be able to detect infinitesimal quantities of these substances diluted in enormous volumes of water. The final hypothesis is that the fish has a genetic memory. Marked parr from Norwegian eggs artificially hatched in the upper reaches of the Allier, in France, have been found in their river of origin five years later. Some salmon arrive at the spawning beds in the winter, between October and January. Known as winter salmon, these are the largest and their weight can far exceed 10kg. They stay in fresh water for a year, and tend to settle in certain pools. Others, spring salmon (also called grilse) arrive in June or July. These are smaller and rarely exceed 3 kg. They ascend the river very quickly. The fish frequently pause for a few days in resting pools on the way up the river.
In our waters, the ascent is becoming more and more difficult. Nets are placed in the estuaries, weirs may not be equipped with fish ladders, or are poorly provided, (a fish ladder is not necessarily used if the placechosen for it is not on a migration path, because there is too little water, for example), then there is extraction of sand and gravel, and a great deal of pollution. By the time they reach their breeding

➤➤➤

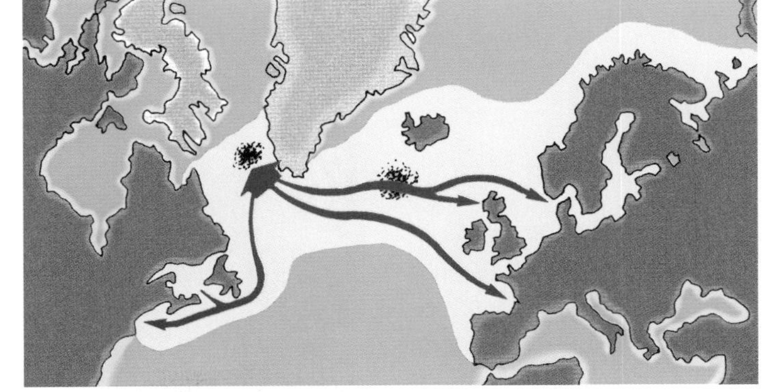

■ *The principal zones where salmon fatten are off the Faeroe Islands and Greenland.*

■ *Ascending salmon make use of specially created fish ladders to circumvent barriers such as weirs.*

Fishing with prawns

Cette technique est particulièrement efficace lorsque les eaux se réchauffent et s'éclaircissent. C'est sans doute la seule qui puisse tenter un saumon « calé » au fond d'une fosse.

■ *Mounting a prawn.*

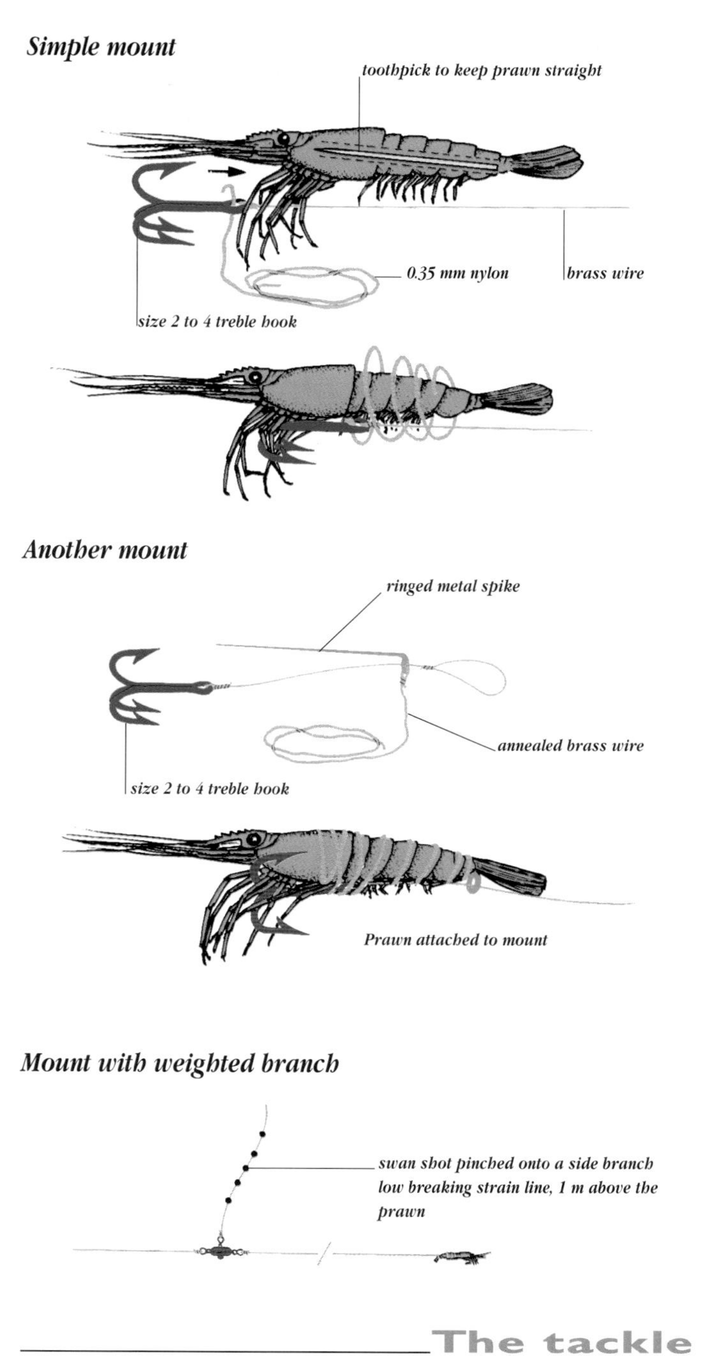

The tackle

The tackle described in the section on spinning will do, but fishing really deep water is easier with a long, supple 13-16 foot (4-5 m) rod that gives better control of the bait.

A light spinning reel is recommended, with a wide spool loaded with 325 feet (100 m) of 0.28 to 0.35 mm nylon line, according to the river.

➤➤➤

grounds the unfortunate fish have lost half their weight and a third of their number: anglers only account for a minute fraction. If urgent measures are not taken to improve the management of the few salmon rivers remaining in France, in a few years' time we will be able to say goodbye to this magnificent migrant. This is a devastating comment, considering that metropolitan France possesses one of the richest hydrographic resources in all Europe.

A report published in 2000 in the UK states that salmon are extinct in six small rivers in Scotland.

The mysterious behaviour of the salmon raises many questions. So far nobody has been able to define the factors that trigger its anadromous migration with any precision. The salmon apparently obeys some kind of impulse that drives it to return to its native river even though it has not reached sexual maturity. Thus it is not just a matter of a simple internal or external sexual stimulus. Recent studies in Scotland have cast some doubt on the theory that salmon always return to the river of their birth (homing). Fish marked in a certain river were found in another river in the breeding season, at a time when low water precluded ascent of the first. Thus salmon do not always follow the rules, but change their behaviour according to the conditions around them.

Other observations, of Baltic salmon, show that they habitually ascend their native river three times in a single lifetime (rare in their fellows), and that they feed in fresh water.

This curious behaviour may be explained by the slight difference in salinity between this inland sea and fresh water. One theory has been advanced that the death of the parent fish some weeks after the task of reproduction, or during their descent to the sea, may be due to causes other than exhaustion. The stress caused by adapting to differences in salinity may also have a harmful effect. Finally we can refer to the very interesting experience of American investigators working on the King, or Atlantic salmon. Introduced to the Great Lakes, this anadromous migrant has adapted perfectly to life in fresh water and

■ ***A male pink Pacific salmon, its body deformed as the spawning season draws near.***

■ *A fine silvery King salmon from the river Karluck (Alaska), taken spinning with a Blue Fox spoon with its vibrating bell.*

completes its whole life cycle therein. Thus, just like the marine lamprey that has colonized these areas, this salmon migrates up small tributaries to reproduce, but remains in the great expanses of fresh water during its period of growth, apparently unperturbed by this radical change in lifestyle. The sockeye, another Canadian salmon, can reach adulthood and reproduce when landlocked in fresh water.

A symbol of our fresh waters and the wealth of our fishing heritage, the salmon is gradually giving up its secrets. Many questions are still without answers, but surely it is not surprising that this, our handsomest, noblest fish should be slow to reveal the secrets of its amazing biological potential?

■ *Mudbank formation.*

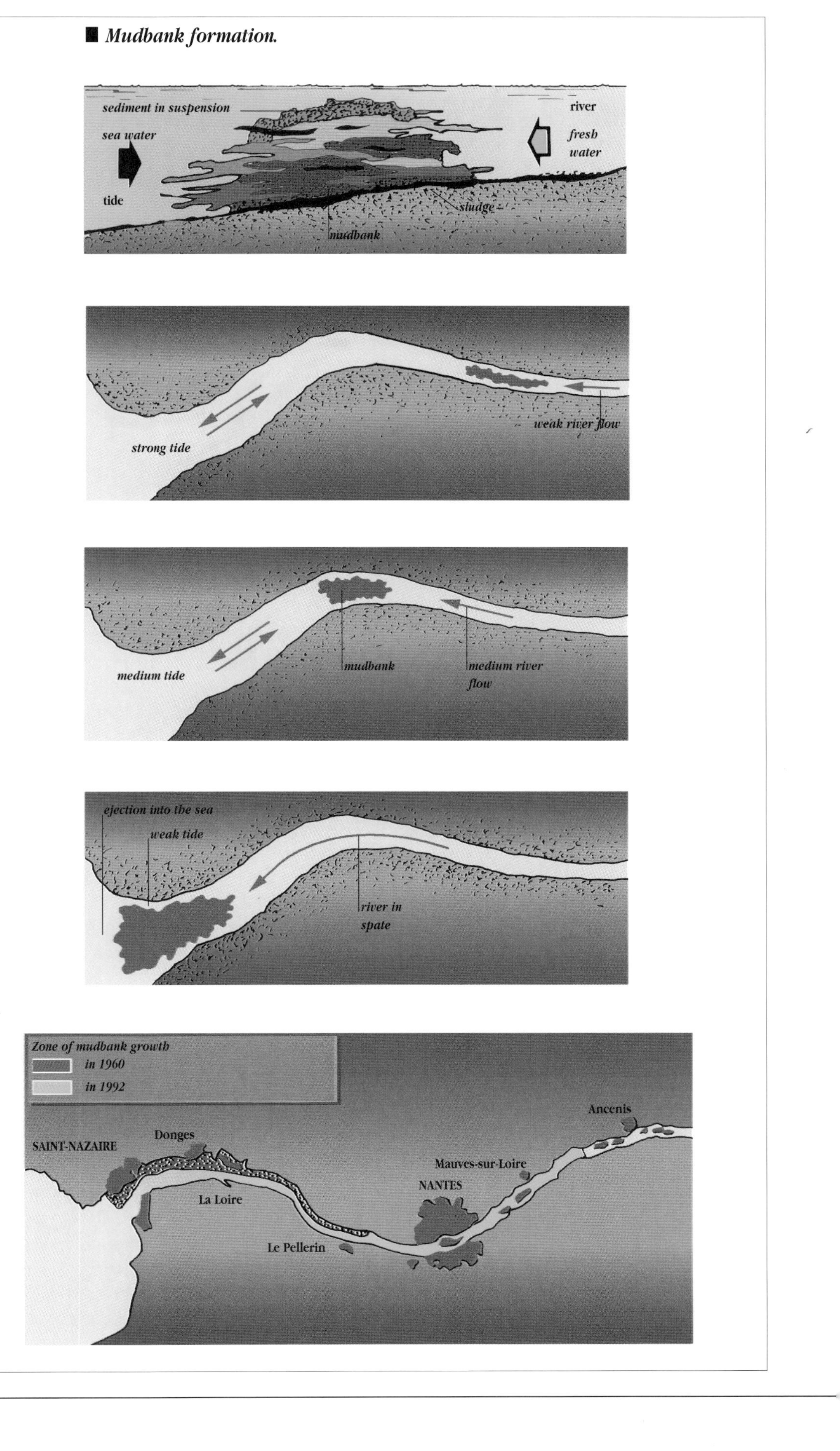

■ *Jean Luc-Martin's "mouse" or prawn-style devon.*

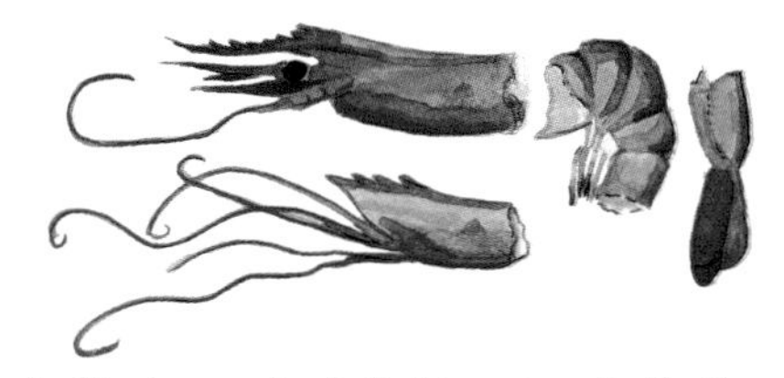

1 - The prawn is shelled to separate the thorax and antennae, the front legs attached below the head, the body, and the tail.

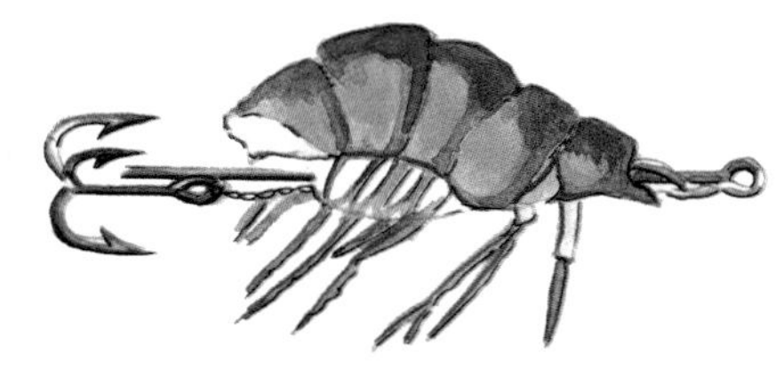

2 - The body is assembled on the shank, the axis of the devon mount.

3 - The part below the head is fixed under the body, up against the treble.

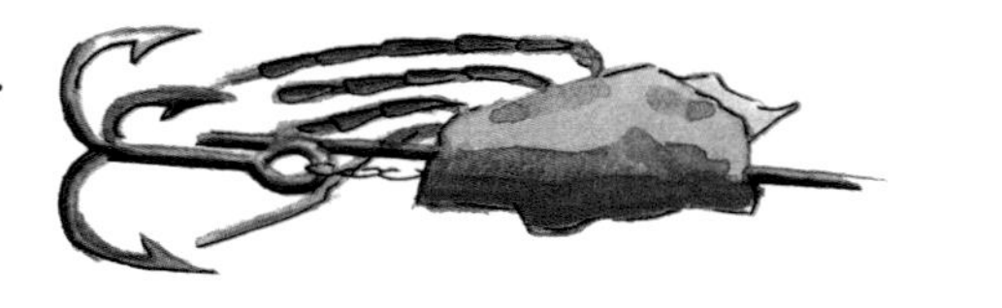

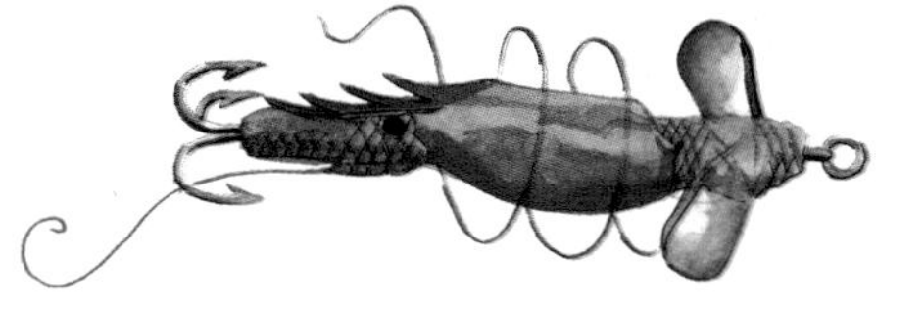

4 - The whole is securely bound.

5 - The rigid thorax is placed over the assembly and tied.

Prawns

Prawns 2-3 inches (6-8 cm) long or grey crayfish are suitable. They are preserved in pure glycerine, kept upright in the jar by means of a matchstick passed up through the body from the end tail segment to the thorax. There are various systems for mounting the prawn on the treble hook (naturally they all make the prawn swim backwards). The simplest consists of impaling the prawn on a fixed metal pin bearing a ring through which the line passes. The ring holds the tail of the prawn with the fin removed. Some pink brass wire is wound around the prawn from the ring down to the treble. The end may be passed through the head of the prawn. Fixed in line some 30 inches (80 cm) above the prawn is a paternoster swivel which takes a 2-2.5 inches (5-6 cm) length of low breaking strain nylon (0.22 mm) weighted with two or three swan shot.

■ ***Success in one of the most famous pools in the world: Rich Pool, at Ballina on the river Moy, in County Mayo, Ireland.***

Fishing method

Cast above the presumed lie and allow the bait to sink to the bottom. Guide it so that it drifts towards where the fish lies, working the prawn like a fly, holding and releasing it to imitate the jerky swimming movement of the crustacean. It is important to make the bait work close to the bottom. If a fish has been seen, make the bait skip about on the spot close by to aggravate the fish's curiosity or merely to irritate it into action.

Worm fishing

Although worm fishing horrifies fly purists, it is nonetheless very subtle. It also disturbs a salmon lie a great deal less than noisy hardware and for this reason is often tolerated on stretches intended solely for the fly when the water is coloured. The tackle and mount are the same as described for the prawn, with a heavier reel and line (from 0.35 to 0.40 mm). A single size 2 hook weighted with a side branch is baited with two fine black-headed worms. Cast to a likely spot, taking care to fish close to the bottom. The bite is often signalled by barely perceptible tugs. Give the fish plenty of time to bite and only strike when you are sure the line definitely moves up- or downstream.

■ ***When the water is coloured, the earthworm or "garden fly" is indispensable.***

Fly fishing

To aesthetes fly-fishing for salmon is the height of the art, the only method of capture truly worthy of such a noble adversary. Most effective when the waters are warm and become low and clear, it can also be considered, using big tube flies, at the start of the season.

The tackle

To the beginner the choice of a rod is not obvious. Single-handed? Two-handed? How long? So many difficult questions to answer. Generally speaking, the choice is affected by the width of the river and the physical constitution of the angler. Those who are slight of build will have difficulty handling a 20 foot (6 metre) cudgel for a whole day, although the materials in use today (carbon fibre or graphite) do permit such fancies. It must also be remembered that a long rod gives better control over the way the fly drifts, which is something to be recognised when the wide counter-currents to be cast over cause the line to snake. However, try to borrow some rods to see which suit you best.

For small British or Irish rivers a single-handed rod of 10–12 feet (3–3.50 m) with a No. 8 or 9 line is sufficient.

In North America, fly-fishermen much prefer to fish for salmon with a single-handed rod, "just for fun".

Pyrenean rivers and rivers like the Allier require tackle better suited to long casts: a two-handed 16–20 foot (5–6 m) rod designed for use with a No. 11 or 12 line.

Moderate quality is unacceptable in that essential piece of tackle, the reel. The large capacity spool should take a 40 yard (36 m) DT9 to DT12 line, joined to about 220 yards (200 m) of 30 lb (14 kg) breaking strain Dacron. All systems must be completely trustworthy, especially the drag.

There is a line to suit every set of conditions depending on the height of the water and the season. For fishing in big holes and deep pools at the start of the season, a line that sinks or has a fast-sinking point is needed. Following the spring, when the water temperature rises and goes over 10 °C, the salmon are more willing to leave their positions to take a fly in mid-water or close to the surface. At this time, a floating double-tapered line is recommended. One can also fish with a greased line i.e. about 10 inches (25 cm) below the surface.

The thickness of the monofilament cast depends on the size of the fly. It should be chosen with care since it greatly influences the way the fly drifts, allowing it to move freely or, if not suitable, holding it back. For flies tied on size 8 to 10 hooks, use 0.24 to 0.26 mm nylon; for hook sizes 2, 4, and 6 use 0.30 mm, and 0.40 mm for the largest flies. The cast is generally not more than 10 feet (3 m) long; remember that the longer the cast, the deeper the fly will sink.

Flies

Choosing flies is a real headache; there have been so many books on the subject, each more comprehensive than the last, there's no point in enlarging on the matter. One basic observation emerges from all these studies: no fly is infallible and all may take a fish one day or another; the skill and manner of presentation, in the right place, at the right time, count at least as much as shape and colour.

All flies are tied on hooks with upturned eyes. Unlike those intended for trout, salmon flies are not supposed to imitate an insect, more a small fish in flight, a prawn or some other little beast which is hard to reproduce like anything you might find in our waters.

These lures, then, are designed to move about in fairly deep water and must have a certain degree of flexibility and translucence that render them lively and attractive. The choice of tying materials is fundamental. Some anglers use nothing but animal hair that moves very

■ *Various English and Scottish streamers created for the Atlantic salmon.*

■ *A fine Atlantic salmon from the Sainte-Marguerite river (Quebec).*

Dark water, dull colour.

■ ***English streamers are often armed with double hooks.***

Tube fly

Bomber

Brittany

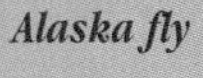

Alaska fly

naturally in the water and does not clump together. Others use feathers of different stiffnesses to suit slower or faster waters. Various cunning mixtures of fur and feather of different texture can be thought up depending on how bulky a fly is to be (thinly dressed for low water, heavily for coloured water), or on the movement it is to be given in the water. There is soft hair (squirrel), stiff hair (deer), and bristle (boar, badger). The best feathers are relatively soft and are chosen from species such as partridge, pheasant, peacock or grey heron.

The slower and deeper the water to be fished, the more all the elements of the fly must work in response to the least prompting from the angler. In such places, one might think of using a fly whose body is dressed in boar bristle and the wings and hackles in pheasant or peacock feather. Flies entirely dressed with hair are mostly intended for rapid waters.

Colour also seems to be fairly important – shades of blue, and red, yellow, black or reddish-brown are the most appreciated. In this context, some swear by the "country fly", thinly dressed in neutral colours and highly effective when in expert hands.

Some flies are famous. For low, warm water, there are the Jock Scott, the Silver Doctor, and the Lemon Grey, tied on size 4 to 8 hooks with hair or feather, depending on whether the water to be fished is fast or slow. Tube flies are mostly used at the start of the season. They come in four sizes: 25, 35, 45, and 50 mm (the Scandinavians use them up to 80 mm long). They consist of a light plastic tube, or something heavier, in aluminium (bronze is very heavy and difficult to fish, but also used). Depending on the appearance and action hoped for in the water, the head of the tube is dressed with a tuft of hair forming a crown, or with the fibres left long. Tube flies are always armed with a treble hook.

Finally, it has to be accepted that there is no miracle fly. Some flies are suited to certain light levels (for example, dull designs are suitable in overcast conditions) and to the state of the water, but equally or perhaps even more, to the fish's imagination. Size is important too. As the season passes the flies used become smaller. It is difficult to make a choice: a good fisherman will change his fly several times in the course of a day's fishing.

Certain flies have long been proven effective, but others have not, and of these, how many are still sitting in the box without ever having been tried, just for a lack of faith?

Don't be shy to ask your ghillie or the local fishing club which type of fly you should tie, or buy. The range is enormous and each river, and even individual beats of the river, has its own special fly, tried and tested by the local fishermen. Give it a try!

Real purists land their fish by hand.

Fishing method

Managing a two-handed fly rod does not present any special problems, and may even seem easier to the beginner than an apprenticeship with a single-handed rod. The action consists of casting the fly at right angles to the opposite bank, or slightly downstream, depending on the strength of the current, and making it sweep a particular area in an arc. It is important not to make false casts that could scare a fish in its lie: the line is lengthened gradually by shooting it a little at the end of each sweep. The line should be cast as straight as possible so the current acts on the line right away, moving the fly and making it fish from the moment it enters the water.

Small movements of the rod tip can make the fly more attractive. Hold a loop of about 25–30 inches (65–80 cm) of line with the right forefinger or between the thumb and forefinger of the left hand, for use when there is a bite. At the end of the drift, when the line is taut and parallel to the bank, lift it with a clean, strong movement to shoot an extra metre or two, and sweep a new area downstream.

In the heart of Ireland, finally a dream comes true!

Short casts are all the more effective because they give perfect control over the way the fly drifts. There is little point in casting 115 feet (35 m). A good distance is between 50 and 65 feet (15 and 20 m), hence the usefulness of waders for reaching a swim. Nor is there any point in persisting with a fish that is not biting; it will only take fright. After two or three passes, carry on fishing and come back later and offer it a smaller fly, or one of a different colour, whatever strikes you at the time.

Though fly-fishing for salmon fishing is relatively easy in running water, the same does not hold for dead water, in holes and slow pools, when the method is only effective if there is a strong wind or rain to ruffle the surface. Here you should cast downstream and create a false drift by retrieving the fly in arm lengths, giving it some movement with the tip of the rod.

■ ***A fine setting for the king of fish on his last journey.***

■ *This Norwegian salmon fell for a wobbling spoon. Belly up, it is brought carefully to the bank.*

When fishing with a greased line, i.e. near the surface, the bite can sometimes be seen as a slight swirl. In deep water it may show itself in various ways: a pull, a heavy tug, a violent check, a movement of the line. Some salmon fishermen do not strike, others may strike on the bite. On the whole it seems preferable to let the fish take the line held in reserve (the aforesaid 25-30 inches / 65-80 cm) before raising the rod in a vigorous strike.

A salmon may take the fly in different ways. It can come up directly on the lure, or approach it sideways while turning, sometimes making a complete turn.

How long the fight lasts depends on many factors: the size of the fish (obviously old male fish are more combative than grilse), the width of the river, and the temperature of the water (the defence is less energetic in cold water). One golden rule: never try to dominate the fish. When it heads at full speed for a worrying obstruction downstream, simply breaking contact by slackening the line may be enough to make it stop and return upstream. The salmon is played with the rod raised until, its energy drained, it comes to the end of its strength; the final rush is often fatal.

The final stage should be conducted in a manner appropriate to the dignity of this noble adversary. Remember, you may wish to relaease this fish, especially if it is a hen salmon, therefore it should not be damaged or totally exhausted.

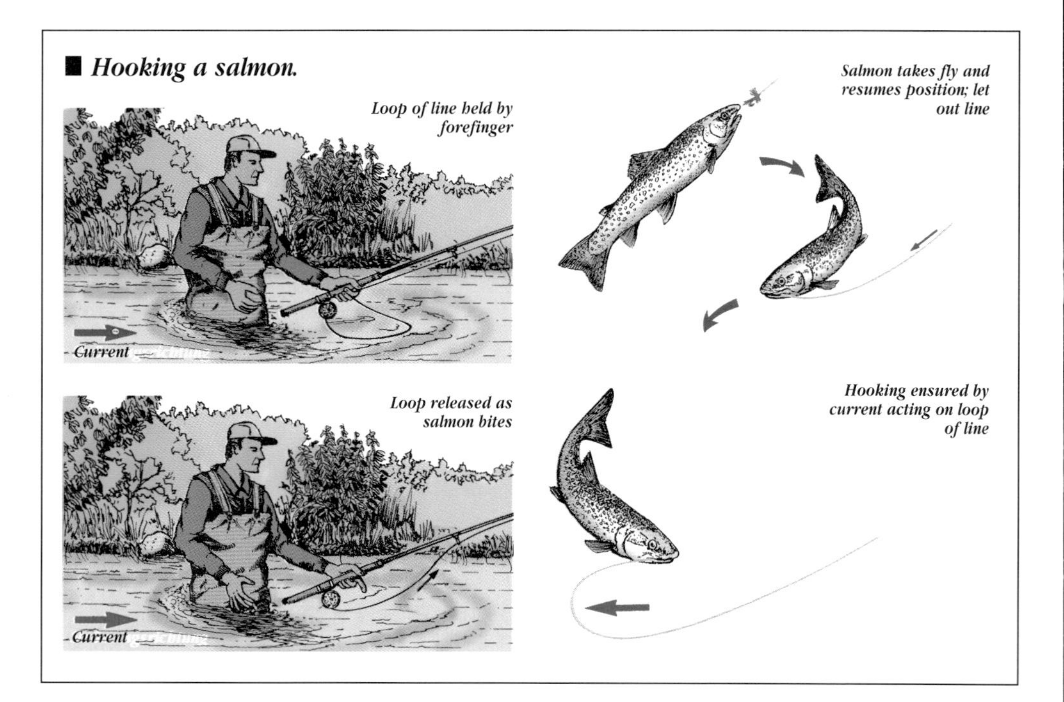

■ *Hooking a salmon.*

Why do salmon bite?

There has been a succession of theories to explain the curious phenomenon that leads salmon, which do not feed in fresh water, to succumb to skilfully presented natural baits (worms or prawns). If this behaviour does not involve the feeding reflex, what other explanation can there be? Aggression, curiosity, territorial defence, the memory of feasts at sea, are other probable hypotheses. Above all, when they enter the coastal rivers, the fish are aggressive. They are setting off to discover a fundamentally different, unknown and hostile environment and may feel an overwhelming need to impose themselves within a certain perimeter by chasing off intruders. This aggression fades as they ascend, giving way to concern about the coming spawning and the need to rest in deep pools. It is reawakened whenever the fish's environment suddenly changes, as in a sudden flood for example, stirring the idling fish to continue its journey upstream and explore new territory.

How do salmon show themselves?

Salmon show themselves in a spectacular manner by leaping, by smacking the surface of the water with their tails, by rising and by 'porpoising'. When a salmon comes up from deep water and makes several jumps in different places, it is the act of a settled fish not generally in biting mood. On the other hand, a fish that rises quietly or makes slight swirls on the surface is often irritated and may bite. In this case, take it on without delay. You may have just the fly to tempt him to make that fatal snap.

When do they bite?

It is an indisputable fact that salmon bite whenever they move on. Any piece of water may undergo a radical change and induce them to attack when presented with a lure or a bait. The best time is around midday, and in summer the evening can be good too. Weather conditions also play an important part. When the sun shines out of a cloudless sky, the results are not always too good. By contrast, a shower can be propitious, especially if it comes with a west wind that ruffles the surface of the water. Salmon seem to dislike a flat calm; at a pinch a storm is to be preferred. Some anglers hold that salmon fishing is totally unproductive when there is no wind. In fact the ideal weather would be cloudy, or with sunny spells alternating with showers driven by a west wind. The water level is also important. A slow spate is promising. When the river turns into a raging torrent carrying along branches and debris, there's no point in fishing. A generally very favourable time is when the water is clearing after a spate.

Where do they bite?

Salmon always ascend the same rivers and make use of the same runs, sheltering behind permanent obstacles such as rocks, the foot of a cliff, a bridge pier, or a sunken tree, according to the water level. They have two major worries in fresh water: security and comfort. The first depends on having an adequate depth of water, the second on the presence of some obstacle that deflects the current efficiently. Good positions are those that conform to these criteria.

Regularly successful anglers are perfectly familiar with such places. They can locate them with much greater precision when the water is cold (below 7 °C the lure really has to pass right under the fish's nose before it will occasionally condescend to grab at it).
It is always worth finding out what the name of a pool means: some of the most famous bear names connected with the salmon lies. Apart from such standard places, a salmon will generally bite when travelling: at the head of a pool when it is getting ready to surmount an obstacle, or at the tail of a pool just after a difficult passage, above a fall, for example. A salmon rarely bites when resting deep in its hole.

■ *A magnificent Chum salmon, a Pacific strain, taken at Clear Creek, Alaska.*

Sea trou

Fishing for sea trout has its ardent followers who consider it the most sporting catch of all, leaving the salmon far behind. It has to be admitted that this fish puts up a spectacular, almost unreal defence as it makes a succession of astonishingly fast leaps, seeming to spend more time out of water than in its own element. Among real purists, the height of the art is fly-fishing for sea trout at night. The practice of night fishing, unfortunately forbidden in France (but not in Great Britain and Ireland) is however tolerated for half an hour before sunrise and two hours after sunset, thanks to Article 14 of the fishing law that allows the Republic's commissioners to make such decisions. This exceptional arrangement is the first time allowance to be made for the individuality of the sea trout, an anadromous migrant mainly active at night.

Taken on the fly, the sea trout is an amazingly active game fish.

The peak of game fishing

Latin name: *Salmo trutta trutta*
Family: Salmonidae

SPECIFICS OF SEA TROUT FISHING

The sea trout does not lead an exclusively nocturnal existence. When the water is coloured, or if the sky is overcast, it will bite in broad daylight. It is only active for very short periods at such times, rarely more than an hour, which means that the fisherman has to be there at the right moment.

Close to the sea, the sea trout is much more active in the flow of the rising tide. Here one can also take advantage of fresh runs of migrating fish. The places occupied by sea trout are typical: usually areas where the water is deep, in pools with a sandy or gravel bottom with plenty of weeds and various obstacles such as logs and rocks, where the bank is hollowed out and trees give shade in the summer. In the summer they like to lie below falls and cascades, at the bottom of dams and the level places at the edge of sudden changes in the slope of the river bed.

Weather conditions and the state of the water most decidedly affect the behaviour of sea trout. They are particularly active when the water is clearing during the days following a spate, but not during the spate itself when the water is high and full of debris, at which time they stick to the bottom behind some sunken obstacle.

Though a violent storm will bring about a cessation of activity, they seem not to mind fine, continuous rain, apparently quite the reverse, in fact.

As with most fish a north wind is unfavourable, the opposite of a west wind. As they are nocturnal in habit, sea trout are best fished for early in the morning or late at night.

The method of fishing more closely resembles that used for trout rather than that adopted for salmon. Too many anglers make the mistake of persisting for hours at one pool, always in the same place. To have luck on one's side in catching sea trout, it is better to fish in as many known places as possible, and not to wait too long in one spot. Being thorough does not mean persisting senselessly. This fish largely positions itself in deep water. Whether fly-fishing or spinning, it is vital to retrieve slowly to ensure that the lure works at the right depth.

■ *The acrobatic defence of a sea trout hooked on a streamer.*

■ *Sea trout are mainly active at dusk and reward the lucky fisherman with good sport.*

■ *Sand eels make a good bait for sea trout.*

■ *Sea trout can also be fished by trotting using natural bait.*

Fishing with natural bait

The tackle

A long, robust, ringed telescopic or sectional rod 16–20 feet (5–6 m) long.

A light fixed-spool spinning reel, the spool loaded with 330 feet (100 m) of 0.24 to 0.35 mm nylon line, depending on the size of the fish.

Size 1 to 10 single hooks, or two-hook Stewart tackle for worm fishing.

Baits

Sea trout take various natural baits, among them worms, prawns, minnows and even sand eels.

Fishing method

Fish the standard sea trout lies (under steep eroded banks, below dams, in deep runs cluttered with rocks and obstacles, and close to tree-lined banks with overhanging foliage). Cast towards these places and if the current allows, with the pick-up open let the bait drift along, skimming the bottom.

Some anglers leave the bait on the bottom for a few minutes, twitching it from time to time, and repeat this all the way. Worm fishing is mostly used when the water is coloured. On the other hand a prawn is preferable when fishing the deeper holes in clear water.

Prawns or grey prawns do very well, alive or dead. The method of fishing is a little different when using prawns. The crustacean is fixed on a special weighted mount and cast well above the deep part so as to swim at the right depth when it reaches the lie. The bait should drift slowly and be given some movement by alternately holding it back and releasing it.

When there is a bite, which may sometimes be barely perceptible, strike vigorously. All these baits can also be fished using a float on the line, especially in places where there are eddies.

Fishing with a dead minnow

This method is much used in the rivers of Calvados, France, and is most effective at dawn and when the water is low and clear.

The tackle

A 2.50 m spinning rod with a stiff top is needed.

A light fixed-spool spinning reel, the spool loaded with 100 m of 0.22 to 0.26 mm nylon line.

Mounts

Any minnow mount will do, though the type with a cap is useful when fishing deep lies.

Fishing method

Cast three-quarters upstream or straight across, then allow the bait to sink close to the bottom. Slowly retrieve the minnow giving it some movement, and speeding it up near likely places (not always very visible in deep water) such as weed banks, logs and rocks. This is where the angler's skill, his feel for the water, and his knowledge of the place all come into play.

Spinning with artificial lures

This method is deadly when the water is high and slightly coloured, especially a few days after a spate. At dawn and during the day it is often much more effective than fly-fishing.

The tackle

A powerful rod from 8 to 10 feet (2.50 to 3 m) long (of the type used for pike or zander), with a tip stiff enough to cast relatively light lures (10 g).

A fixed-spool reel for pike or light salmon use, the spool loaded with 500 feet (150 m) of 0.22 to 0.35 mm nylon line, according to the size of the fish.

Lures

The most attractive spinners are white with black tips in sizes 2 and 3, spoons with long willow leaf blades, or tandem spoons with the smallest spoon at the front. These are often weighted at the head with a boat shaped (Wye) lead or swan shot, or under the blade. The smaller spoons (size 1) are undoubtedly the most effective. Unfortunately, to make them work properly requires nylon too fine for the average-sized fish in some rivers.

■ *A nice basket of finnock, sea trout around 15 inches (40 cm) in length that have only spent a few months in the sea.*

The wobbling spoons preferred are those with long, thin, shiny blades.

Small heavy devons 1.5–2 inches (4–5 cm) long are excellent. With them, large pools sheltering migrating fish can be fished thoroughly and at the right depth.

Half-sinking plug baits between 4 and 6 g are also extremely effective.

Fishing method

Seat trout and salmon fishing are alike in that the cast, which is three-quarters upstream, is followed by a very slow retrieve close to the bottom, allowing the lure to drift and work in the current. The lure should be held back and released, and the retrieve speeded up, making it swim and flutter irregularly. There is no point in persisting too long in the same spot. Maximum caution is called for when moving about, when casting and dropping the lure in, since the sea trout is a very suspicious fish that will stubbornly refuse the best presented spoon if it has noticed a presence, or anything unusual. At the start of the evening and as night falls it may pay to fish lighter lures just below the surface or in mid-water. The fish actually leave the depths and it is not unusual to catch one a few centimetres below the surface. A 3 lb (1.5 kg) sea trout taken at dusk in Ireland this year made a rush of 16–20 feet (5–6 m) with its back out of the water and seized the lure between the boots of an angler friend who was fishing a size 00 flyspoon on very light tackle.

While on this subject, on all the rivers in the north of Ireland, we found that very light spinning The tackle with size 00, 0 or 1 spoons on 0.12 or 0.14 mm nylon worked very well with sea trout. They attacked the lures equally well in clear or coloured water (as with grilse at other times), alas, with inevitable breakages on large fish.

■ *A fine sea trout caught on very light spinning tackle, on the river Glen in County Donegal, Ireland.*

Fly-fishing

This fascinating method is most rewarding in the evening, when it is better than all the other ways of fishing, especially after nightfall. This is wet fly-fishing, using large lure-flies or streamers that imitate small fish such as sprats, herrings or sardines. On summer evenings dry flies such as sedges or three-coloured (grey, red and black) palmers tied on a size 12 hook may produce results.

The tackle

A powerful 9½, 10 or 11 foot (2.8, 3 or 3.4 m) rod.

A large capacity centre-pin reel carrying 300 feet (100 m) of backing and a sinking tip fly line with an 8 foot (2.5 m) cast in 0.22 to 0.28 mm nylon.

Flies

Various types of wet fly with single or double hooks can be used. A friend who is very successful with sea trout makes his own highly coloured flies, in violets, yellows and reds with tinsel bodies, that imitate a swimming sand eel.

In coloured water brighter-coloured flies are the most effective, including the sinking lures mounted in tandem recommended by Hugh Falkus. Sombre models are preferable in clear water. Of all the imitations on sale, some of the most famous creations are: Connemara Black, Blue and Claret, Hairy Mary, Silver Doctor, Black Pennel, Touques, Jock Scott Special, Special Doctor, Alexandra, Lemon Grey and Silver Blue.

A two-handed rod allows better control over the drift. The method of fishing a river in Norway.

■ *Marc Sourdot, a sea trout specialist, with two fine specimens in Scotland.*

Fishing method

Since fly fishing is primarily effective at night, the first thing to do is to carry out a reconnaissance early in the evening to locate the positions occupied by sea trout, and make a mental note of the "dangerous" sections such as deep water or any obstacles, as well as fords and places of access to the river. If the river is rough and the bottom particularly uneven, it is best to avoid wading or risk an involuntary bath at some stage. Extreme caution is essential. If, when it is getting dark, you come across some semblance of activity, there is no point in scaring the pool by attacking fish that are not biting and which will only really "dine" once night has set in. Wait for the right time, then, as soon as the sun has set, position yourself at the head of the pool. Cast three-quarters downstream and allow the fly to sink and sweep right across the river, giving it little jerks with the rod tip or by tugging at the line held in the left hand (the line should always be kept taut to avoid missing strikes). When the line reaches your side, do not lift it; instead retrieve it slowly, making the fly work somewhat like a dead fish. One tends to forget that there are as many sea trout on one's own side as there are opposite, and they are more likely to bite because the lure is working better and deeper. Retrieve right up to the rod tip, for there can often be a bite at the last moment, just as the fly reaches the bank. The renowned bite shows in two ways. When the fly is still close to the surface, it can be seen as a swirl followed by a vicious pull. If it is deeper, the bite is signalled by a sudden stop or a light tug. Strike with a full movement but not too violently; the lightning departure of a big fish can result in a breakage. There follows a fine tussle, almost unreal in a nocturnal setting where one is guessing at rather than witnessing the fantastic leaps of this wonderful fish. Unhooking is frequent, especially with fish fresh from the sea that still have tender mouths, but what ecstasy to fight such an adversary !

The use of a head lamp is strongly advised for night fishing. However the beam must be kept well clear of the water, for fear of arousing the suspicions of the sea trout, which would immediately cease all activity.

■ *Hooking a sea trout that was lying close to the bank.*

A wet fly for sea trout.

■ *A selection of three excellent streamers for sea trout. In clear water blue shades are suitable. On the other hand, more neutral colours are best when the weather is dull and the water slightly coloured.*

Cinnamon Sedge wet fly.

Carnivores and predators of the depths

Since the sudden explosion of the zander population in 1970 there has been an amazing increase in interest in fishing for predators in general, with the appearance of specific tackle, new techniques and original lures. After this tremendous interest in the zander, it is the wels' turn to stir the passions. This fish is gradually colonizing all our waters and attracting a growing number of enthusiasts. And now we have the bass fishermen, these funny anglers with their American tackle, casting rods and strange lures, who have founded their own association – Black-bass France. Yet another aspect of fishing, rather fun and decidedly modern. But if sometimes emotion prevails over reason, who's complaining?

The unnerving bearing of the pike, our great freshwater predator.

Pike

A serial killer

Latin name: *Esox lucius*
Family: Esocidae

The pike is unquestionably our handsomest freshwater predator – and the most interesting to fish for. Its capricious nature, its violent defence and the impressive sizes it can reach make it a prize adversary. The prime characteristic of a pike fisherman is perseverance. He must get used to the behaviour of a fish whose eating pattern is as varied as it is unpredictable, and adapt to it. A pike may keep its mouth tight shut for several days, then throw itself with gusto on every lure or bait passing its door. So far nobody has been able to establish any proper rules that cover the rhythm and timing of its activities. The fish may bite mainly at daybreak, at midday or at the end of the evening, at the same lake, during the same period. It is this that lends interest to a kind of fishing in which the successful never lose hope. The second attribute needed in a pike fisherman is a certain morality regarding his adversary. He must return pike smaller than 2 feet (60 cm) to the water or he cannot call himself a good fisherman, conscious of a duty to care for his fishing heritage. On days when there is a feeding frenzy, reason must prevail and only the minimum needed for personal consumption be taken. People who slaughter 18 inch (45 cm) pickerel using small trout spoons will never be fit to join the noble brotherhood of predator fishermen. The third quality needed, when practising this art in winter, is the determination to carry on, even in the coldest weather, and never to lose heart.

LIVEBAITING

The oldest, but one of the best ways of overcoming the vigilance of large specimens.

The tackle

A good pike rod is relatively long 11–16 feet (3.5–5 m) with a stiff tip. The quality and spacing of the rings is important, and they should be large.

The size of the reel depends on the line to be used. If the line is no thicker than 0.30 mm, a light, strong spinning reel with a reliable drag can be used. Beyond this, a medium weight spinning reel is preferable. The line can be between 0.26 and 0.35 mm, depending on whether the water is free of snags or not.

For the cast an 11–18 lb (5–8 kg) steel trace 16 inches (40 cm) long is essential, to avoid an almost certain break when the line comes into contact with the pike's sharp teeth. There are some remarkable, extremely supple casts available that can be knotted quite easily. Single, double or treble hooks are generally used.

■ ***A pike taken on livebait. The rig includes a float with a vane insert.***

■ ***A small pickerel in ambush at the edge of a lake, ready for a fish or an insect.***

■ ***The pike's jaws are armed with about 700 razor-sharp teeth!***

FLOAT FISHING

The float chosen depends on the livebait, which has to be able to tow it around swimming naturally without taking it down too deep. The weight should be precisely adjusted so that the float's buoyancy does not arouse the pike's suspicion when the fish is seized.

The ideal rig consists of a sliding float, adjusted to the correct height and weighted with a 15–20 g olive resting against a swivel clip. The single, double or treble hook comes at the end of a steel trace 16 inches (40 cm) long which is fixed on the swivel. The size of the livebait depends on the resistance offered by the float. Do not hesitate to use large livebait (25 cm and more) which can catch big specimens.

■ ***Pike like to lie near weed beds and submerged branches.***

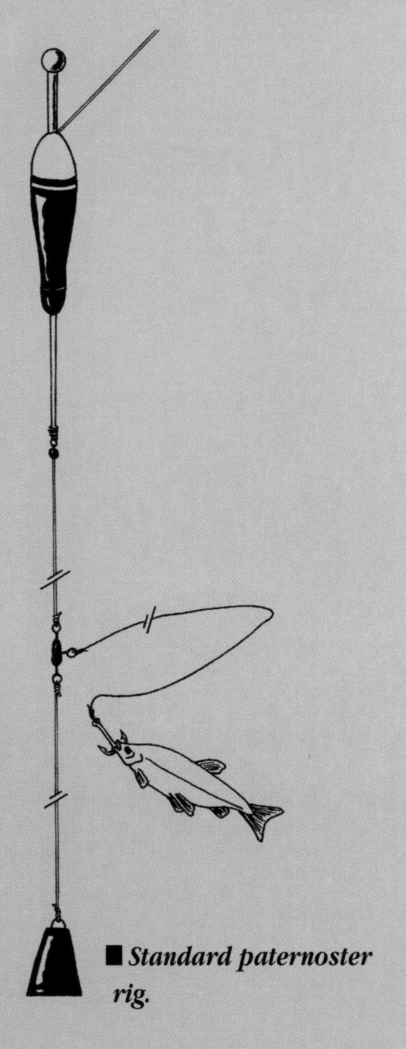

■ *Standard paternoster rig.*

The paternoster rig

This rig can be used to fish in the very deepest places, such as in reservoirs, or to keep the livebait in a predetermined area, which may often be somewhere surrounded by weeds. A triple swivel is fixed to the line. To its side eye is attached a 16 inch (40 cm) steel trace with a single, double or treble hook. The whole is weighted with a 20 or 40 g lead on a weaker piece of line 24 to 27 inches (60–70 cm) long which is attached to the lower swivel eye.

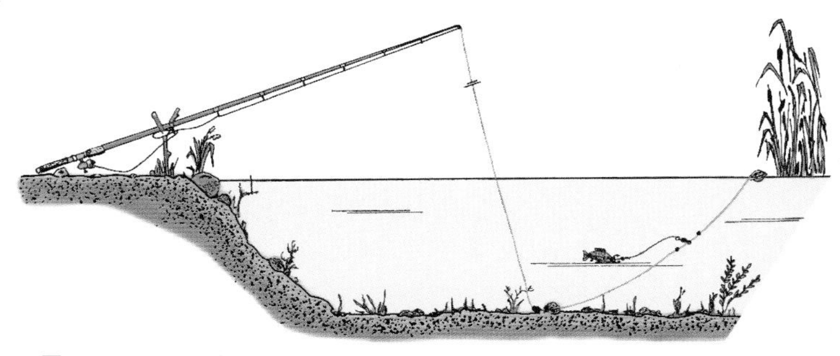

■ *Fishing with a paternoster.*

Fishing method

Having located a promising spot, cast the livebait with extreme care so as not to give it a jolt that might lessen its activity, the essential factor for success. The vibrations put out by a healthy fish are more easily detected than those emitted by a fish dying on the end of the line. Change the fish frequently if it becomes less active.

The rod is placed on its rest with the pick-up open and the line held on the ground with, for example, a pebble so there is no resistance to the bite and the slightest pull will take line out.

The bite is often announced by irregular movements of the float due to the frenzied activity of the livebait, The pike is there, perhaps a few centimetres away, examining its prey with care. Then the float dives, and the line moves towards open water. The pike has taken the livebait crosswise and is taking it away to a place best known to itself. When it decides to eat its prey, it turns it to swallow it head first. At this moment the float re-appears, then dives again. This is the time to strike. Very excited because he does not know what he is up against (it could be the fish of a lifetime), the angler takes up his rod, closes the pick-up and strikes firmly with a full movement. There follows a fight in which the result depends on where the hook has lodged, on the size of the pike, its strength and its guile. If the hook is deep in the throat, the predator is obliged to open its mouth

■ *Baiting a livebait through the back.*

Baiting livebait

There are many different ways of fixing the livebait on the hook. Through the throat, usually with a single hook, or through the back, piercing the muscle with a treble hook, which allows the fish to be hooked as soon as it bites.

One of the most reliable ways of attaching the livebait is to fix the hook high on the side, using a baiting needle to pass the trace under the skin from the tail to the neck. This "surgical operation" should be carried out carefully to avoid wounding the fish. In this case the pike must swallow the livebait completely and the strike must be delayed.

Advice

Lastly, some advice and observations:

The pike is a very wary fish. This was proved the other day on a lake particularly rich in pike, in the company of some rather boisterous friends. Once the livebait lines had been set, we started fishing systematically using lures and deadbait, with much laughter and running about on the bank. Despite the excellent conditions (calm November weather) there were no bites, and we decided to abandon this activity and devote ourselves to duck hunting in the reed beds towards the tail of the lake. Returning after a short absence, we found all our livebait lines stuck in an inextricable muddle close to the bank. Only one small pike on a deadly treble hook had failed to escape. This scene was repeated for the whole of the two days we spent at this lake: the bites came in our absence. The lesson to be learned from this misfortune is that when fishing for pike and especially when moving about, one has to be absolutely quiet.

Another piece of advice concerns hooks: they must be perfectly sharp to be able to pierce the pike's tough mouth. Lastly, the choice of livebait: knowing that a pike can swallow a prey one-third of its own size, use large fish. This eliminates the possibility of taking small pike which are often fatally injured, and stakes everything on catching "the dream pike"!

■ *Two proud young fishermen and their catch: two superb pike.*

when pulled, causing it to "drown" faster. Some have just one aim, to reach the nearest snag, take refuge and break the line, an unfortunate manoeuvre that is difficult to prevent with a big fish. Whatever the case, it is vital to avoid treating the fish violently. As long as the pike is unaware of the situation, its defence is not spectacular. When it sees a landing net or a gaff, or senses the presence of an angler, in its headlong flight it displays a brute force that can be difficult to control. The angler should therefore be careful not to reveal his presence, nor should he bring his prey close to the bank until it is exhausted. At the moment of netting he should free the drag to prevent any final attempt to escape, and failure at the crucial moment. If a pike bites and reaches a snag under the bank, it is best to strike right away to avoid the risk of losing a good catch.

Deadbait fishing

Pike fishing with a deadbait has undergone a considerable boom in recent years, owing much to the development of techniques designed for zander. An attractive method because of its itinerant nature, it calls for a perfect feel for the water, and an appropriate knowledge of the haunts and habits of the fish. As with any method of fishing that necessitates arousing the hunger of a fish of fickle nature, it requires endless perseverance. It is one of the most deadly methods.

The tackle

For good control over the deadbait and better hooking, the use of a rod with a stiff tip intended for zander in deep water is often recommended. These tip-action rods, though very useful in reservoirs or gravel pits, can with advantage be replaced with more flexible rods when fishing in shallow water where there is a lot of weed. A powerful rod is chosen so the pike can be presented with good-sized fish and the risk of catching small pike avoided. The rod can be between 8 and 10½ feet (2.50 and 3.20 m).

A light or medium weight fixed-spool spinning reel with a wide spool loaded with 500 feet (150 m) of 0.24 to 0.30 mm fluorescent nylon line, depending on the degree of clutter in the water. The pick-up arm is not indispensable, and may be replaced with a finger pick-up. Given the frequency of casting, a light model with a reliable drag is recommended.

A pike this size is best released.

Fishing a reed bed, where pike love to lurk.

A worked deadbait can still be counted on when pike fishing.

■ *In lakes pike like to patrol near the bank.*

Mounts

There do not seem to be enough different types of mount on offer, because hardened handymen devise their own mounts which can be equally effective. Anyway, the simplest are the best.

Mounts fall into two categories: those with an axial lead that swerve, such as the Ariel, effective in the current and in fast eddies, and jointed mounts with weighted heads such as the famous Drakhovitch, which are suitable for deep calm water. These are always attached to a steel trace about 6 to 8 inches (15 to 20 cm) long with a breaking strain of about 18 lb (8 kg). Pick a very flexible trace that does not interfere with the action of the bait.

For the deadbait, streamlined species with bright scales such as roach, bleak or small chub are generally chosen. The fish should be killed cleanly just before it is used. In this way its freshness will be preserved and its action that much more natural.

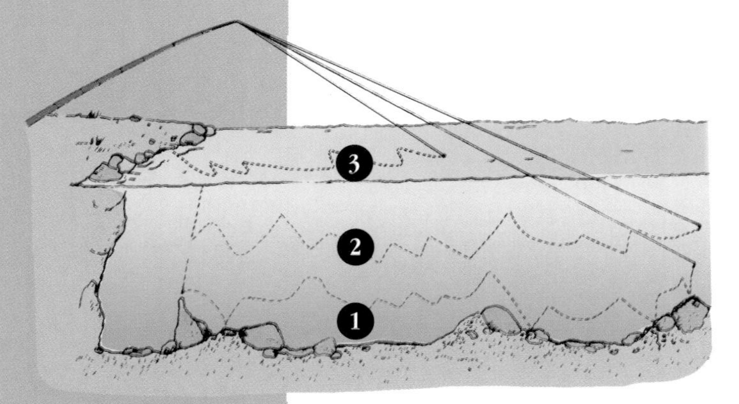

■ *The usual way to work a deadbait: first on the bottom (1), then in mid-water (2) and finally close to the surface.*

Fishing method

The idea is to arouse the pike's desire and stimulate its aggression by offering it a fish with all the appearance of a weak or sick individual, which is why it is important to work the bait correctly.

The cast should be gentle to ensure that the bait reaches the water without tearing the fish or arousing the suspicion of the pike with too noisy a landing. Wait until the tension in the fluorescent line relaxes indicating that the rig has reached the bottom. With the rod low, pull gently on the line to raise the deadbait and give it some movement, making it swim in irregular jerks. Allow it to sink again, and repeat the process, at times moving the fish on the spot. The aim is to use the rod tip to make the dead fish appear alive, changing its direction suddenly and making an irregular recovery with alternate gliding, zigzags and somersaults. Increase the size of the jerks until the retrieved bait reaches the surface. A sudden halt and a feeling of heaviness on the line generally indicate a bite.

When the line slackens, it may be an unusual movement of the line and pass unnoticed. This fine fish demands constant attention. It calls for a perfect knowledge of the usual haunts: cluttered banks covered by arching branches and foliage, drains, sunken trees, pontoons, tributary inlets, the proximity of an island, a strip of water weed and so on.

The strike is made immediately anything abnormal is detected. In the fight that follows, the first rule is never

■ *The best time to fish for pike is twilight – in the early morning or late evening.*

to treat the fish with violence. This is to avoid terrifying it and inducing it to head for areas full of snags. When you arecertain it is exhausted, bring it to the bank and gaff it or slide it into a landing net. Be wary of a pike that comes in too quickly: as soon as it spots danger its unpredictable reaction may be a lightning departure. If care has not been taken to free the drag at the moment of landing, the result will inevitably be a breakage.

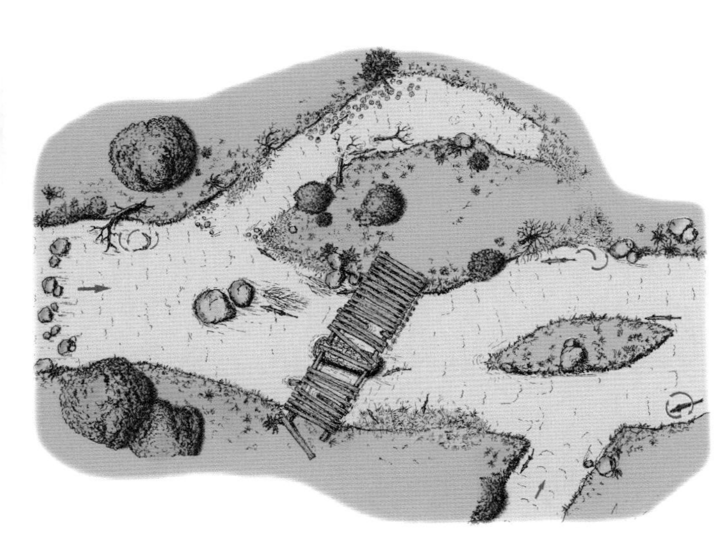

■ *Typical positions for pike in a river.*

Spinning, and casting lures

Casting metal spinners or plug baits is widely practised. It allows a great deal of territory to be covered, and on some days is indispensable. The thickness of line used is generally less than that used for livebaiting, giving scope for spectacular battles worthy of such a fine opponent.

The tackle

A rod 8–10 feet (2.4–3 m) long, capable of casting 10 to 30 g is recommended. For more accurate casting, better lure action and the possibility of casting light lures such as floating plug baits, choose a more flexible rod than is used for fishing deadbait.

A light or medium-weight fixed-spool spinning reel, or a rotary reel (little used in our country), with a very reliable drag, is loaded with 500 feet (150 m) of 0.24 to 0.35 mm nylon line, depending on the likelihood of snags in the place to be fished.

Lures

The spinners must possess certain characteristics. First, they should be a large enough size (Nos 3, 4 or 5 depending on the type) to avoid hooking small pike. The blade must spin rapidly from the moment it hits the water (as well as when it is allowed to sink), and it should also spin at very low recovery speeds. Types vary according to the shape and position of the weight, and the thickness of the blade. There are two principal types to remember: those with an axial weight, under the blade, for use in shallow water, and those weighted at the head for fishing in deep water. Some are adorned with a red pom-pom or a flexible lure to provide a visible focus for attack. Though not much used, wobbling spoons are nonetheless very effective, especially for big pike. During a stay in Ireland, we had almost no bites on spinning blade types, while the wobbling spoons were regularly attacked. The variety of blade shapes, different actions and weights enables any spot to be fished. Do not be afraid of using big lures, say 2½–3 inches (6–8 cm), that allow the largest pike to be taken. In still water, choose thin, light blades of the willow leaf type. When there is a strong current and you want to fish in large holes or very deep places, it is best to use a wide, heavy, blade that will sink more rapidly. There are some lures over 8 inches (20 cm) long, designed for trolling in the Irish lakes. These "shoe-horns" are very effective. After reaching the bottom, the spoon is retrieved slowly and jerkily (worked like a deadbait) occasionally pausing for a good while to let it sink, twirling as it falls. In addition to these movements of different lengths, give the lure sudden changes in direction using the rod tip.

Floating or sinking, plugs make excellent pike baits. Their only disadvantage is high cost, which discourages anglers from always using them. However they are very useful. The floating type (which returns to the surface when retrieval is halted) can be fished in very cluttered places where a spoon could not be used. They swim and dart in different ways depending on the position and shape of the lip, but all are remarkably similar to natural fish, and

■ *The spinner is an excellent lure to catch pike.*

Golden rules

If you want luck to be on your side, there are some golden rules to be respected. There is no point in casting distances so great that you can neither control the way the bait swims nor the strike. In likely places, always try to fish "short" but accurately. The speed of recovery is equally important, and should be slow, since pike do not like to chase after the bait for more than a few metres. When the spoon is spinning correctly, a resistance and gentle vibration can be felt. After casting, wait for the spoon to reach the bottom, then retrieve it slowly and jerkily, alternating pulling and letting go and working the lure with the rod tip. Sudden changes in direction produced by moving the rod may prompt a reluctant pike to bite. The bite is marked by a sudden stop followed by a powerful departure. Strike immediately and with some force, to make the hooks penetrate the pike's tough jaw. The hook points should be checked regularly and sharpened when the need is felt.

Too often neglected, the spinner is still one of the best lures for pike.

so can be used anywhere, in all conditions. Of all the types available choose large lures up to 6 inches (15 cm) or even 8 inches (20 cm) in length. They are all made of balsa wood or rubber, armed with two treble hooks, and have fixed or movable lips of different lengths. The deep-diving models frequently become snagged. To avoid squandering one's entire fishing budget in a couple of sessions, it is advisable to use thick line. Plug baits are often magnificently decorated. In fact their shape, type and ability to dive, which must be appropriate to the conditions, are a great deal more important than their colour.

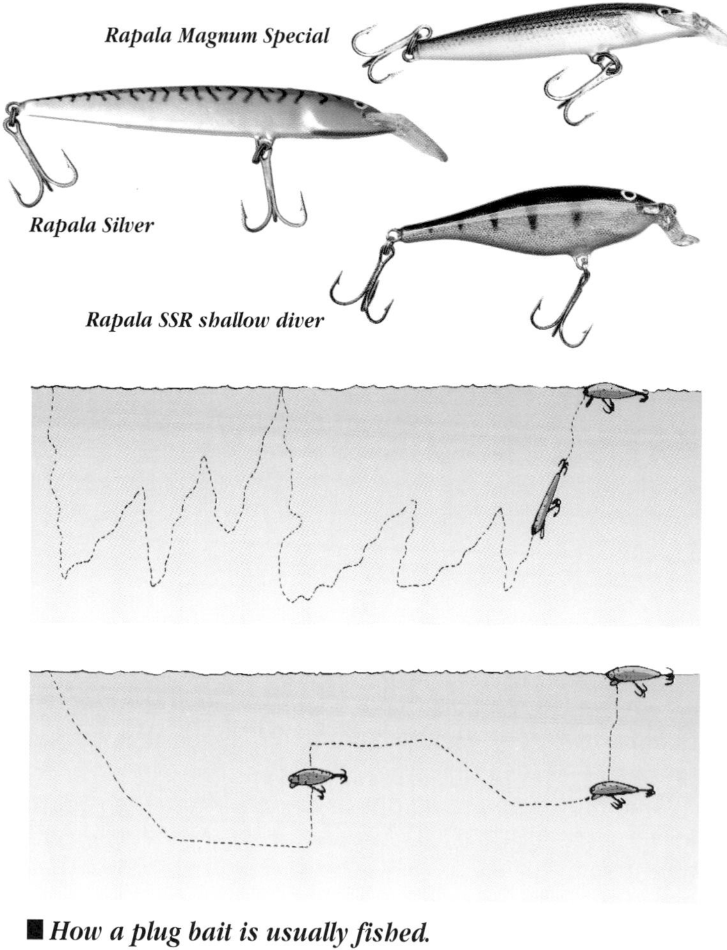

■ *How a plug bait is usually fished.*

A classic pike streamer.

pike family, fly-fishing offers the same chance of success as other methods, because it is aimed at different fish, in other, particular locations.

Fishing in large weed beds during the summer would be inconceivable except with a streamer on the surface. The lure is made to swim lazily enough to tempt a sulking, sleepy pike that up to that point has been refusing baits and lures that were much too lively for it.

■ *Even big pike can fall victim to a fly.*

Fly-fishing

Dapping is increasingly popular among confirmed fly-fishermen, who can carry on their pastime in a season not normally favourable to them. Sea fly-fishing techniques, in which large flies are offered to bonefish, barracuda and even swordfish, have contributed to this development.

The effectiveness of this way of fishing needs no further proof – pike, even big ones, take flies. It has been said that the largest pike ever caught in Scotland was taken on a fly, and weighed some 80 lb (36 kg). Whether this is true or legendary, in waters normally populated with fish of the

Why is the pike disappearing?

Pike numbers in our waters have seen an alarming decrease in recent years. Many theories have been advanced to explain this phenomenon, which has alarmed predator fishermen and above all upset the balance of cyprinid populations. Competition for food with the zander has been mentioned, but this is certainly not reason enough.

The pike, despite its daunting highly predatory appearance, is actually a fragile species that requires very strict ecological conditions to reproduce. The organic pollution rampant for many years favours eutrophication (due to the spreading of agricultural products based on nitrates and phosphates, and household waste rich in detergents) and has tended to silt up our waters and smother the weed beds that are prime spawning sites. In addition, the management of large stretches of water such as reservoirs has been a catastrophe. Sudden changes in level during spawning destroy the pike's eggs, which are stranded when the water level falls by even a few centimetres (unlike those of the zander, which are often laid in some metres of water). In some areas fishing regulations ill suited to the fish's biology are responsible for a decline in the pike population. The opening of the season in April, at a time when many pike (in colder regions) are still breeding is a threat to the survival of the species. The completely ridiculous minimum legal size (18 inches/45 cm) includes some small pike that have never reproduced. A pike worthy of the name measures at least 24 to 28 inches (60 to 70 cm); all the others should be returned to the water.

A number of disturbances to the ecological niche of the pike have had dramatic consequences: drainage operations, the drying out of wetlands, the disappearance of areas liable to flooding, and the resizing of watercourses with harmful effects on weed beds. These have not only affected wildfowl (duck and coot) populations, but by suppressing the weeds necessary for spawning and the development of the fry, they have also seriously compromised the reproductive potential of the pike. Fishing clubs have tried to compensate for these attacks by releasing pickerel (2½–2¾ inches/6–7 cm fingerlings) but, as with game, it is totally unrealistic to attempt the renewal of a species unless the right environmental conditions have been re-established. In addition, these large-scale introductions have very often been badly managed, the small pike all being left together in the same place, then eating each other. The few that escape and struggle to reach 16 inches (40 cm) will fall victim to murdering spoons. Then again, stocking with fry is a lot of trouble; the cultivation of pike is a particularly delicate business. The fry will not accept anything but living, moving prey, so zooplancton have to be produced on the spot. At the age of a few weeks, confinement drives them to eat each other. This cannibalism reaches the point where an entire batch can be reduced to nothing in a matter of days.

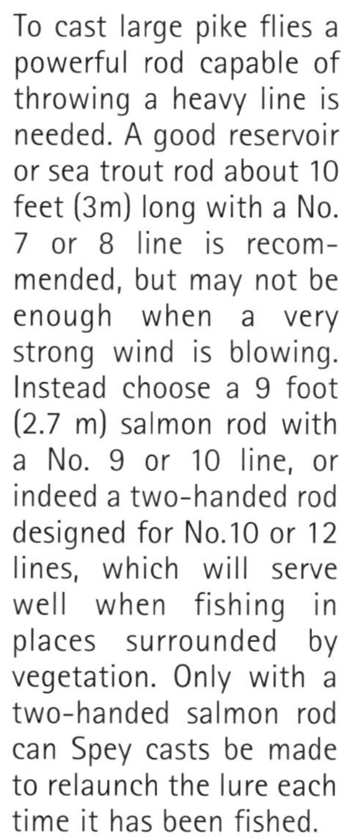

Fishing a pike fly is very effective in weed beds.

The tackle

To cast large pike flies a powerful rod capable of throwing a heavy line is needed. A good reservoir or sea trout rod about 10 feet (3m) long with a No. 7 or 8 line is recommended, but may not be enough when a very strong wind is blowing. Instead choose a 9 foot (2.7 m) salmon rod with a No. 9 or 10 line, or indeed a two-handed rod designed for No.10 or 12 lines, which will serve well when fishing in places surrounded by vegetation. Only with a two-handed salmon rod can Spey casts be made to relaunch the lure each time it has been fished.

The reel can be a reservoir or sea trout type.

A heavy line is essential for casting pike flies. Depending on the season and situation, choose a floating line (to fish weed beds in summer, just below the surface) and a medium or sinking line with which you can seek out *Esox* in 10 or 13 feet (3 or 4 m) of water in the winter. Forward taper lines will cast further than double taper and are preferable.

The short 6–8 feet (2–2.5 m) cast in 0.26 to 0.30 mm line, depending on the amount of clutter and surface weed, is attached via a barrel swivel to a very flexible steel trace with a breaking strain of 15 to 22 lb (7 to 10 kg).

A well-filled box with a variety of streamers for pike and black bass.

Flies

Pike flies bear no resemblance to the very many standard wet and dry imitative flies in existence. They are flies that vaguely imitate some sub-aquatic creature: a newt, a tiny fish or any other long, coloured creepy crawly, a product of the fly-tier's fertile imagination. The aim is to trigger the pike's feeding or territorial instinct, which is to dislike intruders. All the flies currently on sale have one major defect: they are most often intended for sea fishing and are therefore too heavy (and provided with impressive hooks), too dense, and too bulky. Casting these lures is an acrobatic exercise, and even impossible when the wind takes a hand. The only solution is to tie them oneself.

Pike flies can take different forms, depending on the tier's imagination, but they are generally very long. They are assembled from fur, feathers, silk, material and so on, anything you like and which you think might be successful. The single or treble hooks are of fine wire, making it easier for the barbs to penetrate the predator's jaw. These lures can never be overdressed, and are tied on size 1 to 5/0 hooks according to the way they will be used. The bulkiest (streamers 4 to 6 inches (12–15 cm) in length with long strands of deer hair) are fished on the surface. As with metal lures, an extra touch of a lively colour (red or orange) may catch the pike's attention and provide a focus for attack.

Fishing method

In the summer the weed beds and areas covered in water lilies that are never fished by spinning are just right for the fly-fisherman, who can fish on the surface with a floating or medium-sinking line. Having despatched the fly into the midst of the vegetation, retrieve it in short pulls, 8 to 12 inches (20 to 30 cm) at a time, holding the rod low. Alternate retrieval with fairly long pauses in the clear spaces between the weeds, twitching the fly on the spot with the rod tip. With this kind of fishing, the bite is a real plus. The pike shoots to the surface like lightning and grabs the lure in a shower of spray. Only strike when there is a definite pull on the line held in the left hand; the pike does not immediately let go of a fly.

The attack is so violent that there is always a tendency to strike too soon, before the pike has seized hold of the lure properly.

Where to fish for pike

Pike readily take large streamers.

Rivers:
In winter pike like slow deep eddies, deep holes, steep banks covered in vegetation with overhanging trees, areas cluttered with rocks, backwaters and dead water. As the water gets warmer, they gradually take over more oxygenated areas where the fry they eat are found. They can be encountered in the current, sheltering behind a big log or a rock, in a fast eddy, or by belts of vegetation growing along the bank. They also hunt close to small tributaries emptying into the river.

Lakes:
In the winter pike seek out the depths: in the middle of open water, close to the embankment, especially along the wall in a dam, and basically anywhere the branches of trees hang over the water. They can also frequently be found under pontoons and barges tied up at the bank. Though these are all useful locations, they are not the only places pike occupy in the summer. The predator lies in ambush in the reed beds and strips of vegetation taken over by shoals of cyprinids, or in the shade of water lily leaves, or of small willows growing on the banks.

Reservoirs:
The whole secret of success lies in a perfect knowledge of the bottom. Specialists in lake fishing for pike have sometimes photographed the entire area when the lake was emptied, so locating trees, constructions, and various submerged obstacles such as drains. The entrance of a tributary is always an excellent spot.

In short, a good spot for pike must satisfy at least two conditions: somewhere to hide, and a high enough concentration of potential prey.

Winter fishing

In the winter pike must be sought where they lie, that is, very deep, and this requires the use of a line with a sinking or rapid sinking point. Cast the fly beyond the place to be fished and when it has reached the bottom, retrieve it in short bursts interspersed with quite long pauses during which the rod tip can be used to make it skip about on the spot and move from side to side. Arousing a sleepy pike at this time of the year may take several passes in his immediate neighbourhood. This type of fishing is not about speed; the lure is most effective when it works slowly. The number of attacks is never related to the number of casts but to the way the fly moves and the accuracy of casting.

The comm

Still known as the Striped Beauty, the perch loves underwater obstacles such as dead wood and stony rubble.

The ferocious appetite, curiosity and aggressive nature of the "Striped Beauty" indubitably make it the commonest catch for those on the track of predators. Its highly diversified diet presents the angler with many possibilities and with a little imagination and creativity, permits the use of countless techniques.

Perch often move about and hunt in fairly dense shoals. Their hunts, especially in still water, are particularly spectacular: these small predators literally charge the shoals of fry, which burst through the surface to escape their executioners. The fry are pursued by much jaw snapping, and in their panic some will not hesitate to run aground.

The angler must know how to find the shoals and be persistent in places that show promise, for it is not unusual to catch several in succession. It often happens (but not as a rule) that a fish coming unhooked at the last moment spreads panic and confusion through the shoal, which then makes off for less dangerous parts. In such cases it is useless to persist, so try elsewhere.

This roving type of fishing is far more rewarding than static methods, particularly in running water, because the perch are sought out.

Perch are attracted by any shiny object; an observation that has led to the perfection of techniques exploiting this behaviour, especially fishing with a metal lure, which is unbeatable in cluttered spots. It's a pity that nowadays this has fallen from use.

on perch

An appetite with stripes

Latin name: *Perca fluviatilis*
Family: Percidae

■ *The mayfly larva has an irresistible allure for the greedy perch.*

FLOAT FISHING FROM THE BANK

The perch is particularly fond of live natural baits. Its ferocious appetite and predatory instincts lead it to throw itself greedily at many different prey, especially in motion or swimming irregularly. However, perch do show a preference for certain baits such as mayfly larvae, bloodworms and young fish.

Fishing with mayfly larvae

This is the larva of the celebrated mayfly *Ephemera danica* well known to fly-fishermen. Much sought after by perch, this insect is especially prized at the end of the winter. Collecting them is a chancy business since the small watercourses that harbour this magnificent ephemerid are becoming increasingly rare.

The tackle

A ringed telescopic trout-type rod 13 to 20 feet (4–6 m) in length with a soft top-section will do very well. When fishing spots far from the bank, it is preferable to use a rod of the English type that allows longer casts.

Depending on whether one is fishing close to or far from the bank, a simple rotary reel or a small light or very light fixed-spool reel is used.

The spool is loaded with 165–330 feet (50–100 m) of 0.14 to 0.16 mm nylon line.

The rig is quite simple: a small, fine elongated float that can slide on the line is weighted with enough soft dust shot to balance the very fragile bait.

The cast in 0.12 mm nylon terminates in a size 12 to 14 fine hook.

Baiting

The mayfly larva must stay alive or it loses all effectiveness. To avoid damaging the larva, the point of the hook is passed through the last segments of the tail or under the rings of the thorax, behind the head.

Fishing method

The whole difficulty lies in finding places that shelter perch. Sometimes a lengthy search is necessary, in the first place carried out in the vertical plane. When the bottom has been carefully plumbed, the bait is gently immersed and the water column explored at different depths until the bank is reached. If there are no bites, there's no point in continuing, so move on. The grub is given some animation by pulling it up and releasing it, using less movement than one would with a worm. These enticing movements are very important and can often persuade even sated perch to bite.

A bite is indicated by the abrupt departure of the float, to which the best response is to yield for a few seconds. The subsequent strike should be sharp but not brutal. When a shoal of biting perch is encountered, it is as well to exploit the feeding frenzy to the maximum since it may not last long. Speed (in unhooking the fish and casting in again) is an essential factor in success.

The mayfly larva often tempts large perch, which though they may not put up a very violent resistance, still give plenty of excitement on a 0.12 mm line.

Perch are often very active at dawn and dusk. These are special times when even the largest fish occasionally get careless and make that fatal mistake.

Worm fishing with a float

The tackle is essentially the same as that just described, with a stronger set-up. The main line in 0.18 mm nylon ends in a cast in 0.14 or 0.16 mm nylon to which is attached a size 8 to 12 hook, according to the size of the bait. The stubby float is weighted with an olivette that has been scraped with a knife blade to make it shinier.

Fishing method

The float is positioned so that the worm (a small earthworm or blood-worm) just scrapes the bottom. It is very important to give it enticing jerks to get the perch excited; it will be attracted by the glitter of the olivette. If, after having tried various depths in one spot, there is no result, it is pointless to keep on. Stay on the move and you will see just how effective worm fishing can be.

Livebaiting with a floating line

A small livebait or young fish is the prime choice for catching large perch; they are often solitary and are best looked for in areas that have the most snags and obstacles.

The tackle

Identical to that used for worm fishing, but stronger, matching the weight of the set-up. A telescopic or sectional trout-type rod with rings and a stiff tip, about 15 feet (4.5 m) long, will do for fishing close to the bank or from a boat. When fishing on rivers where there are long runs, an English-style rod may prove to be more useful.

The light fixed-spool reel of a good make should have a reliable, sensitive drag. Sometimes a pike will take the initiative and seize the livebait, hence the importance of tackle able to counter a vigorous defence.

The spool is loaded with good quality 0.12 mm nylon for the main line. A spindle-shaped sliding float is weighted with bunched shot or an olivette. The cast, of 0.18 mm nylon, ends in a single size 8 hook or a small size 14 treble. In waters where there are plenty of pike, it may sometimes be necessary to use a flexible steel trace instead of the nylon to avoid being broken by what might be the "fish of the year". Unfortunately, adding this metallic trace appreciably reduces the number of bites by perch.

Livebait

It is well known that all shiny objects attract perch. Some fish with silvery scales flash in the water, especially when very skilfully worked. The most effective are small dace 2 to 2½ inches (5–6 cm) long, Heckel's bleak, small roach, small bream or young chub. Minnows also do very well: their size appears to suit the perch's "build".

Fishing method

In closed waters or reservoirs (in the latter, fairly deep water calls for the use of a sliding float), one proceeds by trial and error. Having cast in a promising spot, begin by trying close to the bottom, jerking the livebait up and down, giving it nervous twitches and sharp sideways movements. The float is moved gradually down the line, working the small fish at different depths until it nears the surface. When fishing from a boat, keep on going right up to the hull. Perch often follow the bait right to the surface, then conceal themselves under this convenient shelter. Again, rather than spending time in places that contain few fish, it is better to roam about to try and locate the good-sized shoals more quickly.

On a river, allow the current to take the bait and give it a jerk each time it passes some likely spot (a tree blocking the current, a belt of vegetation on the bank).

The bite is signalled by the slow, continuous departure of the float as the perch roughly seizes the bait before swallowing it. Wait a few seconds then strike; the further away the float, the harder the strike should be.

It is also possible to livebait using a bullet sinker. This shiny weight is fixed on a link swivel to which the cast is also attached. The livebait is put in over snag-filled spots just beneath the rod tip (a bottom strewn with obstacles: logs, branches, rocks) and waggled about close to the bottom, then gradually raised without stopping the teasing movements. The shine of the sinker in combination with the irregular movements of the bait prove irresistible to big perch.

JIGGING

This technique is based on the fact that perch are attracted by all shiny or unusual lures when they are moved in the right way.

Sinker fishing

In the old days the weight used was a bullet, lovingly polished to a brilliant shine. Today there are commercially available sinkers designed for perch fishing that have their surface nickeled to increase their powers of attraction. They do have one disadvantage however: the small range of weights, which only goes up to 8 gm. This is not enough when exploring waters of considerable depth and strong currents (eddies and holes in rapid rivers). A home-made sinker is easily produced: just take an olive of the right size and cut it in half through the middle to obtain the right weight (15 g, 20 g, 25 g).

The tackle

Depending on whether one is fishing from a boat or the bank, the rod will be a different length (from 10 to 13 feet/3–4 m in the first case, 16 to 20 feet/5–6m in the second). Fitted with rings, and telescopic or sectional, it should always have a rigid tip to optimise the action given to the bait, to give better control of the relatively heavy rig, and above all ensure an immediate and effective strike.

The light fixed-spool spinning reel is loaded with strong line: for example, fluorescent 0.24 mm nylon for the main body of the line. Two or three 5 cm droppers are fixed to the line 8 inches (20 cm) apart, with the first 10 inches (25 cm) from the sinker at the end. The droppers can be in 0.18 to 0.20 mm diameter nylon with size 6 to 12 hooks, depending on the size of the bait.

main body of line in 0.14 to 0.16 mm nylon

swivel clip

bullet sinker

15 cm cast in 0.16 mm nylon

size 12 to 16 hook

■ *Two mounts for fishing with a bullet sinker.*

■ ***The minnow is one of the best livebaits for perch.***

Perch haunts

Generally, perch like any spot cluttered with obstacles that offers the possibility of shelter or somewhere to hide. In rivers they are found downstream of masses of branches or tree trunks blocking the current, under waterfalls, along deep banks with holes hollowed out, near water inlets (small tributaries, canals, mill races), and in pools and large, slow eddies.

In lakes perch like to be near the bank (especially if it is planted with trees whose foliage reaches over the surface), in the vicinity of outlets, and banks overgrown with vegetation (banks of reeds, mats of water-lilies), stream inlets, piling, pontoons and the remains of old boats and landing stages. They are often encountered under moored boats.

In reservoirs, perch are often to be found near feeder streams, piles of stones, along sheer walls and among sunken trees that break the surface. Places where there is a change of slope or a step on the edge of deep water can be excellent.

Baits

The most commonly used baits are earthworms or small bloodworms, pierced close to the head so that the body hangs free and wiggles. A combination of worm, small fish and mayfly larva could be considered.

Fishing method

Put the sinker into the water just below the rod tip and let it sink vertically to the bottom. The line goes slack. Engage the pick-up then start irregular jigging movements, first close to the bottom, then working progressively to the surface. Sideways movements can be added to this irregular jerking to increase the effect of the shiny sinker and simulate the escape of the bait. The bite is a sharp tug and the fish generally hooks itself. It can be allowed to struggle for a few moments to stimulate aggression in the other perch, but the best tactic for making a good "bag" is speed. With the shoal localized, the perch usually bite with a will, sometimes attacking all three hooks at once. It is best to pull them out and unhook them as quickly as possible, so that you can profit from the feeding frenzy before the shoal moves off.

With the sinker areas full of snags can be fished. Don't hesitate to drop it into thick weed or submerged drains that may often shelter a big perch or, why not, a fine zander or a pike?

Fishing with metal lures

Fishing with metal lures has largely been forgotten, and this is a pity, because they are effective and rarely rejected by perch and pike. In some big alpine lakes jigging is performed with metal lures or plug baits. These may include Sting silda spoons, Zazous and Stromers.

■ ***A fine pair, taken on a jig.***

■ ***A metal lure or a heavy Zazou spoon fools even the largest perch.***

The tackle

A ringed rod about 10 feet (3 m) long for use in a boat, or 16–20 feet (5–6 m) when fishing from the bank, provided with a soft top-section to absorb the damaging impact of a sudden pull on the lure. A light fixed-spool spinning reel is loaded with a robust 0.24 to 0.26 nylon line. This diameter is necessary because of rapid line wear at the point of attachment to the lure, and the ever-present possibility of catching a fine pike.

Metal lures differ according to whether they are for use in still or running water. In the first case, highly attractive light, flat types are preferable. When fishing in eddies where there are strong currents these lures are too light. Carried away by the water they cannot go deep enough in the places chosen. In such cases denser, thicker, egg-shaped lures are preferable. Depending on the type, metal lures are armed with double or treble hooks at the head end. They are fixed to the line at the tail.

Fishing method

Drop the lure in lure directly below the rod tip and let it sink to the bottom, near a snag or in a promising place. Next, give the lure a sharp tug, some 20-24 inches (50–60 cm) or so and let it go again, moving the rod tip sideways to avoid snagging the line with the hook. Repeat the operation level by level, still moving sideways, alternately tugging – as though striking automatically – and releasing. A sudden stop when pulling, or a sudden slackening indicates the bite. Be sure to strike immediately. This "sideways jigging" is a particularly effective method.

■ *This young angler is proud of his capture taken on a Vibrocast by Ragot, a lure well-suited to jigging.*

Jig fishing with droppers

This technique is mainly used in big lakes where the perch is hunted by sight on the surface. However, it would be a pity to limit it to such situations alone, knowing that fishing with droppers is also undeniably effective in reservoirs though, when adapted to this environment the method is slightly different.

The tackle

A spinning rod 2.5–3 m long, as used for dead baiting, will generally suffice as long as it has a definite tip action.

A light, fixed-spool spinning reel is loaded with 0.28 to 0.30 mm nylon for the body of line, which ends in a 20–30 g weight. This last may be replaced with a large metal lure or a sinker.

From three to five special little lures fixed on 2–4 inches (5–10 cm) droppers of 0.26 mm nylon are attached to the line about 16 inches (40 cm) apart. These are brightly coloured teats (red is very fetching) or flies representing small fish.

Fishing method

The line is put in directly under the rod. When the weight reaches the bottom, close the pick-up and retrieve 6 feet (2 m) at a time, jerking and moving the line sharply from side to side. The aim of this rising movement is to find the level at which the perch are circulating. As soon as the first bites are felt (and it can happen that all the lures attract attention at the same time), retrieve the line as quickly as possible by "pumping" (hence the need for strong line) so as to take maximum advantage of the feeding perch. Sometimes the fish follow the lures right to the surface, then take refuge under the boat. In this case, moving the lures about on the surface close to the hull may take in even the most cautious individuals, but be extremely quiet when moving about on board.

One can equally well hunt perch on sight. Cast the rig to the other side of the shoal then retrieve it on the surface with the rod raised so as to bring the lure through the middle of the shoal. At this point jerk the rig and move it from side to side. The perch will then throw themselves on the lures.

An appetite with stripes

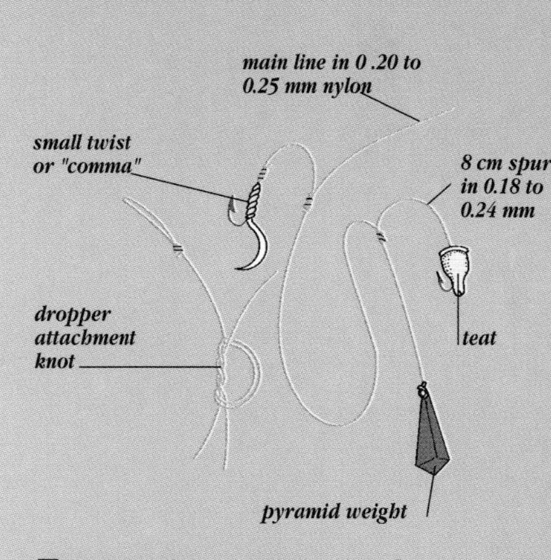

■ *Using droppers: a rig for fishing at a distance and retrieving line.*

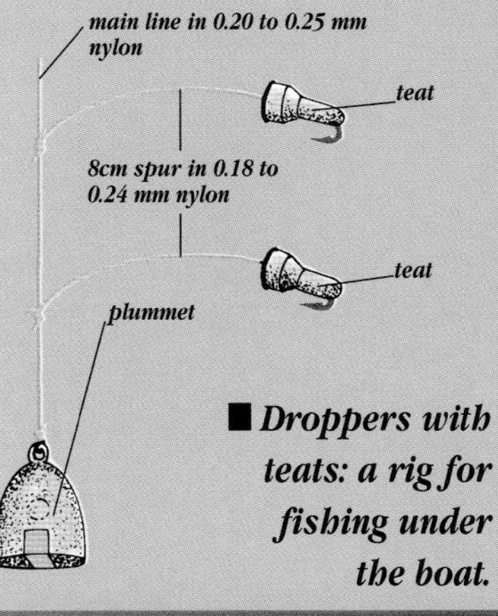

■ *Droppers with teats: a rig for fishing under the boat.*

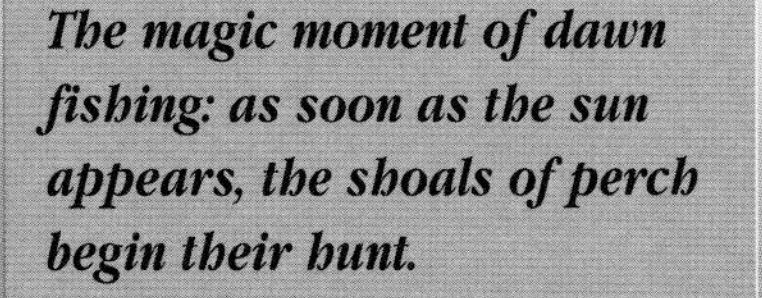

The magic moment of dawn fishing: as soon as the sun appears, the shoals of perch begin their hunt.

FLY-FISHING

Streamers and fly-lures

Though fly-fishing for perch is little practised, it can nonetheless bring pleasant surprises when the fish are inshore chasing fry in shallow water. To the implacable fly-fisherman it is an agreeable and rewarding pastime in dam or reservoir throughout the summer.

The tackle

A classic 10 feet (2.80 m) fly rod or an 11 feet (3.3 m) reservoir rod, with a No. 5 floating silk line, or a line with a sinking front end for deep waters.

An 8 foot (2.5 m) cast ending in a 0.16 to 0.18 mm nylon.

Flies

Streamers and other fly-lures are the best for this type of fishing, especially if they are in bright colours (red, orange, blue). Since these are generally rather sparsely clad (like pike flies), it is as well to dress at least the body with tinsel to give them a more brilliant effect.

Fishing method

When fishing shoals that are visible, simply cast beyond them then retrieve the streamer below the surface, giving it some life by jerking the line sporadically with the left hand, or by using the rod tip. In deep water all promising places should be explored at different depths. Here the action is completely different from the classic method used for reservoir trout, since the lure must be made to swim in the wildest fashion, creating the maximum commotion and stimulating aggression in the perch. Pulling, releasing, sideways movements, trembling on the spot, and simulated flight toward the surface, all are movements that rarely leave the predator indifferent.

A fly is quite likely to tempt a big perch.

Most streamers imitate young fish or small crustaceans.

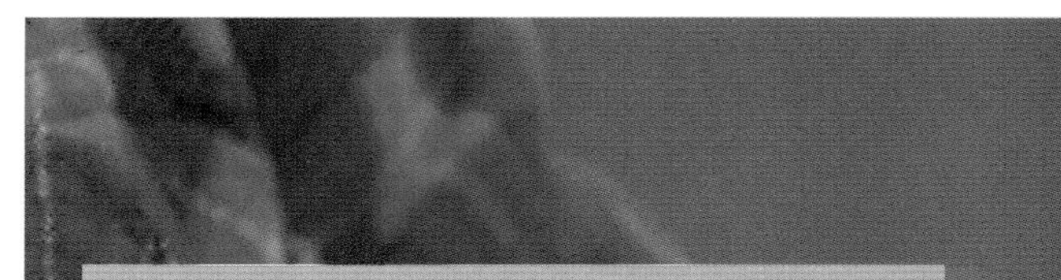

Perch, like black bass, love the unusual, and spoons with the hooks decorated with feathers, fur, or fringes of rubber strip are occasionally just too irresistible.

The Vibrocast, a good perch lure in pond or lake.

■ *Willow leaf spinner with a flexible plastic fish.*

■ *A fancy heavily-weighted spinner for fishing very deep.*

■ *A spinner with the axis passing through the blade.*

SPINNING

Light spinning

This technique is just as fascinating as that used for trout because of its itinerant character, and the knowledge it requires of the subtleties and habits of the fish involved. It is most effective when practised in small rivers where there are plenty of obstacles.

The tackle

More or less identical to that used for trout.

A rod of medium power (150 g) capable of casting 5–8 g, with a length of 6 to 7½ feet 1.8–2.2 m.

A light fixed-spool spinning reel is loaded with 330 feet (100 m) of 0.16 to 0.18 mm nylon line. As regards the choice of lure, most size 0, 1 or 2 spinning spoons are suitable provided they turn slowly and flutter perfectly when retrieved slowly. Some wobbling spoons are equally alluring, as are minnow spoons, floating or sinking plug baits, and flexible lures, mixed lures and jig mounts. When fishing waters that are deep or whose depth varies, it may be useful to add an interchangeable boat-shaped lead at the head of the lure. In waters where there are plenty of pike, the addition of a metal trace may also be useful, even if it may sometimes interfere with the action of the lure. However, small specimens are most likely to be taken, since a contest with a pike of a legal length of at least 2 feet (60 cm) on 0.16 mm nylon is very risky. In running water one can also use a size 0 Drachkovich dead bait mount, or a waggling or capped mount. A small bleak or a dead minnow are both very effective baits – as confirmed by the innumerable perch bites one gets when fishing for zander.

Even if the fish are not very active, the magic surroundings make a trip to the water's edge worthwhile.

Fishing method

Cast towards likely spots (the edge of weed beds, close to obstacles such as logs, dead trees, rocks, submerged drains, the mouths of tributaries, and pontoons and piling. Let the lure sink, then bring it in very slowly, brushing the bottom and close to any obstacles. Spoons with blades that flutter with the minimum of traction are very useful because they emit vibrations and flash as they sink, and begin to work and "beat a retreat" before they are retrieved. Perch may follow without biting.

To stimulate their aggression, it is essential to impart an irregular swimming action to the lure by jerking and releasing it during retrieval. Sudden changes in direction produced by moving the rod tip are very attractive, especially when close to the surface. They simulate attempts to escape that very few predators can resist. The bite usually comes when the lure is released or when it changes direction. It is not particularly violent, though sometimes the perch shakes its head angrily, and may become unhooked by tearing its delicate jaw membrane.

■ *A magnificent double taken on a spinning spoon, from a lake in the Bourbonnais district, (Allier) France.*

Ultra-light fishing

Lethal during the summer and entertaining because of the lightness of the tackle used. A rod rated at about 80 g is fitted with an ultra-light reel of a good make (possessing a reliable brake, good recovery speed and a wide spool to avoid frequent tangles with fine nylon). A line of 0.12 mm nylon 330 feet (100 m) in length is sufficient. The lures correspond to the classic types: fly spoons with minute red pom-poms,

predominantly bright red, orange or blue streamers, natural baits (weighted worms, caddis and small fish).

The fishing technique is identical to that recommended in the chapter on "ultra-light trout fishing". This technique is particularly well suited to the mouths of dam feeder streams. In fact, when deciding to ascend one of these streams in search of trout, to get your eye in, why not first catch a few "zebras" round about where the entry of the stream produces a habitat that particularly favours perch.

■ ***The tiny spinners used in ultra-light fishing are most effective in shallow water, for example, along the bank.***

Black bass readily swim in shoals, especially when of medium size. They love to hide among submerged branches or under boulders so need to be enticed out.

Relatively unknown in France, the black bass is a magnificent sport fish, long the darling of millions of American anglers. The Americans, inventors of the craziest lures, have made a real cult of the largemouth. It has to be admitted that the black bass's desperate, spectacular defence, its quirky character and unpredictable reactions make it the sport fisherman's quarry of choice. It is also truly the most combative of all the carnivorous fish. This is why some amateurs are willing to travel considerable distances in search of places where this extraordinary adversary flourishes. It appears to be worth the journey when one hears reports of these trips.

Black bass

Cut out for combat

Latin name: *Micropterus salmoides*
Family: Centrarchidae

■ *The plug bait is an excellent lure for black bass.*

FISHING FOR BLACK BASS WITH NATURAL BAITS

Black bass rarely refuse a well-presented bait as long as great care is taken in overcoming its vigilance. One can thus avoid going home empty-handed when all other techniques have proved fruitless. In the summer, black bass often stay close to the surface at the hottest time of day. Lying in wait, they will remain frozen in rock-like immobility for hours, apparently unaware of the roundabout of fry surrounding them. There is no apparent explanation for this unexpected behaviour. Large solitary black bass that live in the weeds are difficult to fool. Maintaining the essential element of surprise calls for extreme caution, particularly when first sighting the fish, which though it may feign indifference, has spotted the angler at the same moment. To persist when this happens will only annoy it and cause it to flee. Shoals of smaller black bass remain at various depths and occupy different locations according to the time of day and the season. In addition to the classic spots (close to water lilies, weeds, or different obstacles such as logs and dead trees), stretches of open water should be explored at various depths, because if a black bass refuses to bite at the surface, his fellows down below may not behave in the same way.

The tackle

An English rod or a spinning rod 8 feet (2.5 m) long, capable of casting 12–15 g will allow fishing at some distance from the bank.

A light fixed-spool spinning reel is loaded with about 330 feet (100 m) of 0.20 to 0.22 mm nylon line. There is little point in fishing with line of greater diameter that can interfere with casting and may arouse the fish's suspicion, unless dealing with big black bass in areas full of snags (in which case, use 0.24 to 0.26 mm line).

Fishing with frogs

This method, which is very effective in summertime, can be used to catch fish lying in ambush just below the surface, close to water lilies. A bubble float on the end of the line can be used to propel the frog and control its movement.

A dropper of about 8 inches (20 cm) about 3 feet (1 m) higher up the line ends in a size 4 or 5 hook.

The frog, attached by the throat, or the back, if a double

■ *In summer the black bass hunts among the weed beds for small fish, insects and frogs.*

■ *Favorite spots for black bass, close to snags and where there are obstacles to hide behind.*

Introducing black bass to a lake

A study carried out by M.J. Wurtz Arlet of Paraclet makes the following recommendations: To obtain the fry of one summer, put in a dozen good parents about three years old weighing about 450 g together with 150 6 inch (15 cm) parent roach for "fodder fish", for each hectare of lake. At the end of October or early in November some 3,000 to 10,000 young black bass 2–4½ inches (5–12 cm) long can be harvested.
Cyprinid and black bass populations are perfectly compatible: like the pike, the black bass is no blind predator that eliminates all small fish. To a lake that is regularly fished every year and produces about 330 to 440 lb (150 to 200 kg) of fish per hectare, add 300 young black bass one summer old (4–6 inch/10–15 cm long, with an average weight of 25 g), 100 carp of 500 g. and 200 parent roach about 6 inches (15 cm) long. At the end of the following year, the yield will be 250 black bass of about 200–250 g, 100 carp of 3 lb (1.5 kg), and some 4,000 or 5,000 young roach bred from the parents. In good conditions black bass grow rapidly. They reach between 10 and 50 g in the first year, from 150 to 200 g in the second, 350 to 400 g in the third, 500 to 850 g in the fourth, and from 750 g to 1.2 kg in the fifth year. Association with other predators must be carefully avoided, particularly perch, which hunt the breeding grounds and devour the fry around their nests.

■ *A fine Spanish black bass taken on a flexible lure.*

or treble hook is used, is then cast to a likely spot (water lilies, weed beds, dead trees or logs), then very slowly retrieved, making it skip on the surface (equally good results can be obtained with a plastic lure).

The bite of the black bass is most spectacular, marked by a violent attack and a leap that often hooks the fish without the intervention of the angler. The frog can also be fished using a sliding lead. One last point: keep informed of any regulations in force concerning the taking of frogs; these may vary from one place to another.

Worm fishing

This method can be used at different depths. Bass in deep water can be taken on a worm fixed on a mount of the type used for zander. Equally well, a bubble float almost full of water can be used in mid-water or near the surface. To this is attached a 16 inch (40 cm) dropper ending in a size 4 or 5 hook. Cast it out towards the chosen spot, then bring it in slowly, alternating jerks and stops. Take care not to cause too much commotion by jerking the bubble float too hard. When the black bass have gone to the bottom, the classic rig with a sliding lead can be used. The main body of line is 0.22 nylon, with a 15 g sliding olive, a stop lead, a swivel and a 16 inch (40 cm) cast in 0.20 mm nylon ending in a size 5 hook.

Black bass make spectacular leaps as soon as they are hooked.

Black bass fishermen are keenly enthusiastic about American casting tackle combined with the multiplier reel.

Fishing with crayfish

Only the use of the American crayfish is authorised: this cannot fail to satisfy a fish with transatlantic origins.

The bait, hooked through the last tail segments, is cast with the aid of a bubble float, then slowly retrieved so it moves about close to the chosen spot. Another technique is to cast the crustacean using a rig identical to that used when worm fishing with a sliding weight. Cast it out and wait until the bait reaches the bottom. Retrieve it a foot or so, then stop and wiggle the crayfish. Alternate between jerking, relaxing and wiggling movements. When there is a bite, leave it a few moments then strike sharply.

All the other natural baits suitable for carnivorous fish (live fish, Planer's lamprey, and possibly flexible lures) may be useful.

■ ***A black bass caught on a plug bait.***

CASTING

Much used by black bass anglers because it is so effective, this method involves a variety of lures each more exotic than the next.

The Americans, past masters of the subject, produce absolutely incredible designs, resembling monsters created by a science fiction author more than lures intended for serious fishing.

Here we are entering an unreal world; the black bass is surely the only fish with such curiosity that presenting it with almost any kind of strange-shaped "imitation" can have a real chance of success. Thus it comes about that one black bass angler, a skilful jewel setter, successfully catches black bass in his lake using a floating Mickey Mouse lure.

The tackle

A spinning rod of 7 to 8 feet (2 – 2.5 m) with a stiff top, capable of casting about 12–15 g is recommended.

A light fixed-spool spinning reel (or a small multiplier, much used in the United States), loaded with 330 feet (100 m) of 0.20 to 0.24 mm nylon line, complete the outfit.

Spoons

Though most types of lure are suitable, highly coloured ones are the most attractive. As with a fly, dressing a spoon with a red tassel or a flexible plastic teaser seems to increase its effectiveness. Fixed-blade weighted spoons also give good results, especially when the fish are deep down. When the size of fish and the habitat are suitable (no large fish and little weed), ultra-light casting is recommended. The black bass can be presented with fly-lures or fly-spoons that are highly attractive in the summer when retrieved close to the surface. Unfortunately this technique does not always allow one to reach places far from the bank.

Fishing method

Cast towards chosen spots (never on top of the fish!) avoiding too much noise when the lure hits the surface, then retrieve slowly in jerks. When the fish bites, strike firmly and control it to prevent it from regaining the weeds. Because the fish's defence is spectacular, unhooking is frequent, but can be limited by keeping the hooks perfectly sharp. Blunt points do not pierce this predator's tough throat at all well.

Designed for a fight

■ *Spanish fishing guide Javier and a fine catch on spinning tackle.*

■ *Shads and other twist lures for black bass are favored by "Dr Manu".*

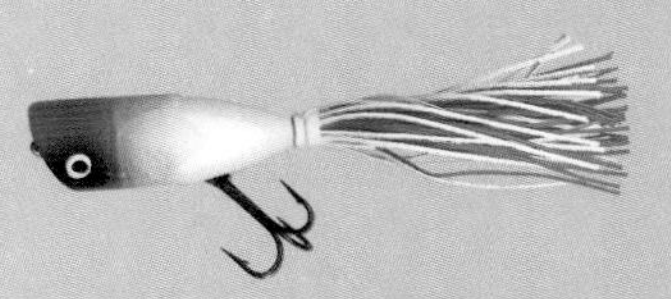

Skiperoo casting popper by Ragot

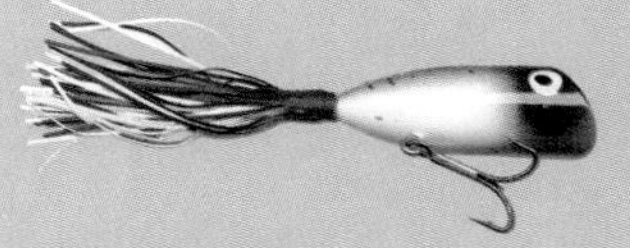

Astucit popper

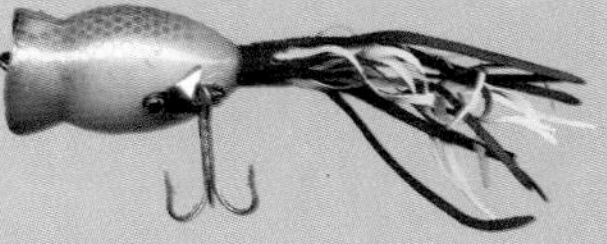

Hula popper

Astucit popper

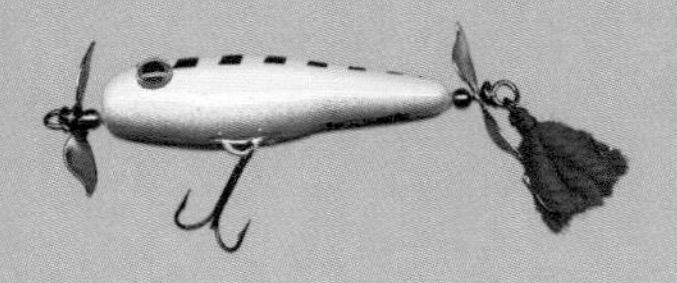

Big Big

■ ***Originally designed for sea bass fishing, propeller lures are now popular for surface fishing for pike and black bass.***

■ ***The slug is an excellent black bass lure.***

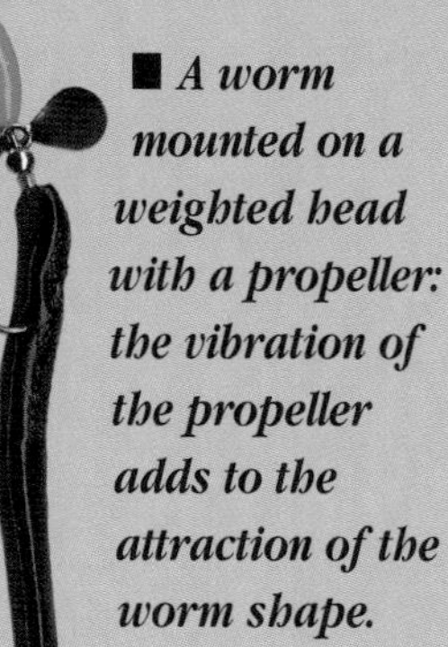

■ ***A worm mounted on a weighted head with a propeller: the vibration of the propeller adds to the attraction of the worm shape.***

Wobbling spoons

Many types of wobbling spoon have been created to satisfy the American market and are not available in France. However some models that approach the transatlantic ones in appearance are to be found in specialized shops. These are long spoons ending in a single hook or a treble dressed with strands of plastic or a tuft of coloured feathers.

Fishing method

The wobbling spoon is especially effective in wintertime when the black bass have retreated to deep water.
Cast in likely spots (sunken trees, underwater boulders), then retrieve the spoon slowly, giving it a lively action. Strike vigorously when there is a bite.

Flexible lures

Compared with other flies and spoons designed for black bass, flexible American lures lack nothing as regards unlikely creations. They more or less resemble large worms, grasshoppers, shrimps, fry, tadpoles or frogs, and the models designed for surface fishing are only lightly weighted. Others have a front weight disguised as a helmet, allowing the lure to be worked close to the bottom. Sometimes they have appendages or false feet aimed at stimulating the black bass's curiosity, and are also often fitted with a useful anti-weed device allowing them to be used in the thickest tangles.

Fishing method

For the weighted types, the method is identical to that recommended for flexible lures. The light lures are cast over weed beds and retrieved in jerks. It is worth leaving the lure motionless a few moments, then making it move on the spot with trembling movements of the rod tip.

American mixed lures

These were created by associating a spoon blade with a flexible lure or some strands of plastic forming a plume. The shape of these lures may seem absurd, but the famous "Roland Martin Spinnerbait" was still voted the best black bass lure in the United States!

Fishing method

This type of lure is of interest because it can be used to seek out black bass at all depths. Bass attack these lures violently, perhaps indicating curiosity as much as pure naked aggression.

Plug baits

Of all the types available, plug baits 3½–4¾ 9–12 cm long in wood or balsa are the most effective. The Rapala fat rap and shad rap types are particularly good. Deep diving plugs are equally effective for black bass in deep water. Older models such as Floppy and Plucky are still good and as effective as ever. Typically American small plug or bugs are also telling baits. One-piece or jointed, with a lip or spirals, they come in an infinity of shapes and colours.

Fishing method

Floating plugs are very effective during the summer. Cast in promising spots and agitate the lure on the surface by moving the rod tip, then recover it 8–12 inches (20–30 cm) at a time. The plug dives, then reappears on the surface as soon as recovery stops. The attack often takes place at the very moment the lure dives. Occasionally savage, the attack may also be marked by an unobtrusive swirl followed by a hard bite. Misses are frequent: they are due to striking too slowly or gently, but more often to blunt hooks or to the fish lashing out. Because black bass are so suspicious, avoid casting noisily right over the fish.

■ ***Crayfish mounted on a hook weighted at the head.***

■ ***This type of crayfish lure is fitted with an anti-weed device.***

FLY-FISHING

No fish that is so sporting and whose natural curiosity excites it to seize the oddest of lures, can escape the wiles of the fly-fisherman. The black bass fights madly and uses every means at its disposal to escape.

■ ***The mouse makes a good surface streamer.***

The tackle

A powerful 9–10 foot (2.7–3.0 m) tip-action rod is recommended.

The reel is the classic manual type, loaded with a nylon backing line then a size 6 or 7 silk double-taper or single forward taper floating line to which is attached a 6 foot (2 m) braided cast.

Surface fly-fishing

The black bass never ceases to astonish trout and grayling purists, who use exact flies in perfect imitation of aquatic insects. The most hideous, brightly-coloured specimens are the ones that actually appeal most to this fish. Flies for black bass are large, and with or without feet. The most effective types are classed as sedges. Panama flies are also excellent.

Fishing method

Drop the fly close to a chosen spot or near a fish, then retrieve it slowly, making it work. The rises are sometimes very quiet and constant concentration is needed. Strike firmly when there is a bite.

Streamer fishing

All designs more or less resembling a worm, an insect or a fish are suitable. They can be used to take black bass on the bottom or in mid-water. The use of a silk line that floats perfectly is advisable. When sinking lines are used, some of the less obtrusive bites may go undetected.

Fishing method

Cast to chosen places such as over a weedy bottom or by immersed trees and retrieve slowly in jerks, tugging the line with the left hand. The line slips between the fingers of the right hand and the rod handle. The bite, which is occasionally almost imperceptible, is indicated by a slight movement of the line, a check, a swirl or a violent attack calling for an immediate strike in response.

■ *The crayfish makes an excellent streamer.*

■ *A rabbit fur streamer.*

Fishing with poppers

These extraordinary lures are most effective for black bass when fished on the surface with a fly rod. They more or less represent large insects, beetles or dragonflies, and their particular advantage is that they can be used to fish the densest weed beds. Their design largely eliminates the risk of snagging.

Fishing method

Every typical location should be carefully explored, particularly areas where weeds are plentiful. At certain times of day, during heat waves, black bass seek out the shade offered by foliage overhanging the banks. To exploit these places it is essential to wade or better, use a boat. Casting a popper does not call for it to be plonked down arousing the fish's suspicions; a simple, quiet, cast is enough to alert it. The line is held taut in the left hand. A sharp tug of about 4 inches (10 cm) will make the lure dive suddenly. As the movement stops, the popper rises again. Alternate this tugging and slackening with trembling on the spot produced by the rod tip, as well as intervals of immobility. The black bass often attacks when it thinks the lure is about to escape, or when it is motionless. The bite, occasionally spectacular, is often subtle, the black bass seizing the popper with some delicacy. Any suspicious swirl should elicit an immediate vigorous strike. Misses, which are frequent, are due to slow striking through not having detected the bite in time, or to blunt hooks.

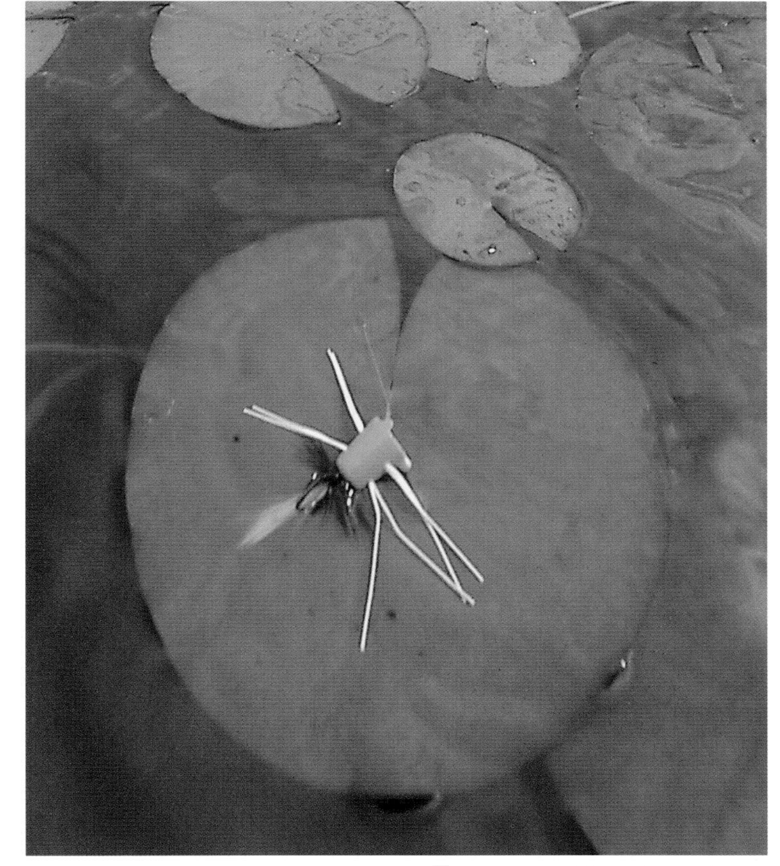

■ *A popper placed on a lily leaf: it can be towed on the surface among the weeds.*

Popper construction

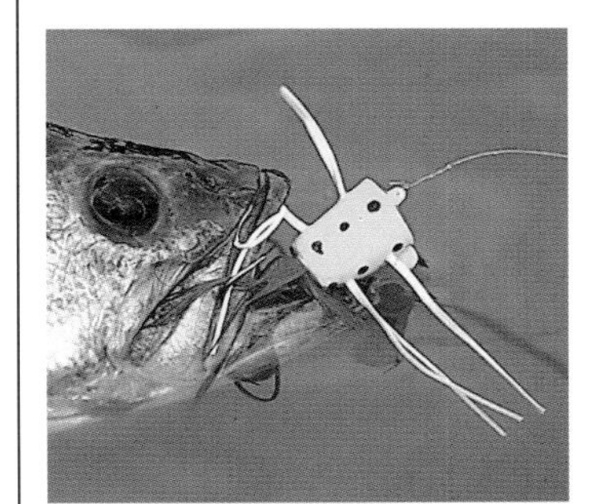

■ *This popper has literally nailed the black bass's wide mouth.*

This lure is made out of a cone-shaped piece of cork or balsa, with the wide end at the front. This latter is somewhat hollowed out and bears the eye to which the line is attached. The whole is completed by a size 4 to 8 hook with a long shank and downturned eye, together with a tuft of feathers or thick fur and long strands which terminate the lure. One can add eyes, antennae, legs (fetching, and useful for balancing the lure) or wings, or not. Everyone can give free rein to his or her own imagination!

The mounting of a simple anti-weed device is strongly recommended. Lighter poppers can be made of dense polystyrene. The weight should not be more than1g.

The zander has been actively fished for since its sudden appearance in the 70s. Moreover, it has largely been the cause of a new craze for predator fishing with its own group of enthusiasts.

The increasing scarcity of pike has led most hunters of predatory fish to fall back on the zander, another predator of reasonable size that until recently was spreading rapidly.

In about the 70s Albert Drakhovitch and Henry Limouzin, two French anglers with such an international reputation that they need little introduction, were the forerunners of a veritable piscatorial revolution. At a time when the behaviour of the zander and techniques for catching it were relatively unknown, they revealed their secrets and popularized the use of the famous Drakhovitch deadbait mount, which was the start of the boom in using this method.

With their enlightened advice, they helped to create a movement that brought new enthusiasm to many an angler disillusioned by continued setbacks and ready to hang up his rods.

Zander

A very popular predator

Latin name: *Stizostedion lucioperca*
Family: Percidae

■ ***This fine zander will soon return to its element.***

LIVEBAITING FOR ZANDER

Above all, livebaiting for zander means being able to persevere, since the activities of this very temperamental fish are completely unpredictable. The zander may provide the angler with genuine pleasure by biting furiously for a certain time (sometimes not more than a few hours), then it will remain with its mouth buttoned for several days, even weeks, without it being really known why. It is impossible to formulate any strict rules about the influence of light or climatic conditions on the aggressive behaviour of this fish: however, a cloudy sky accompanied by a west wind seems more favourable than bright sunlight and a north wind. Changes in the water are particularly favourable, especially if they are gradual, but precede an appreciable rise in level (autumn spates, for example). If the influence of meteorological conditions is poorly understood, it is an established fact that success depends 80 per cent on the reconnaissance of likely spots, failure being due to fishing in deserted waters! To locate the haunts of this fish in vast stretches of water such as gravel pits would be impossible without an echo sounder that allows the shape of the bottom and the shoals of fish to be seen. Diabolical when used well, this device is forbidden in free waters.

■ ***Wintry weather does not deter the zander enthusiast from fully enjoying his favourite pastime.***

Float fishing

If a fixed float is satisfactory in a shallow pond or river, it is less so in a reservoir where one may be fishing in 16 feet (5 m) of water. In this case, exploration at the desired depth can only be achieved by adding a sliding float or an English waggler type float to the line.

The tackle

Choose a ringed telescopic or sectional rod not longer than 16 feet (5 m), rated somewhere between a model intended for trout and one recommended for pike. For an English rig, use a 13 foot (4 m) English rod in three sections.

A light fixed-spool spinning reel is loaded with 330 feet (100 m) of 0.22 to 0.26 mm fluorescent nylon depending on how cluttered the location is.

In the set-up, the float is kept just at the surface with an olivette. The zander's teeth do not call for the use of a steel trace. The nylon cast, not longer than 20 inches (50 cm) ends in a single size 2 or 3 hook through the lips of the live bait, or in a treble hook fixed in its back at the level of the dorsal fin. These rigs, which lend themselves to immediate hooking in cluttered places, may be made lighter (with hooks smaller than the recommended size) when fishing in areas with fewer snags.

Livebait

Any white fish sized between 2½ and 4 inches (6 and 10 cm) will do, preferably a species clad in brilliant scales such as bleak, roach, rudd. Unlike pike, zander seek small prey, though there are exceptions, as proved by a bream of just over 1lb (500 g) found in the stomach of a 6½ lb (3 kg) zander.

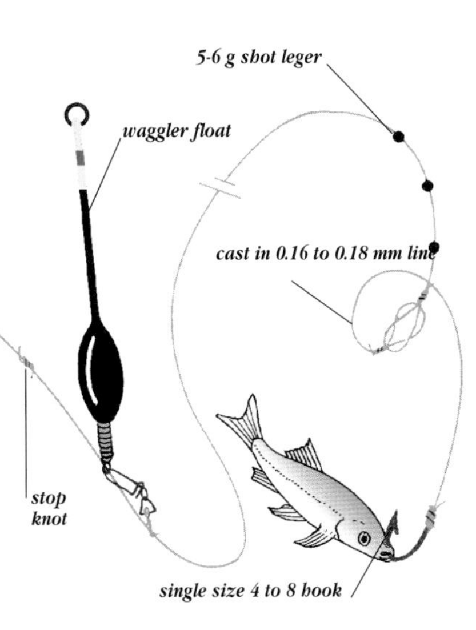

■ ***An English rig for livebaiting for zander with a float.***

■ *Fluorescent line often permits even the quietest bites to be detected.*

■ *A well earned break for these anglers, after taking a trophy zander.*

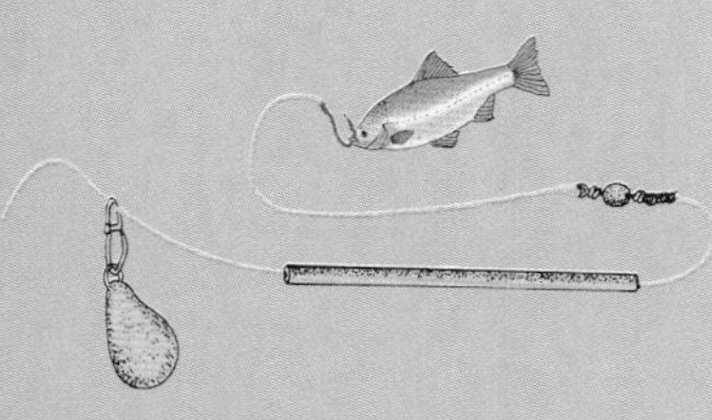

■ *A long-distance livebait rig.*

Fishing method

Having found a likely spot, carefully plumb the depth and adjust the float accordingly, because zander always feed near the bottom. Cast the livebait in, gently. If fishing where there is no current, place the rod on a rest with the tip towards the water and the pick-up open. Avoid forming an angle between the line and the rod and creating resistance that would inevitably arouse the fish's suspicion. The line is lightly held in a clip, or with an elastic band or a pebble, to ensure that the livebait does not take line from the spool. Rods should always be positioned with great care. Avoid heavy steps on the bank, noisy casts, and rods rattling together on the rod rest.

In cluttered places, where immediate hooking is necessary, close the pick-up at the least unusual movement and strike vigorously with a full action. The fish is lifted off the bottom without undue ceremony, and hauled to the surface as quickly as possible.

When it is possible to delay the strike, the zander must be given time to seize the bait, though without allowing it the interval recommended for pike. The bite is signalled by a sharp tug, a halt, then another tug. Strike at the second movement.

Leger livebaiting

With this method the livebait can be kept in a slight current that would carry a float away; long distances can be achieved in huge stretches of water such as gravel pits. The weight, some 20–40 g, is attached to the main body of line above a link swivel, and separated from it by a sliding length of plastic.

Fishing method

Cast the livebait gently to avoid injuring it, or becoming unhooked when it hits the surface. The outgoing line is braked with the index finger to avoid tangles and ensure the rig is presented correctly. When a slackening of the line indicates contact with the bottom, the line is held in a bite indicator and pulled up at the least unusual movement.

If no such device is used, a pebble or an elastic band will do just as well. A bite is indicated by trembling of the rod tip, followed by a rapid departure. Let the line go a few meters then take up the rod, close the pick-up arm and strike with a full movement. It sometimes happens that the fish takes the

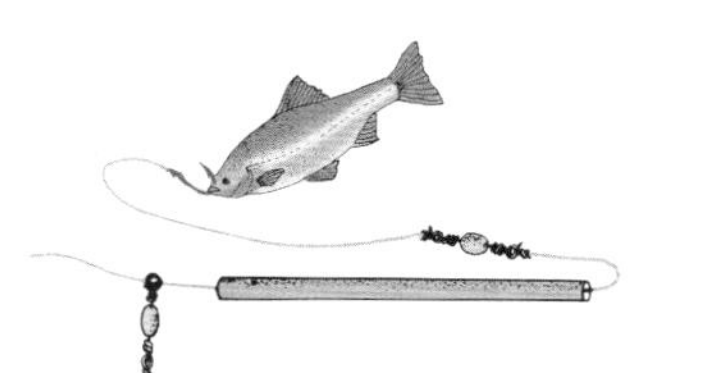

■ *A livebait rig with drift weight.*

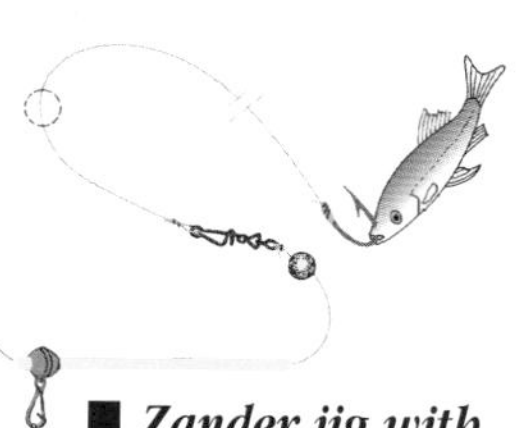

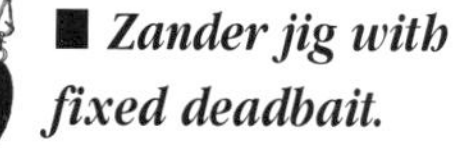

■ *Zander jig with fixed deadbait.*

A very popular predator

A zander taken on a flexible lure.

bait just as you pull the line in at the end of a long and fruitless wait. At the least sign of an unusual stoppage, open the pick-up again to allow the predator time to seize the bait, then strike sharply.

CASTING WITH NATURAL BAITS

Worm fishing

Casting the worm is an effective if little known method that allows the zander enthusiast to follow his passion throughout the close season for pike.

The tackle is the same as is used for deadbait fishing, except for the rig to hold the worm. The main line in 0.28 mm fluorescent nylon bears a link swivel above which is fixed a shot of about 8 g. The 20 inch (50 cm) cast ends in a size 6 to 8 treble hook, or a single size 2 hook. Choose a large black-headed worm and impale it just behind the head on all three points of the treble with the body hanging free. With the single hook, the worm is pierced twice behind the head and formed into a loop.

Fishing method

Gently cast in the direction of a likely spot, braking the descent of the bait with the forefinger on the outgoing line so as to avoid tangles and a violent landing that could break up the worm. Keep some tension on the line throughout the descent. When the bait reaches the bottom (the line slackens slightly), close the pick-up and retrieve any slack with the rod tip down. Raise the rod tip sharply to jerk the bait nervously for a foot or so, then lower the rod tip again and let it go slack. Alternate these movements with a trembling of the rod tip, always keeping in touch with the bait, and change the speed of retrieval to give the worm an intermittent swimming motion, constantly regaining contact with the bottom. The bite is a sudden check, which should be answered with an immediate strike.

Mention should be given here to an even more effective bait than the worm: Planer's lamprey. With the point of the hook passing immediately under the skin to avoid injury, the lamprey is pierced twice immediately behind the head so that the body forms a loop. The fishing action is the same; the only problem is in finding this little lamprey.

Likely spots for zander are in calm, deep water away from the main river current, especially where there are objects such as submerged trees. This is just as true in reservoirs, where the environment is particularly suitable for this fish.

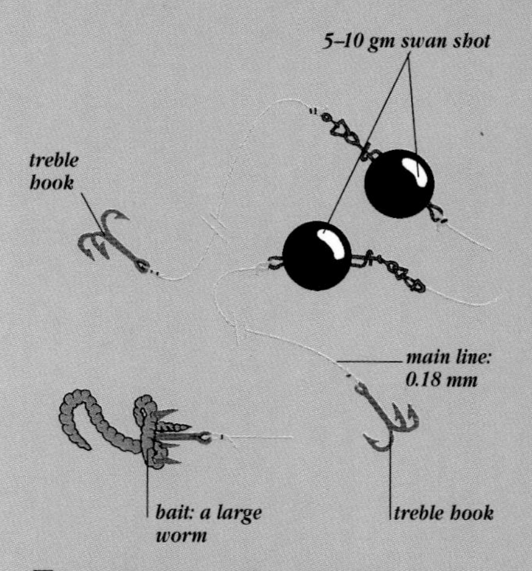

■ *Worming rig for zander.*

Likely spots for zander

In rivers zander like deep, calm water, the bottom cluttered with obstacles that can provide refuge. Big, slow eddies with submerged trees or logs, deep banks full of holes, and sheer rock walls are all equally good places. In deep water zander shows a distinct liking for places where the slope changes at the edges of large holes. In the summer they sometimes hunt in fast, shallow water.
In canals, zander are found in the deeper parts towards the middle, near locks, and in wider sections such as basins.
In lakes they can be encountered close to any embankment, and especially near sluice gates, and in deep areas of open water.
In reservoirs zander are found in the deeper parts where there are obstacles such as sunken trees, logs and rocks. Other good spots are where the slope suddenly changes, near masses of submerged rock, on gentle slopes leading to a steep incline, old riverbeds and tributary inlets.

■ *Deadbait fishing from a boat calls for a minimum of coordination by these two anglers.*

■ *A fine display of yellow pike, the Canadian zander, taken by expert fisherman Daniel Sabatini.*

Deadbait fishing

This fishing method is one of the most suitable for a fish that hunts slowly in the depths. If it seems biblical in its simplicity, the method is nonetheless one of the most difficult in practice. This is because it demands total involvement: constant concentration to be able to detect the smallest abnormality, an excellent knowledge of the bottom and the fish's haunts and habits, perfectly sharpened reflexes, and unfailing persistence – such qualities make a real angler out of an amateur. The active nature of this pleasing method also adds to its appeal.

The tackle

The rod should have a number of characteristics. 8 to 11 feet (2.5–3.4 m) long, depending on whether one is fishing from a boat or from the bank, it will be necessarily quite stiff, with a pronounced tip action. In fact, and this is especially so in reservoirs, this rigidity will only just be enough to convey the nervousness of the movements imparted by the rod, as well as making sure that the strike goes home and is not absorbed by the flexibility of the top section and the length of the intervening line. Carbon measures up to these criteria, with the added advantage that because of its light weight it can be wielded all day without excessive fatigue. Another benefit is that the angler can be sure that any abnormal behaviour of the line will be better transmitted, hence the greater sensitivity of the tackle.

The light fixed-spool spinning reel with a very reliable drag system – since this will be heavily used when striking.

■ *Fixed and running rigs for leger livebaiting.*

■ *Deadbait is worked along the bottom.*

The spool, which is wide to avoid excessive twisting when casting long distances, carries 500 feet (150 m) of 0.26 to 0.28 mm fluorescent nylon. This diameter can be smaller when fishing in lakes or rivers that are relatively shallow, but not in the depths found in reservoirs.

In fact some of the nervous movement imparted to the deadbait is absorbed by the length of thin, stretchable line, and this may render the bait less attractive. Coloured line is not just recommended, it is essential, because it allows the movement of the bait to be followed and the contours of the bottom to be assessed as well as alerting the angler to anything unusual while it is sinking, or being raised or lowered.

Mounts

Not without a certain irony, some Irish anglers claim that all salmon flies are good as long as they are black.
The same goes for deadbait mounts, they are all good as long as they hold the fish perfectly, bear two fine size 8 to 10 treble hooks and are provided with a changeable weight, are jointed at the head. in short, if they are identical to a No.1 or No.2 Drakhovitch mount. The mount is an essential element in this type of fishing, and true zander fishermen know it well, making their own models in the greatest secrecy, These models however always more or less resemble the "Drakho".

The fish

Zander seem to have a preference for small, very shiny fish. Species such as bleak, small roach, chub, gudgeon or rudd should be chosen, between 3 and 4 inches (8 and 10 cm) long. Kept live in a pail, they are killed with a flick on the neck before being used. This ensures an appetizing freshness and longer attachment to the hook. If necessary frozen fish can be used, but these stay on the hook only moderately well.

■ *Some of the crew of the "Pêcheur de France" at work: Mark-Antoine and Natalie Colle, on a water in Normandy.*

Fishing method

This consists of presenting the zander, with the dead fish at different depths; when made to somersault it will have a lifelike appearance. Having chosen a promising spot, the dead fish is cast in and, with the rod pointing at the water, close attention is given to its descent. It is essential to maintain constant control through light tension on the line because, as the fish spirals to the bottom. there may be a bite, betrayed by some slight movement of the line.

When it reaches its destination (marked by a slight slackening of the line) close the pickup immediately and raise the rod with a sharp movement, then jerk the rod tip up about a foot, so as to imitate the agonies of a sick fish. Lower the rod tip again and repeat the process, keeping the line taut and watching for any abnormal movement, and above all, maintaining regular contact with the bottom.

From time to time these irregular movements may be performed on the spot, as with a lure, to arouse the desire of a sated or sleepy fish.

The bite is signalled by a sudden check followed by a strong pull. In such unmistakable cases it pays to reply with an immediate strike. Sometimes the bite is barely perceptible, betrayed only by a slight movement or gliding of the line. When there is the slightest doubt, always strike. The whole art of this method of fishing lies in being able to identify quiet bites, having a feeling for the water and knowledge of the fish's haunts. On a reservoir or a gravel pit, this can be really difficult, which is why a good guide or good on-the-spot advice is so important so don't hesitate to ask at the local angling club.

■ *A superb zander seduced by a deadbait. Note the remarkable colouring of this fish caught in very clear water.*

■ *The Drakhovitch mount, with its jointed, changeable weight, was a mythical object in the 70s, and is just as effective today.*

JIGGING

Invented by zander specialists, this technique is also effective for deep-water fish such as char, but comes into its own when fishing for zander, above all when they are much fished over.

The rig and technique are biblical in their simplicity. The rig consists of a 10–15 g olive resting against a silicone tube that protects the knot of a link swivel. The 0.22 to 0.24 mm nylon cast is armed with a single size 4 to size 6 hook through the nose of a live bait about 4 inches (10 cm) long.

The whole art of this method consists in allowing the livebait to move along the bottom, alternating intervals of immobility with gliding about, somersaulting and jigging movements on the spot.

Rods with thin, sensitive tips of the quiver-tip type are used in this form of fishing, sensitive enough to detect the gentlest bite. The method can also be used with a worm or even a flexible lure.

■ ***In some circumstances, especially in summer when zander hunt in the current or approach the bank during an autumn (or spring) flood, they may be tempted by a well-presented streamer.***

FLY-FISHING

The zander can be fished for with the fly, though this method is primarily intended for ponds not much more than 10 to 13 feet (3–4 m) in depth. In fact, we know that this fish essentially feeds on the bottom. It would be impossible to work a streamer effectively in a gravel pit or reservoir deeper than about 30 feet (10 m).

Likewise in rivers, strong currents rule this method out since the lure must pass close to the bottom, and very slowly at that.

One solution is to weight the streamer to make it sink all the faster.

This is no cure-all, even if it may prove effective in some cases, since the weight renders the swimming action of the lure less attractive. Not only this, great depths call for relatively heavy weights (from 2 to 4 g) which make it difficult to handle a reservoir or sea trout fly rod correctly.

One can also use an extra-fast sinking fly line, but it can only be used to maximum effect in waters less than 10 feet (3 m) deep. This would be in lakes, or downstream along the edges of some rivers.

To fish the best places in a reservoir, the use of a boat is essential; the least visited spots are in open water. This is where the fish are likely to be found.

LURE FISHING

The completely new flexible lures that have invaded the market are effective when used for zander: on certain days, the "commas" and other spangled fish prove more effective than live or dead bait. They are not miracle lures, however, as was believed when they first appeared.

They are effective because their design allows them to be weighted very quickly, giving a slow, attractive swimming movement (thanks to the comma-shaped tail) close to the bottom. All the other metallic lures (spoons for example) are not as attractive because they swim too fast and do not work deeply enough.

The tackle

A ringed rod about 10 feet (3 m) long is chosen, with a more flexible tip than is used to work a deadbait.

The reel is a light fixed-spool type, its spool loaded with 500 feet (150 m) of 0.26 mm fluorescent line.

Lures

Most effective are lures weighted at the head, or commas. In those with a jointed weight at the head, the weight can be varied to give better manoeuvrability. Soft fish mounted on a No. 0 Drakhovitch, or tandem mixed jigging rigs are equally attractive.

All these lures more or less imitate a large worm or a small fish. They are variously coloured, some models in brilliant fluorescent colours giving the very prettiest effects. These are reserved for coloured waters; in normal conditions lures in natural colours are preferable.

Fishing method

After casting, it is essential to watch the descent closely, keeping the line in light tension: a good flexible lure is attractive from the moment it enters the water. Watch out for any unusual movement of the line as soon as it submerges. When the lure reaches the bottom, lower the rod and retrieve any slack line. Then raise it with a sharp movement of the rod, giving it a series of nervous jerks before letting it touch the bottom once more. Zander sometimes bite when the lure is released, or is lying still on the bottom. Be ready to strike at any moment.

This choice fishing technique calls for as much care as fishing with deadbait. The comma or flexible fish can also be made to skip about on the spot, especially in a reservoir when it is directly below the boat. The bite is felt as a shock or a sudden check, or much more subtly by an uptake of line or a snagging sensation when slack is recovered after letting the lure sink. Whichever the case, strike vigorously at the least unusual sign.

■ ***The flexible lure: indispensable for catching zander in deep water.***

Is the zander in decline?

■ *The autumn months see a resumption of activity by the zander.*

■ *A flexible lure on a Drakhovitch mount is suitable for fishing the zander.*

Takes of zander seem to be falling, and in many areas do not compare with the excesses of former years.
Are populations decreasing ? The question remains; some observations tend to support the idea, others, on the other hand, seem to blame fishing of such intensity that the fish have become suspicious of the lures and baits offered them. A second theory is based on numerous observations. Zander are encountered in previously deserted stretches of water, proof that the species continues to colonize our waters. Further supporting evidence emerged with the draining of the Neuvic-d'Ussel reservoir in Corrèze, in the autumn of 1989. This location, famed for its predator fishing, had proved disappointing in previous years, at least as far as catches of zander were concerned. However the emptying revealed an
absolutely incredible density of zander of all ages, a significant indication of excellent reproduction activity.
Why had the fish stopped biting?

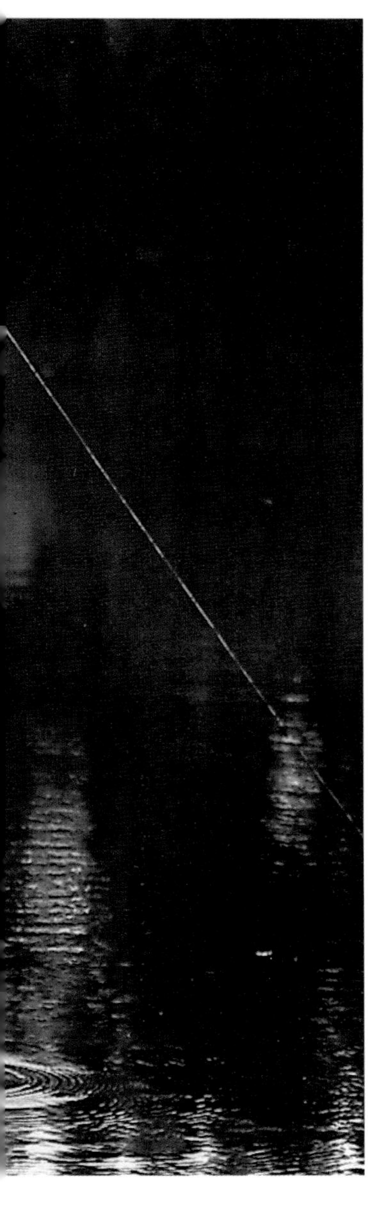

One can't help recalling Albert Drakhovitch's most judicious remark:
"What is happening today is the logical outcome of things. Now the fish choose their anglers!" The apparent reduction in numbers of zander can also be explained by a long- and well-established theory of the biology of all living beings: "The population of an introduced species goes through a phase of exponential growth, followed by an optimal phase, in the course of which a balance is reached, generally at a lower level than during the exponential phase." Doubtless zander populations in most waters have experienced this cyclic phenomenon.
Far from alarming anglers who fish for predators, we cannot mutely pass over the numerous assaults disturbing the biology of these fish that lead some scientists to predict a gloomy future for the species. Above all, there is the pressure of fishing, excessive in numerous places, and at the expense of fish whose minimum legal length of 13–14 inches (35 cm) seems ridiculous, especially since most of the specimens concerned have never reproduced. It must be said that for many years the zander, a victim of its reputation for cruelty, was the object of real extermination campaigns. At that time the capture of young specimens was considered beneficial. The anglers responsible for these executions, ever eager for sensational fishing, and more concerned with filling the freezer than respecting sporting ethics, even set about gatherings of breeding fish at their spawning grounds. The fish, famished and very aggressive, attack any lure within reach. The work of destruction is completed by nets fixed in known places by professional fishermen. No words are strong enough to condemn these actions, especially since in the absence of legislation suited to the fish's biology, half of the total annual catch in many provinces is taken by these sinister individuals – and this during the three or four weeks required for breeding to take place.
Finally, managers of large stretches of water (reservoirs) do not invariably make allowance for the reproductive requirements of the zander. Marling carried out just after spawning has taken place can have disastrous consequences: the eggs either dry up or end up in water that is too deep. In the second case, the results are just as dramatic: the fry with its sac has to reach the surface to acquire an air bubble – a one-way trip, for the unfortunate fish's strength is not enough for the distance involved.
So, is the zander in decline, or are its numbers being maintained at an acceptable level? The more optimistic are inclined to the latter view, and we hope they are right. Nonetheless we cannot ignore the cries of alarm raised by the "pessimists". Whatever the case, every zander angler must respect a certain ethic, release specimens less than 18 inches (45 cm) in length and above all, limit his take. As regards professional fishermen, the case against them is no longer groundless. Only they more or less control the excess populations of bream in reservoirs, and I have personally known some who regularly use small nursery streams to repopulate these lakes with pike. After all, they have as much interest as we rod and line anglers in fishing in rich and fishy waters. They should be reasonable and avoid netting during the breeding season, something that was once the ruinous act of the unlicensed poacher.

The history of the zander in France

Altough the Zander is an extremely unpopular fish in British waters, where the Water Authorities are trying to eliminate it, it has for some years been the most popular and numerous predatory fish in French waters. Unfortunately in some regions of France its numbers have declined significantly owing to a lack of legislation appropriate to its biology. Originating in central Europe, particularly in great rivers such as the Don, the Dneiper or the Danube, it first appeared in France in 1945 following illegal introductions. Real proliferation occurred during the decade between 1960 and 1970, the predictable outcome of the interaction of several factors favouring the species. Pollution, physical as much as organic (domestic refuse, leaching of agricultural fertilizers, extraction of agglomerates) has helped to warm up the water, resulting in increasing eutrophy favouring the profusion of algae, and leading to an increase in turbidity with layers of silt smothering the bottom and the breeding grounds. The zander is well suited to these disastrous conditions, which cause pike numbers to reduce, because it cleans, maintains and ventilates its spawning grounds. Its enormous reproductive potential (a female lays 200,000 eggs per kilogram) enables it to withstand numerous assaults on the species.
The exploitation of sand and gravel from the river bed has also made a fortunate contribution: the creation of ditches up to 33 feet (10 m) deep which, once they were colonized by zander were seen as beneficial, since these fish love the depths. The proliferation of gravel pits that communicate with watercourses when in flood have also contributed to the invasion of the species.

The wels is gradually colonizing all our main rivers. This terrific predator, which, in the right conditions, can grow to several hundred pounds, is increasingly coveted by the sporting angler.

No freshwater trophy can equal this! The wels is enormous, exceptionally so, and calls for the use of robust tackle. Fascinated by the power of this adversary, some anglers fish for nothing else, ignoring other carnivorous fish that cut a poor figure beside this giant predator.

■ ***A good wels will not pass up a carp of two or three pounds.***

FISHING WITH NATURAL BAIT

Sliding link leger

The tackle

A heavy casting sea rod, or a powerful carp or pike rod is recommended. About 12 to 14 feet (3.50 to 4 m) long, it should have a solid, reliable, reel mounting (the fixed type is preferable). The rings should be of good quality, wide and very smooth.

A formidable battery of rods, all set up for livebaiting using floats.

A first class sea or salmon reel is needed. The type with a progressive brake is preferable. The pick-up is not essential and may be replaced by a finger-type recovery system.

From 500 to 650 feet (150 to 200 m) of 0.45 to 0.50 mm line fill the spool. Its condition should be checked regularly and any line that is twisted or has been repeatedly rubbed should be replaced.

The hooks can be single (from size 1 to 4, according to the size of the bait), double or treble, and should be very strong and sharp.

The weight (a sliding olive or a plummet) varies between 40 and 150 g depending on the strength of the current. A steel trace is not necessary.

Wels

Power in murky waters

Latin name: *Silurus glanis*
Family: Siluridae

Rod rests are essential: these are padded to avoid noise when placing the rod. A gaff could also be used, though sporting etiquette calls for the fish to be landed only by hand.

Bearing in mind the extraordinary power of the fish's jaws, thick gloves are also essential. The Waller gaff can only be used when the fish is completely exhausted. Taking the rod in the left hand, wedge the thumb behind the teeth on the lower jaw, using four fingers to hold the jaw closed. Taking advantage of surprise, land the fish quickly, watching out for the powerful, violent blows of the tail that the wels can deliver.

To the tackle described above add an olive of 30–50 g next to a stop weight, above a good quality link swivel. The 20 inch (50 cm) cast ends in a single hook.

Baits

Worms, earthworms, crayfish, and small livebait are the most commonly used baits.

Fishing method

An absolute priority is to be unobtrusive. The wels is very sensitive to sound, and every precaution should be taken to keep it to a minimum (move softly on the bank, use foam-padded rod butts if fishing from a boat). Cast In a likely spot (a depression, sunken hiding place, by a shady bank) then place the rod on the rest and fix it securely. Keep the line horizontal. When hooked, the fish puts up a muscular, if not very spectacular defence. It resists using its size and weight, seeking help from the current and hitting the line violently with its tail or, having decided not to budge, quite simply sinks to the bottom. Pulling up a 44 to 66 lb (20–30 kg) fish is no easy task!

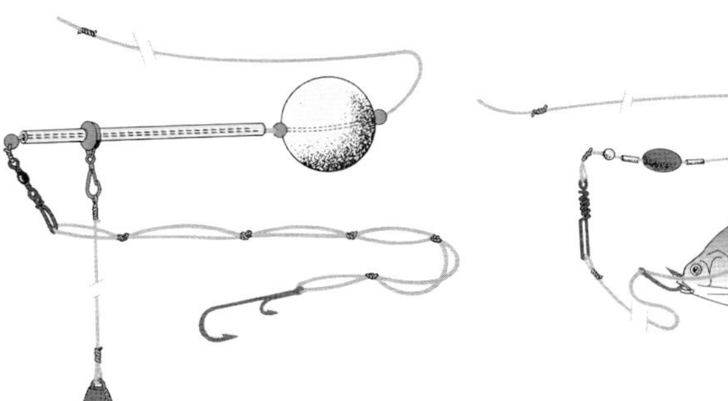

■ *Wels rig for cluttered spots.*

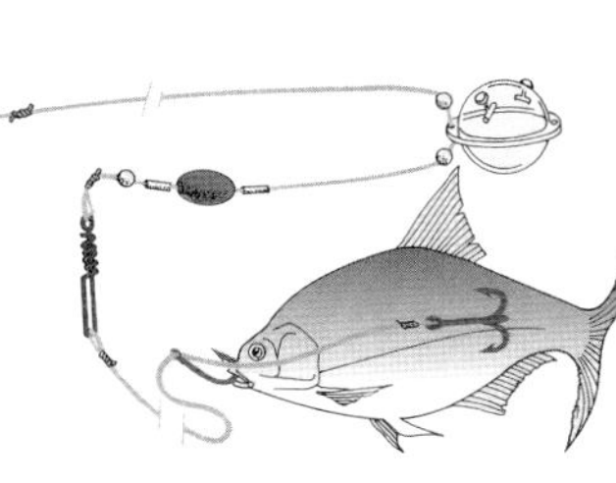

■ *Rig allowing an immediate strike among snags.*

Float fishing

This method is mostly used for livebaiting. The tackle is identical to that previously described, with the addition of a sliding float weighted with a 30–40 g olive.

Paternoster fishing

This consists of presenting a large livebait of at least 450 g in mid-water on a double or treble hook. The hook is attached to a 20 inches (50 cm) spur of 0.45 mm nylon attached to a treble swivel made for paternoster rigs. The weight is a pear-shaped lead of 50–100 g.

Fishing method

Cast where the wels is thought to be. When the bait touches the bottom, put the rod on its rest. When there is a bite, wait a good while (the line may be taken for some distance), then strike vigorously.

■ *Set-up for livebaiting with a paternoster.*

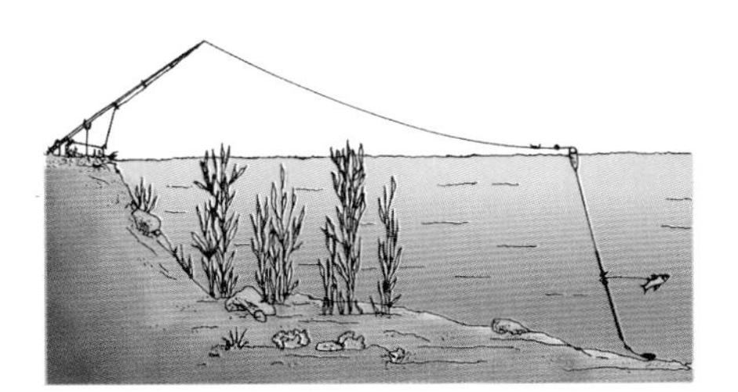

■ *The formidable-looking wels has six prominent barbels around its mouth with which it detects its prey.*

CASTING

Lures and deadbait

The tackle

A medium weight spinning rod for salmon, 12 feet (3.5 m) long. A medium weight fixed-spool spinning reel for salmon, the spool filled with 200 m of 0.4 mm nylon line.

Lures and baits

There are two effective types of lure: wobbling spoons with the blade about 4 inches (10 cm) long weighing from 15 to 20 g, and plug baits that sink to about 30 to 50 feet (10 to 15 m). Dead fish (roach, bleak, chub) are fixed on mounts with robust steel hooks, identical to those used for pike.

Fishing method

Similar to pike fishing. Cast where the wels is thought to be and retrieve slowly, close to the bottom, then in mid-water. The fish may sometimes attack the lure just below the surface or as it reaches the bank.

■ ***Extremely sensitive to sound, the wels is attracted by the noise of a clapper.***

■ ***The wels can be caught in mid-stream on metal or flexible lures, especially during the breeding season. Here, a scene at Mequinenza, in Spain.***

OTHER TECHNIQUES

Roaming the riverbank in search of the wels with a single rod and a livebait, a bunch of worms or a crayfish can be equally effective whether casting the bait or retrieving it slowly along the bottom. The livebait may also be fished from a boat drifting with the current, using a float.

The beast is displayed for the photographer before its release.

ATTRACTING THE WELS

Groundbaiting

This is very important in fishing for the wels; it may act indirectly by attracting small fry whose commotion cannot fail to arouse the hunger of the wels, or directly, if the groundbait is meat-based.

Indirect groundbaiting

Most of the heavy flours usually recommended for white fish are effective. Simply groundbait close to the place the wels is thought to be, and wait until its attention is aroused by the arrival of the fry.

Direct groundbaiting

Consists of attracting the wels by offering it a mixture of chopped fish (bream) and oat flakes, in fairly large quantities (4–6 lb/2–3 kg each time), for about 12 days before fishing.

Calls

Here again the wels reveals its extraordinary abilities. Very sensitive to noise (being endowed with a particularly elaborate auditory system), this fish is attracted by certain sounds which enervate and excite it to seize baits at the end of lines. Thus the Butochkalo, a call originating in Eastern Europe, emits a sound that is attractive especially at night. On occasion the wels will throw itself out of the water in an attempt to seize this strange device, and may even grab the arm of the unfortunate angler!

Romanian calls

The Romanian call is a simple tin vessel shaped like a yoghurt pot, the base fixed on a wooden handle. Striking the water with the inverted vessel attracts the wels.

Yugoslavian calls

The Yugoslavian call is a piece of wood about 2½–2¾ inches (6–7 cm) in diameter, the base bevelled at an angle of 65° and hollowed out like a bowl, with the middle part of the device narrowed by about 3 cm. The bowl is struck on the water at regular intervals (three or four rapid blows every 30 seconds) to attract the predators.

Catfish

The mustachioed gourmand

Latin name: *Ictalurus melas*
Family: Ictaluridae

No angler, however unlucky, can fail to catch a catfish. Its greed condemns it to be the privileged target of the tyro, who sharpens his reflexes on this "moustachioed villain".

It has to be said that apart from undeniable gastronomic qualities – the only favourable thing that can be said about this scourge that has colonized a good part of our water system – the catfish is a real calamity that would be very difficult to reverse! Its legendary resistance to lack of oxygen enables it to live in the worst conditions. Emptying one's lake to get rid of it is useless if any parts stay permanently wet. The fish sink into the mud and can hibernate for many months, then overrun the piece of water as soon as it is refilled. Other undesirable characteristics are its tendency to multiply, and its inordinate taste for the eggs and fry of other fish. Only the black bass manages to control its numbers satisfactorily. If fishing for catfish is within everyone's reach, it is no less unpleasant. The catfish actually swallows the whole bait right up to the float, so every catch involves real surgical intervention, rendered the more dangerous by poisonous spines in the four pectoral fins, capable of inflicting painful wounds.

Float fishing or using a running leger

The tackle

Catfish are caught by float fishing or with a running leger. The first method calls for a 13 or 16 foot (4 or 5 m) telescopic rod to which is attached the main body of line in .16 mm nylon. A spindle-shaped float is weighted with a cluster of shot. The cast, in 0.14 mm nylon terminates in a size 12 hook. In the second method, any classic spinning rod of 6 to 8 feet 1.80 – 2.5 m will do. A light fixed-spool spinning reel is loaded with 330 feet (100 m) of 0.18 mm nylon. A 10 g sliding olive is stopped by a swivel to which is attached a 12 inch (30 cm) cast with a size 10 hook on the end.

Baits

As the catfish is essentially carnivorous, animal baits are to be preferred. Earthworms, brandlings or bunches of maggots will serve perfectly well.

Fishing method

Since the catfish rarely feeds on the surface, the bait should always lie on the bottom. The float should be adjusted accordingly. Groundbaiting can be carried out with blood mixed with the soil from a molehill and sections of earthworm. The bite is unmistakable and an immediate strike is necessary to prevent the catfish swallowing too much bait, which makes it difficult to extract the hook. Large specimens may sometimes be taken on pike lines.

■ ***Though the catfish resembles the wels, it belongs to the Ictaluridae, a different family, known as bullheads.***

In recent years the fishing techniques used for white fish have been greatly refined. This is particularly true with carp, now the object of a real cult among a new generation of anglers equipped with ultra-sophisticated tackle, who adhere to the admirable code of regularly releasing their catch.

The pursuit of white fish in running water has also developed considerably with the appearance of new techniques such as the Bologna method. The cyprinid population in our waters is literally exploding, and offers the angler new and exciting possibilities.

Refined fishing techniques for white fish

Modern English carp fishing methods involve highly sophisticated tackle and a wide variety of baits.

Carp

A matter of initiation

Latin name: *Cyprinus carpio*
Family name: Cyprinidae

Carp fishing has its unshakeable adherents, gathered at the heart of a true brotherhood single-mindedly devoted to the cult of this suspicious and devilishly combative fish. Its power, the enormous sizes it can reach, and its stubbornness and guile in combat make it one of the most difficult fish to control at the end of a line. The recent advent of English techniques has upset the habits of our traditional carp fishermen and, by reason of its sporting character, converted not a few of them. The English respect a certain code, that of invariably returning the catch to the water. In addition the carp is fished for on light, highly advanced tackle, which can be very exciting when dealing with large fish. A new, very wide range of baits and groundbait, the result of scientific research into the role of odours, makes of the angler an expert, if not an informed biologist!
Methodical carp fishing is a demanding discipline, and a difficult test of the angler's tackle and his patience.
More than with any other method, success is only the fruit of long experience and rigorous practice. Only very rarely does the novice obtain consistent results right from the start.

■ ***A fine carp tempted in classic fashion by this young angler with a legered bunch of worms.***

TRADITIONAL METHODS

Traditional methods call for heavy tackle and are aimed at very weighty carp living in waters cluttered with obstacles. Long in use by our fishermen, it regularly yields magnificent specimens.

Legering

The tackle

A powerful 15–16 foot (4.5–5 m) rod is used, with the length and action to permit long casts and provide useful resistance when dealing with a particularly combative fish. It is hard to find the ideal rod because two apparently contradictory criteria must be satisfied: sufficient power to be able to propel weights of up to 100 g, combined with the flexibility needed to cast very fragile baits without damage. The rings, especially the first and last, should be unaffected by nylon.

The reel, of good make, is a medium weight salmon type with a wide spool that can hold about 650 feet (200 m) of 0.35 mm to 0.45 mm nylon line. The drag should be reliable and easy to operate.

Rigs

Depending on how snag-free the water is, and the average size of the fish, the main body of line can be of 0.35 to 0.45 mm nylon. The running lead weighs 30–40 g and is a round, hexagonal or clawed olive. It rests against a small stop weight, or a plastic tube through which the line is threaded, to prevent constant rubbing against the knot attaching it to the swivel clip.

Because the fish is so suspicious, the 24 to 36 inch (60 cm to 1 m) cast can be smaller in diameter (0.30 to 0.40 mm). The size and shape of the hook depends on the bait used.

■ ***Groundbait strategy.***

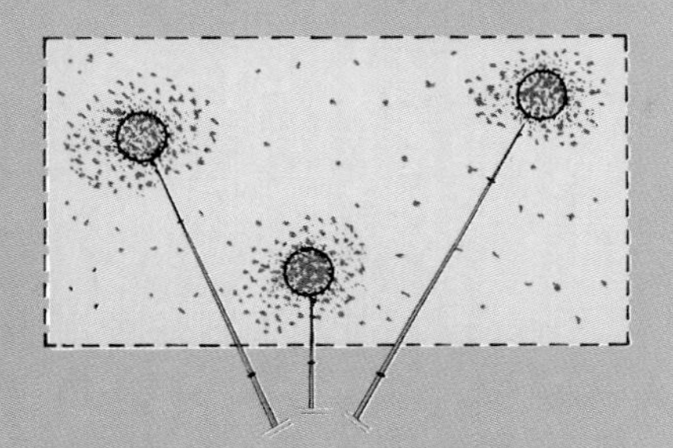

Light all-over groundbaiting with more for each rig.

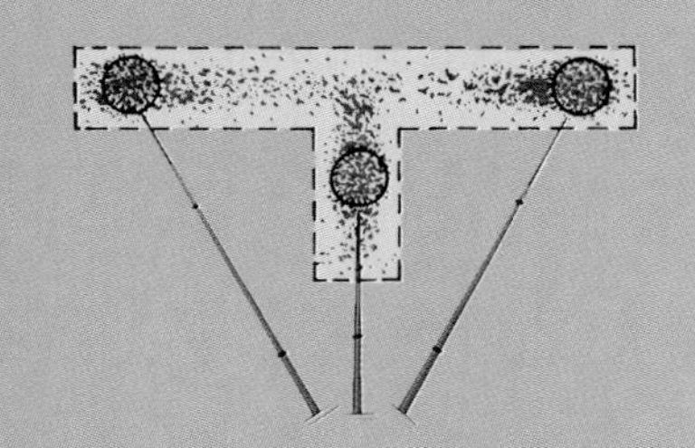

T-shaped groundbait pattern.

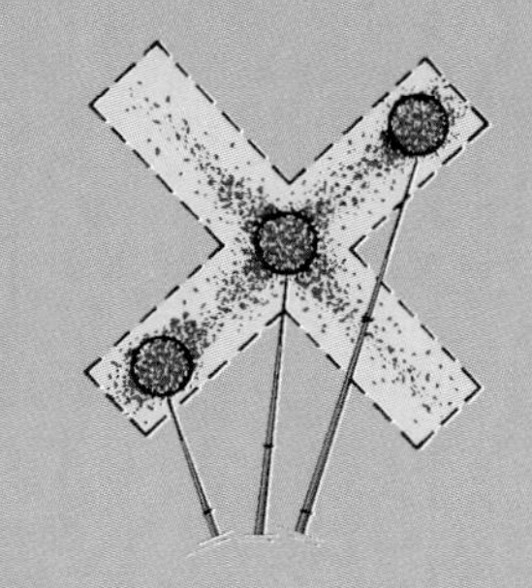

X-shaped pattern.

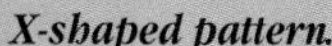

Baits

Traditionally vegetable baits are used; these are particularly well liked by carp, though bloodworms and maggots are sometimes more effective in coloured waters. Baits more currently in use are a cube of potato, mounted on a size 8 or treble hook using a baiting needle (or it will break up when casting), or a grain of maize on a single size 4 or 6 hook. Wheat or a broad bean on a size 1 hook, also kidney beans and peas are very fetching. Carp also appreciate "boilies": different recipes for these are given in the section on "English techniques".

Maggots are often mounted in a bunch on a single or a treble hook. A large earthworm can be put on a size 2 or 4 hook. All the vegetable baits are used so as to form a habit. It is therefore essential to groundbait for several days in advance, using the same materials that will be used during fishing.

Groundbaiting

Groundbaiting is essential when fishing for carp, and is a condition for the success of the projected fishing session. The place to be groundbaited should be chosen with care. It is pointless to groundbait in an unsuitable area not usually visited by the fish. Avoid places where there are dangerous snags close by. Groundbaiting serves to attract the fish into a particular area, but more than anything it is to get the fish used to feeding. Their suspicions are allayed by the regular supply of food, identical in quality and quantity to the bait to be presented later on. The pitch is groundbaited at a certain time for the five or six days preceding the intended fishing session. When the place chosen is fished regularly, a small amount of groundbait is enough. In a new spot, tens of kilos can be thrown in. The night before fishing and on the day itself, a reminder groundbaiting is needed, even if the place is continually fished. Whatever bait is used, the balls of groundbait should not be too large. One can use commercially available flour based groundbait in the form of pellets that swell and acquire a soft texture when wet. To these add a variable amount of the bait to be used when fishing, such as cubes of potato, broad beans, kidney beans, peas, grains of wheat or of maize, maggots or bloodworms.

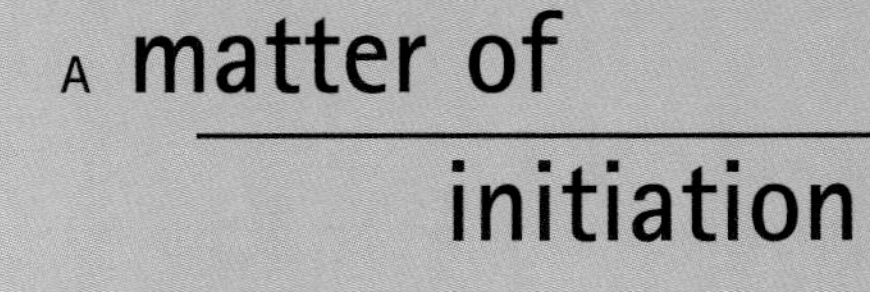

An open day organized for a "carp marathon" at Lake Chambon in the Puy de Dôme region, France. The children seem to handle the fish quite confidently. Perhaps an expert carp fisherman in the making.

Fishing method

The bait is cast accurately into the groundbaited area with some care, because it is delicate. When the olive has reached the bottom, retrieve the slack in the line but leave a certain amount of "give" to avoid arousing the carp's suspicion when biting. A carp will let go of the bait if it feels the least resistance. In running water the line should be kept tight. This disadvantage can be partly overcome by placing a small pebble on the line coming from the reel. The line will come free at the slightest pull and unwind as many turns as there are coiled on the ground by the pebble. The rods are placed on their supports and firmly fixed, with the drag on the reel set very light. The bite may be marked by an abrupt departure, with the fish making off with a few yards of line in a few seconds to the sound of a deafening screech from the reel. Sometimes the bite is just indicated by a slight trembling of the rod tip, or by sideways movements and a gradual tightening of the line. In this case it is as well to wait a few moments before picking up the rod and striking with a full movement. The drag is set very light at the start to avoid treating the fish roughly and getting it irritated enough to jump out of the water and endanger the line. A carp should never be over-controlled (a golden rule in contests of this kind with cunning, powerful fish). Apart from jumping and suddenly heading for dangerous snags, the carp will mount a more stubborn and prolonged defence as a result.

During the fight the drag is progressively tightened so that the fish can only take line by making a sustained effort that will rapidly exhaust it. The rod is kept vertical, its power opposed to the carp's wild defence.

Sometimes a particularly wily quarry rockets towards the angler. This dangerous move often leads to the fish becoming unhooked. When this happens the only remedy is to reel in line quickly to keep in touch with the carp. When the fish seems genuinely beaten, it is brought gently to the bank, close to the landing net.

This manoeuvre must be carried out with extreme care since the very sight of the net may provoke one last rush, breaking the line, which can be infuriating after a fight that may last more than half an hour. Because of this the drag should always be slackened during the last phase of the fight.

Fishing with a maggot pellet

This is a good way of catching big carp, especially if one takes the precaution of groundbaiting consistently for several days in advance, using balls of the same size to be used at the fishing session. When accustomed to looking for these pellets, the carp will not be particularly suspicious if they are presented armed with a hook.

The tackle

The rod, 13 to 16 feet (4–5 m) long is essentially the same as that used for legering.

The reel is a medium weight fixed-spool type. The main body of line, in 0.4 mm nylon, ends in a cast 8–12 inches (20–30 cm) long in 0.30 to 0.40 mm nylon, to which is attached a single size 6 to 8 hook. The weight, a round or a flat olive, is restrained by a small stop weight on either side.

Bait

The pellets are made of a mixture of sieved clay and maggots. They are prepared by incorporating the larvae into the earth, then kneading the mixture to obtain a pliable paste that sticks well to the hook.

■ *A superb mirror carp taken in the river.*

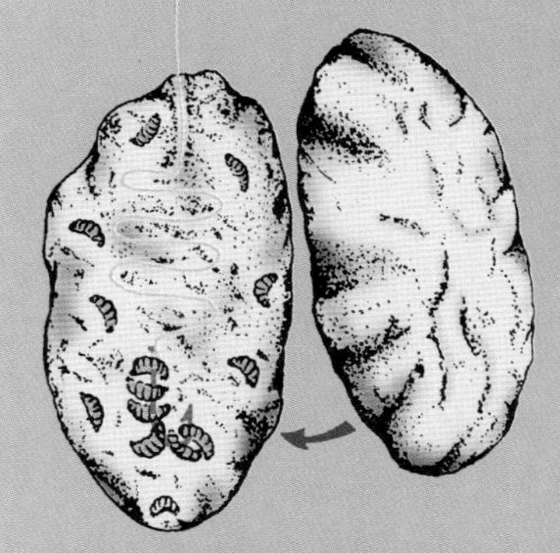

■ *A "maggot pellet", an ancient type of bait.*

■ *This fine carp surrendered after a hard fight.*

Mixed and moulded by hand, the pellets are made the size of an egg, and serve as bait and groundbait.

Carp are very sensitive to aromas. Impregnating the pellets with honey or hempseed oil considerably increases their appeal. More maggots can be kneaded into the pellet when baiting the hook; some of these will drop out and fall to the bottom. This activity cannot fail to excite the carp. The cast and the hook are buried in the pellet: the maggots, so very tempting to the fish, should be allowed to appear on its surface.

Fishing method

Long casts are not possible with pellets because they are so fragile. It is best to use this method close to the bank, or to fish from a boat. The bite is signalled by a trembling rod tip, indicating the carp is breaking up the pellet to get at the maggots. Wait for a definite movement before making a confident strike.

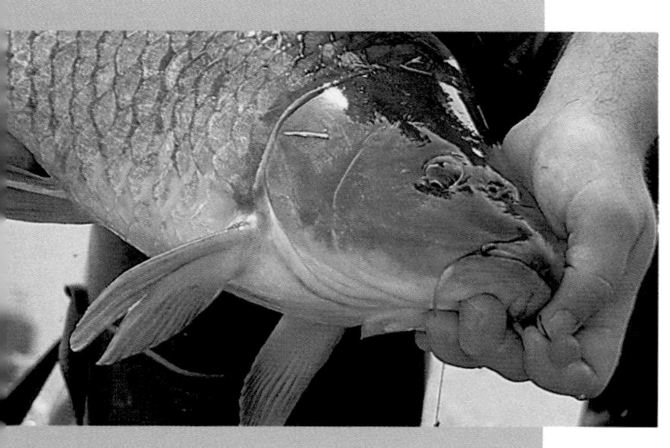

■ *A common carp taken on an English rig baited with two boilies. Unfortunately, the picture does not show what aroma was used!*

Fishing with bread

Throughout the fine season carp move about close to the surface and willingly take floating bread flake. This may be the only method possible when the fish are swimming about right in the middle of thick growths of water lily and pondweed.

The tackle

When dealing with large fish, the rod is the same as that used for legering. For medium-sized carp or when fishing in uncluttered waters, something lighter will do, such as a 12 foot (3.50 m) long English-type rod.

A medium weight fixed-spool spinning reel loaded with 500 feet (150 m) of 0.30 mm nylon line can be used.

The very simple rig consists of a single size 4 or 5 hook on the end of the line. When using heavy tackle, it may be necessary to add some weight to be able to cast the bait easily. For this use a bubble float, or even better, a lump of sugar held in a knot (a single hitch) that will come undone by itself. Having acted as a weight, the sugar dissolves when it reaches the water.

Baits

Use fresh bread flake or the flake from bread kept wrapped in film, which stays on the hook better.

Fishing method

Cast the bread flake to where the carp are swimming close to the surface among the plants. The rod can then be placed on a support, but it is best to hold it because this fish demands constant attention. To attract the carp, groundbaiting with bits of bread flake is advisable.

Making a few final adjustments before what can be a long wait for a bite.

The bite is clearly seen: the carp moves the bread flake, making it dance about on the surface. It is best not to strike too soon: allow the fish time to swallow the bait properly. When it disappears down the fish's throat and you feel a pull, strike without undue violence. The tussle that follows is often risky if the spot is cluttered, especially when a big fish is involved.

Float fishing

Float fishing is mostly practised in still, shallow water, or in summer when carp are found close to the surface. It is generally used for catching medium-sized fish, but can sometimes be useful for fishing in open water when obstructions near the bank prevent the use of the traditional sliding ledger.

The tackle

A English type medium powered rod is chosen, from 3.6–4 m in length.

The light fixed-spool spinning reel is loaded with 150 m of 0.22 to 0.26 mm nylon line.

The rig comprises a sliding float for deep water, or a fixed float for lakes of even depth. The float is adjusted so that the cast and the bait rest on the bottom. The cast, in 0.16 to 0.20 mm nylon, ends in a single size 4 to 6 hook. The line is weighted with a small olive or bunched lead shot.

Baits

Identical to those used with a running leger, but smaller in size. The best are maize, potato, peas or a pellet of dough.

Groundbait

The principle is the same as that described under legering.

Location

Areas rich in vegetation, slow eddies and backwaters.

Fishing method

Cast into the groundbaited area, place the rod on the rest with the pick-up closed and the line slack, in a natural curve. The drag should be set very light. A bite is indicated by a trembling of the float or some sideways movement followed by an abrupt dive. It is as well to wait a few moments before striking; the further away the fish is from the bank, the harder the strike. With a light line the contest can be good sport. Beware of snags and take care never to play the fish in such a way as to produce violent reactions (jumping or making desperate runs). The contest can sometimes last quite a while, which adds a certain appeal to a method that is very effective with very suspicious fish in over-fished waters.

■ *True carp anglers always return their catch to the water after the usual photo.*

THE ENGLISH SYSTEM

A three-rod battery

Introduced some years ago by the English at Saint Cassien Lake in the Var district, France, this system has completely changed the habits of our traditional carp fishermen. It advocates total respect for the fish, which is returned carefully to its element immediately after capture. The sporting code does not end there. The very light tackle used provides unequalled excitement when used against such a powerful adversary. The English style of fishing has given rise to a plethora of gadgets and new baits that excite amateurs fascinated by equipment. The lightness of the tackle precludes its use in places where there are snags.

The tackle

The rod is the classic English ringed type, designed for carp.

The light fixed-spool spinning reel should be a good make, with a spool large enough to hold about 650 feet (200 m) of 0.3 mm nylon line.

The whole is fixed on a special rod-rest that takes three rods side by side, and is equipped with an audible or flashing bite alarm and a bobbin for each rod.

Depending on the length of cast to be made, the line is weighted with a 20 to 50 g sliding olive. This weight is restrained by a small stop weight or a soft plastic tube through which the line is threaded, and which serves as a shock absorber, avoiding repeated shocks to the knot attaching it to the swivel clip. The 20 inch (50 cm) cast ends in a single size 2 to 6 hook or a size 8 to 12 treble hook.

The rigs

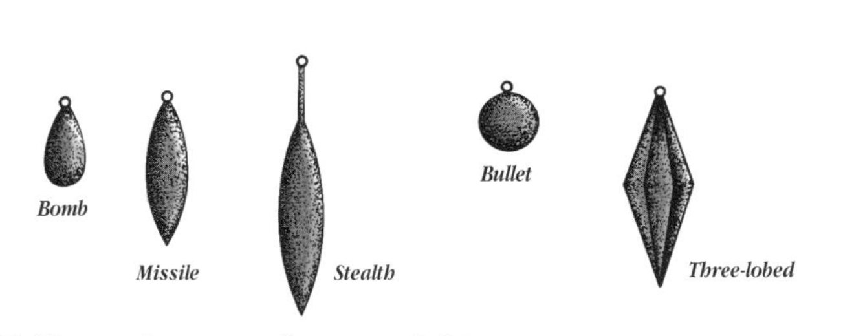

■ *The main types of carp weight.*

Depending on the length of cast to be made, the line is weighted with a 20 to 50 g sliding olive.

This weight is restrained by a small stop weight or a soft plastic tube through which the line is threaded, serving as a shock absorber, avoiding repeated shocks to the knot attaching it to the swivel clip.

The 50 cm cast ends in a single size 2 to 6 hook or a size 8 to 12 treble hook.

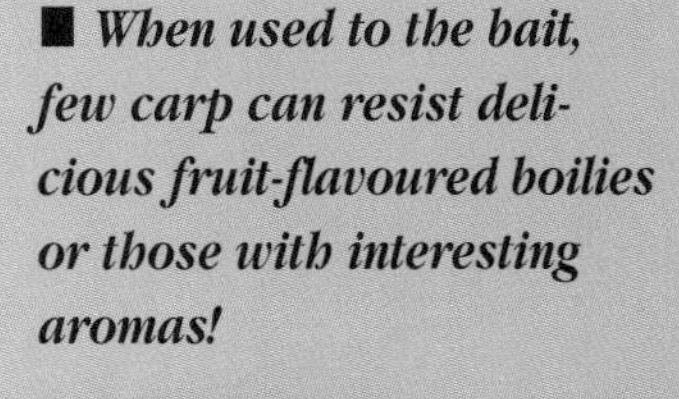

■ *When used to the bait, few carp can resist delicious fruit-flavoured boilies or those with interesting aromas!*

Baiting

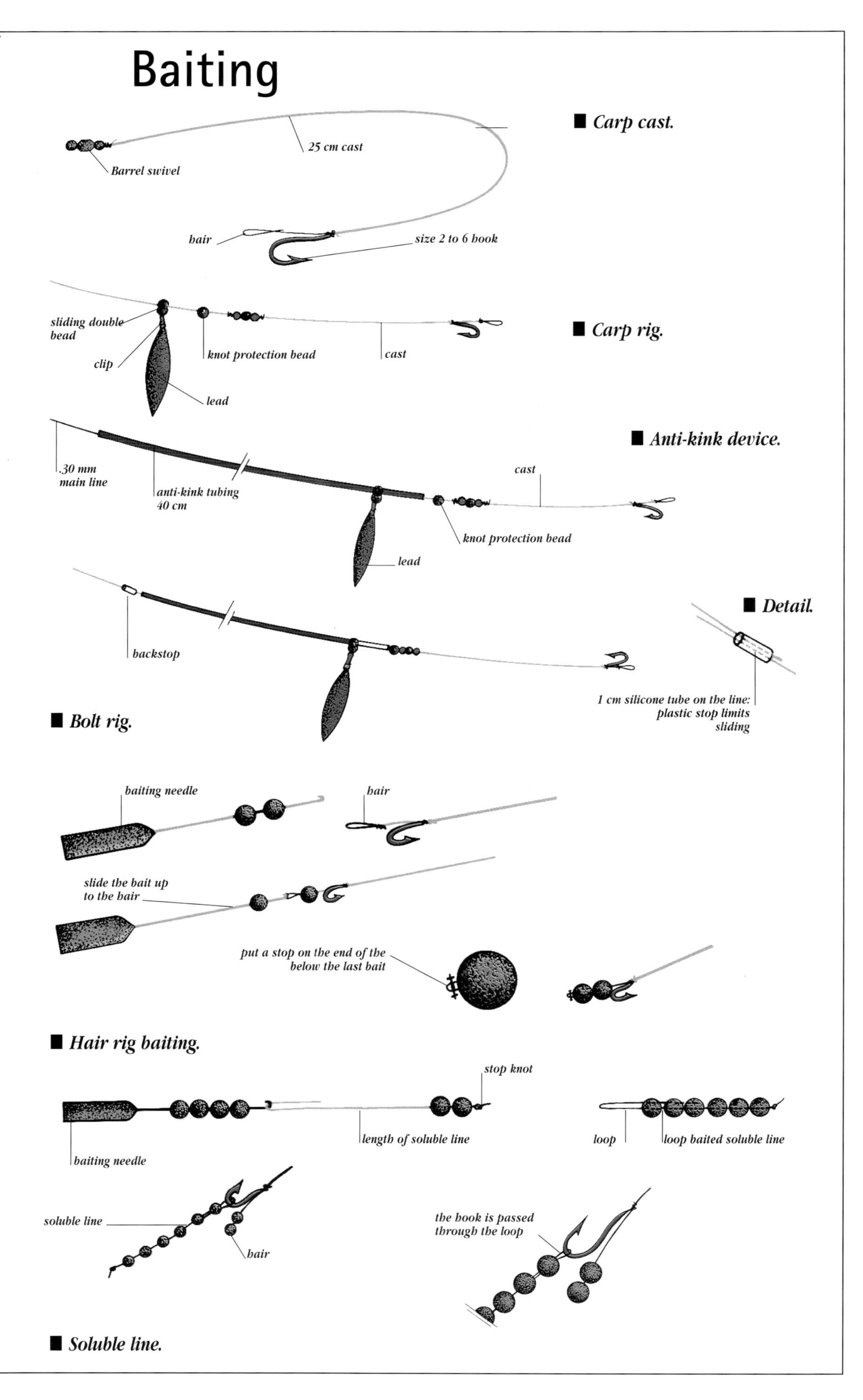

Baits

All the classic baits (wheat, maize, potato, peas, kidney beans, worms, maggots) can be suitable. However it must be stressed that the originality of this fishing method lies in the use of the new synthetic mixtures, in the form of boilies. These small hand-shaped balls stay on the hook remarkably well provided they are hardened by boiling them for several hours.

The preparation of boilies is based on flours and a wide range of ingredients (yeast, fishmeal or ground meat, dried dog, cat, trout or cattle food, soy extract, casein), all very rich in protein.

Other more traditional mixtures will do perfectly well. They can be made with fresh bread flake soaked in hempseed oil (an excellent binder) or mixed with corn-flour or milled hempseed. Honey is also a very good binder, as is egg yolk.

Many combinations are possible, and every true carp fisherman has his own secrets for making the best mixture. By incorporating such subtle and delicate aromas as strawberry, vanilla or crayfish, great heights of scientific and artistic achievement are attained. The carp is undoubtedly a discerning gastronome.

Groundbaiting

The groundbait is based on the same ingredients, then given the same aromas as those to be used in making up the boilies. Some particle bait such as peanuts or haricot beans previously softened in water is added.

The quantity of groundbait to be thrown in depends on the extent to which fish frequent the place, and on the regularity of groundbaiting through the year. During the fishing session, throwing in a few boilies as "reminders" will be enough to keep the fish in position.

For long-distance fishing, groundbaiting with a catapult is almost essential.

■ *A standard battery of English rods but missing, though, are the bobbins, bite indicators and alarm lights.*

Fishing method

When the baits have been cast gently and accurately into the groundbaited area, the rods are placed on the rod rests with the tips pointing towards the water. Each line passes through a bite detector and under a bobbin positioned an inch or two above the ground.

When fishing with an open pick-up, the line is held in a clip. It must never be taut, or the fish's suspicions will be aroused when it swallows the bait.

At the smallest pull by the carp the bobbin rises, the bite indicator sounds and the alarm light goes on.

Some carp fishermen cannot imagine carp fishing without a certain degree of comfort, and take their leisure stretched out on a folding bed or a deckchair.

The English, who have foreseen this situation and distressing awakenings in particular, use a different coloured alarm light under each rod. In this way, the fisherman awakening with a start when there is a bite will not mistake rods.

■ *One of the most valiant adversaries in its class: the leather carp.*

Where carp can be found

Carp fishermen don't cast their lines just anywhere. Relying on certain signs, they can recognise promising areas at the outset. First of all, signs of fish, seen making spectacular leaps out of the water, or as clouds of tiny bubbles betraying the presence of carp rummaging through the mud in search of food.

The general situation of the site is equally important.

In rivers carp are to be sought in the calm deep places: in holes, big eddies, along cliffs and upstream of bridge piers.

In lakes they hang around banks of reed, sluice gates or feeder inlets. In reservoirs they can often be found in the little bays that mark the inlet of a stream, near submerged grassland sloping gently to a depth of 13 to 16 feet (4–5 m), and in water of medium depth where there are plenty of obstacles such as sunken trees.

The carp fisherman avoids the immediate neighbourhood of large obstacles which carp unfailingly head for when hooked, and break the line. He prefers clear areas with easy access so that he can play his fish in complete safety.

Roach

A not-so-easy cyprinid

Latin name: *Rutilus rutilus*
Family name: Cyprinidae

The roach is undoubtedly one of the most popular fish because it is found in most of our rivers and lakes, and because it makes fishing possible in all seasons. It is a very wary fish and the right tackle must be used to catch it. Some fishermen exercise boundless ingenuity in perfecting techniques for its capture, and make a great art of it. The methods employed are at least as subtle as those used in fishing for trout and salmon with the fly, and call for the same qualities in those who are devoted to them, namely, knowledge of the water and the fish's habits, excellent eyesight, perseverance etc, all "non-standard" criteria that hardly match the cartoon image of the portly, grumbling angler sprawled on his folding chair supposedly waiting for a bite. If the definition of a sporting fisherman is as it should be, firstly a matter of ethics, in which the art and method of taking the fish scores over the quantity caught, then without doubt, the roach fisherman falls into this category.

The roach is one of the fish most prized by discriminating bank fishermen.

FLOAT FISHING

Fishing with natural baits

The tackle

A telescopic or sectional rod from 13 to 20 feet (4–6 m) long is chosen according to the distance and depth of the water to be fished. Since the roach is a very wary fish that keeps far away from the bank, some match specialists like to use rods reaching 32 feet (10 m) in length.

Carbon fibre is clearly the only material suitable for making such rods. It pays to handle them with great care, especially if fishing near high-tension electricity lines. Carbon is an excellent conductor of electricity and the risk of electrocution is high.

Generally one uses a canal type rod fitted with an elastic shock absorber that permits fair-sized roach to be more easily handled.

Rigs: extreme care should be taken in preparing, and especially, balancing the rigs. Success depends on it.

■ ***Roach fishing in a backwater of the river Allier, France.***

Fishing for roach

In rivers, roach like stretches where the current is slow and the water deep, with a smooth bottom covered lightly in weed (moss and algae on pebbles). Look for the presence of rocks, or of stone structures such as dams or bridge piers close by, as well as back-washes.

In lakes roach seek out places where the vegetation is abundant (where there is pondweed or there are floating beds of lilies, and alongside reed beds). Depressions and elevations are favoured because they relieve the monotony of an even bottom (roach specialists look especially for faults in the ground. Tributary inlets are also sites that attract interest.

■ *Match fishermen rely heavily on roach to build up their points.*

■ *Preparing groundbait based on bloodworms.*

If the water is still or over-fished, the thickness of the line should not exceed .08 mm. A small sensitive float (the spherical kind is fine) is weighted according to the depth of the water.

In deep water the weight should be grouped, as dust shot bunched together, or swan shot, or an olivette held by the knot joining the line to the cast. A single shot is then pinched onto the cast 4 inches (10 cm) above the hook.

When fishing in mid-water, it is preferable to spread the weights out. The .065 mm nylon cast ends in a single size 18 to 24 hook depending on the size of the bait used.

In a current or water disturbed by waves the use of a squat balsa quilled float weighted with bunched shot is recommended. The main line, in 0.10 mm nylon, ends in a 0.08 mm cast.

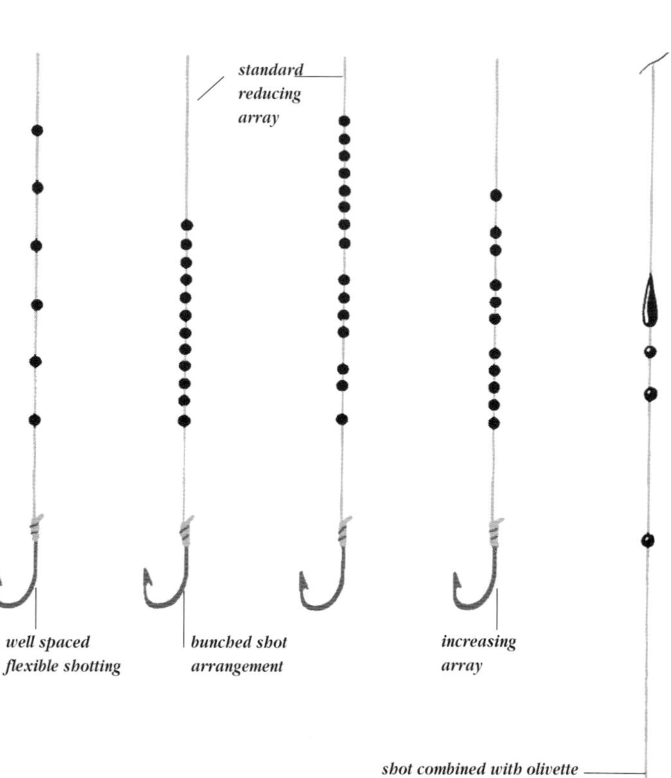

Baits

The bloodworm is one of the most used baits, and rightly so, for it regularly produces the most consistent results throughout the season. One or two larvae are fixed on a long-shanked size 22 fine steel hook.

A white or coloured maggot is just as good, especially during the summer. Fix one by itself on a size 20 hook, or two on a size 18 hook. Brandlings can be used to replace bloodworms. Fixed on a size 18 hook, they are especially effective during autumn or winter spates.

■ *Groundbaiting a roach swim with a catapult.*

Groundbaiting

The roach is no exception to the rule regarding the need to groundbait to attract the shoal. Excellent groundbaits are available commercially. If you want to make them yourself, mixtures of milled hempseed, oilcake, breadcrumbs, and cornflour make attractive recipes. Naturally, the same bait to be used on the hook is added to the mixture. The addition of a mess of bloodworms is particularly appreciated. In running water a variable proportion of clay or sieved clay should be added to the groundbait. This ingredient increases the sticking power of the preparation and makes is heavier, so the current does not carry it away downstream too quickly. Groundbait for bleak will do perfectly well provided one takes care to make it heavy to stop it breaking up when it hits the surface. If the roach swim is not much frequented by fish, it should be groundbaited a few days in advance. If it is, a simple reminder at the beginning of the session (two or three balls the size of an orange) will be plenty. It should be repeated whenever the frequency of bites begins to fall off.

Fishing for roach with a sectional rod.

Fishing method

Whether fishing in still or running water, roach are generally found close to the bottom. It is therefore necessary to plumb the groundbaited swim accurately in advance; this permits the bait to be fished just brushing the bottom. Once the line is in the water, it is a good idea to perform some enticing movements. In the current, this consists of holding it back and releasing it at irregular intervals. In still water it can pay to pull the float along very slowly, as if in a current.

The bite is quick and definite and calls for an almost instantaneous strike, especially when fishing with a bloodworm. With a brandling or a maggot on the rig, the strike can be very slightly delayed.

Fishing with paste

The tackle and rig are identical to those employed when using natural baits. It must be remembered though, that this method calls for an immediate strike, therefore a rod with a stiff top section is needed. The groundbait is based on a mixture of hempseed, breadcrumbs and meal. It should be light enough to disintegrate while sinking, and so should not be too wet. Reminder groundbaiting is essential. Numerous commercially available natural or synthetic pastes are perfectly suitable.

One can produce groundbait oneself, making a mixture based on sugar or honey let down with any grain (maize, wheat) and mixed with an egg yolk and a crushed potato. The aim is to end up with a smooth mixture that stays on the hook well but does not stick to the fingers. It takes a bit of experimentation to get the consistency just right. Shaped into a bullet, the paste is put on a size 18 hook. The bite is lively and calls for an immediate strike.

Fishing with hempseed

Hempseed is the seed of a particular variety of hemp (not Indian hemp) used in the production of textiles.

Commercial hempseed, perfectly cooked and preserved

■ ***Rig for fishing hempseed.***

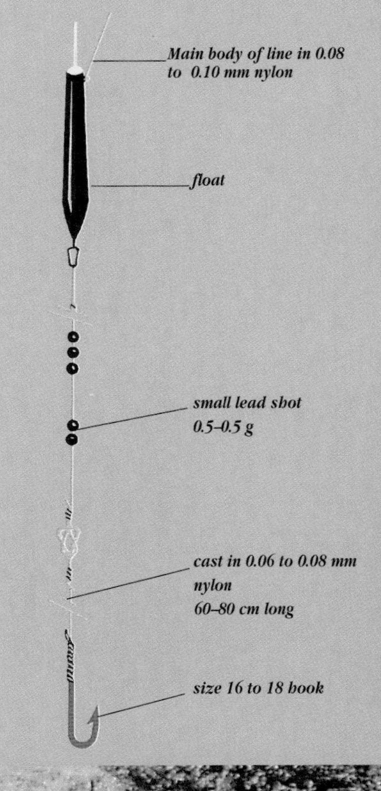

Today's fishermen use rods that can be 32 feet (10 m) and even longer.

■ *Roach fishing in canals is often productive.*

in vacuum packs can be bought, as can the untreated seed. The latter should be allowed to soak for ten hours or so, then rinsed and cooked to make the shoots just appear. Cooking is then stopped and the seeds cooled down rapidly in cold water.

The tackle

Fishing with hempseed is undoubtedly a technique that calls for rapid reflexes, for the bite is fast and fleeting. Use a suitable rod with a strong, rigid top section that allows an instant strike. A canal type rod can be used; its length, from 20 to 30 feet (6–9 m), depends on the distance of the places to be fished.

Rigs

In running water a very stable, stubby quilled float is recommended. This is weighted with a group of shot or with an olivette resting on the knot joining the main line to the cast. In addition to this, two dust shot are placed 4 and 6 inches (10 and 15 cm) from the hook. The main body of line is in 0.10 mm nylon and the cast in line not more than 0.08 mm in diameter. The hook size varies from 16 to 18.

In still water the main body of line in 0.08 mm is followed by a cast in 0.065 mm nylon. The very sensitive float can be a small quill balanced by bunched or spread shot according to the depth of water fished.

■ *The modern bank fisherman's tackle is generally an impressive array.*

Groundbaiting

When a swim has never been fished with hempseed, plentiful groundbaiting several days in advance is essential to accustom the fish to this bait. It should be put in at the same time each day, as hempseed cakes with 3½ pints (2 litres) of seeds mixed in. On the day chosen for fishing, two good handfuls of hempseed will be enough groundbait. Following this, a few pinches every three or four casts will serve as a reminder.

Fishing method

Fishing with hempseed is carried out on the bottom. It is therefore necessary to plumb the swim carefully to be able to position the bait at this level.

The seed should be constantly moved by holding it back and releasing it. These enticing movements considerably increase the bait's appeal. The bite is sometimes unobtrusive (a simple sideways movement of the float may be noticed) and calls for an immediate strike. Because of this, a close watch must be kept for any abnormal movement of the float as it drifts. The hook is baited by sliding it between the two halves of the seed so that the point just appears.

Fishing with wheat

Well loved by the roach, this bait is of equal interest to other fish such as bream, and especially carp – hence the frequent breakages that occur when using this bait.

Standard tackle and rigs are used. The main body of line, in 0.12 to 0.14 mm nylon terminates in a cast in 0.10 to 0.12 mm line. The weights are positioned according to the same criteria as previously mentioned. A size 16 hook is baited so that its point can clearly be seen protruding. A waggler float is used when fishing in the English style, especially in deep water. As regards adjusting the float, fishing with wheat is no exception to the rule that the bait should rest on the bottom. Careful plumbing of the depth is therefore necessary in advance. In a swim where the fish are not used to this bait, generous groundbaiting with cooked wheat mixed with hempseed cake for a few days before fishing is essential. The bite is slow and definite. Let the fish swallow the bait, and strike smoothly.

Fishing with weed

The weeds in question are mosses or algae that grow on piers and submerged rocks. A small tuft of moss fixed on a size 18 hook makes an excellent bait during the summer, especially where there is a lively current.

Rudd

A cousin of the roach

Latin name: *Scardinius erythrophtalmus*
Family: Cyprinidae

RUDD FISHING

Though very similar in form to the roach, the rudd behaves differently; this means a number of different ways of fishing can be used. The rudd is more inclined to feed on the surface or in mid-water.

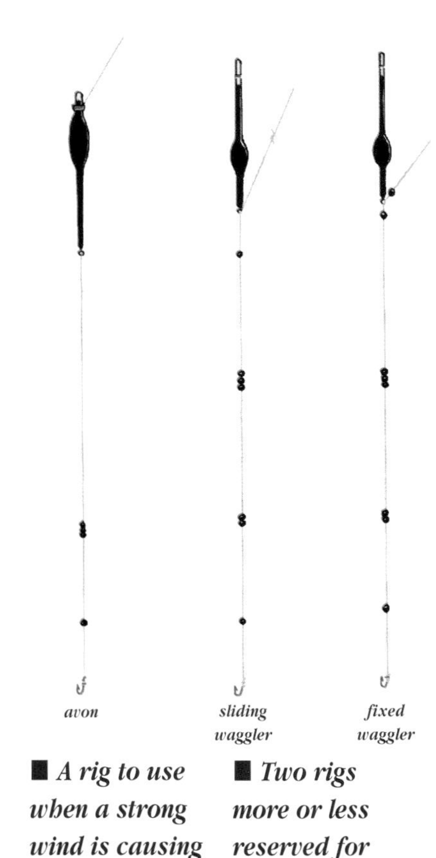

■ *A rig to use when a strong wind is causing ripples.*

■ *Two rigs more or less reserved for calm weather.*

When float fishing, the higher the temperature, the shallower the bait should be fished; a high temperature makes the shoals of fish rise in the water. The rudd is often caught on a bait dropped close to it on the surface (using the same methods as those described in the chapter on chub), or on an insect fished using a bubble float.

It can also be caught on the dry fly, using flies intended for bleak.

An entertaining method of catching the large specimens that stay close to the bottom or swim in mid-water is to employ a heavily dressed neutral coloured (brown-red) nymph imitating a shedding larva. The weight of the lure makes it necessary to use a tip-action rod. The fly line, which should float perfectly, ends in a 5 foot (1.5 m) cast in 0.14 mm nylon.

Cast the line out and let the nymph sink, then retrieve it by pulling it with the left hand, with the line passing between the right index finger and the rod handle.
At the smallest bite, indicated by a slight tug on the rod point or by the line moving sideways on the surface, strike with a sharp flick of the wrist. A bite can also occur as the bait sinks. When this happens, the movement of the fly line or the cast can be seen on the water.

■ *When the rudd is spawning, its colouring turns gold.*

■ *This little rudd is about to return to its element.*

The true bream enthusiast is interested in the great, or bronze bream (Abramis brama)*, not the smaller silver bream shown here.*

Although the bream's defence is weak and of short duration and its insipid flesh is full of bones, it is nonetheless of interest to numerous anglers because of its wariness and finicky character. Enthusiasts must demonstrate their devotion by being very careful when moving about on the bank. The same particular care must be given to the preparation and balancing of the very fine lines used. The new English methods designed for big roach and bream, which like to swim well out from the bank, add further interest to this type of fishing. These deadly techniques make it possible for the exacting fisherman to make large catches in places where this species flourishes.

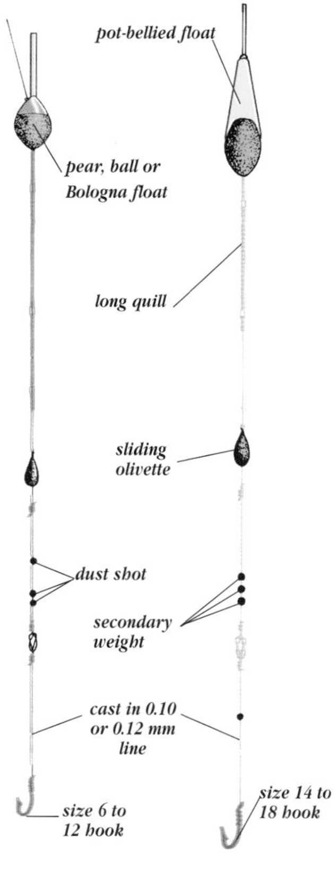

■ *Calm water rig.*

■ *Running water rig.*

TRADITIONAL FISHING

Float fishing from the bank

The tackle

A classic rod 6 m long is suitable, (longer if the swim is far from the bank), made of composition or of carbon fibre, with the top section fitted with an elastic to absorb shock.

Rigs

The choice of float depends on the features of the stretch of water and the presence or absence of ripples due to the wind.

In still waters or stretches where there is no current a thin highly sensitive quill is used, weighted with spread shot going down as far as the cast. Where there is a strong current or if there are waves, a very stable, stubby quilled float is recommended. In this case, more weight is used.

An olivette rests against the knot joining the line with the cast, followed by two dust shot about 4 inches (10 cm) above the hook. The latter is fine, of steel, long-shanked and between size 14 and 20 according to the size of the bait. A cast about 2 feet (60 cm) long in 0.08 mm nylon follows the 0.12 to 0.16 mm line.

■ *The bream is gregarious and moves in large shoals, giving the angler the chance of a magnificent bag !*

Bream

Above all, finesse

Latin name: *Abramis brama*
Family: Cyprinidae

Baits

Bream accept animal and vegetable baits equally well. Bloodworms, brandlings, wheat, and bread flake are the most commonly used. The bream is a fish that takes the greatest assortment of animal (e.g. maggots, bloodworms), vegetable (wheat, paste) and mixed baits (maggots, artificial paste and maggot, bread flake).

Some anglers use different combinations of different colours (for example, white maggots with red artificial paste) to attract the fish's curiosity.

Groundbaiting

Bream love to root about in the mud in search of food. Under cover of dark they often move nearer the bank into shallow water where they suck food from the mud, leaving little depressions called "bream pits". The standard groundbait should therefore be plentiful and heavy so as to keep the fish in position burrowing about in this providential manna and feasting on it with gusto.

Generally a mixture is made of flour (maize), cake (soybean), milled hempseed and sieved earth. Should there be a slight current crossing the swim, the latter should comprise at least a third of the mixture. Some anglers make allowances for the suspicious nature of the bream and are against groundbaiting while fishing. According to them, groundbaiting should be done just once, either the evening before, or right at the start of the session. Others maintain that bream become perfectly accustomed to regular groundbaiting if it is performed discreetly with balls not larger than a mandarin orange. When an animal bait is fished, whatever bait is used on the hook should be added to the groundbait mixture. Bloodworm diggings are particularly attractive.

Fishing method

Since bream feed while burrowing on the bottom, the first thing to be done is to plumb the location thoroughly so that the bait and the whole of the cast can be made to rest on the bottom. The float will thus be slightly slanted.

Unlike with the roach, enticing movements are useless when fishing for bream. In contrast, the bait can be positioned close to the small clouds of bubbles breaking the surface that betray the activities of fish busy digging about in the groundbaited area. The bite of the bream is characteristic: the float lies flat on the surface.

This happens because the fish raises its head and rises after swallowing the bait and takes some weight off the cast. At other times the bite is signalled by a slight trembling of the float as the fish nuzzles the bait warily before biting, or not. Wait for the float to make a definite plunge before striking firmly but smoothly. If it is a large specimen, it will stick to the bottom obstinately, opposing any pull with its weight. Firm contact will be sufficient to avoid any violent reaction; harsh control is pointless. A bream is easily exhausted and soon rises to the surface, allowing itself to be pulled on its side over to the landing net without difficulty.

ENGLISH FISHING METHODS

The appeal of these new, subtle, refined techniques resides in the fact that they permit swims great distances away (130 feet/40 m and more) to be fished that cannot be reached by the standard methods. The fineness of the tackle used and the distances at which one fishes can outwit the wiliest of fish. Bream and roach are the main victims.

■ ***Fishing for bream, English-style. Note the rod tip held under water to sink the line.***

Float fishing

The tackle

The rod is a standard 12 to 13 foot (3.6–4 m) English model in three sections, with at least five rings.

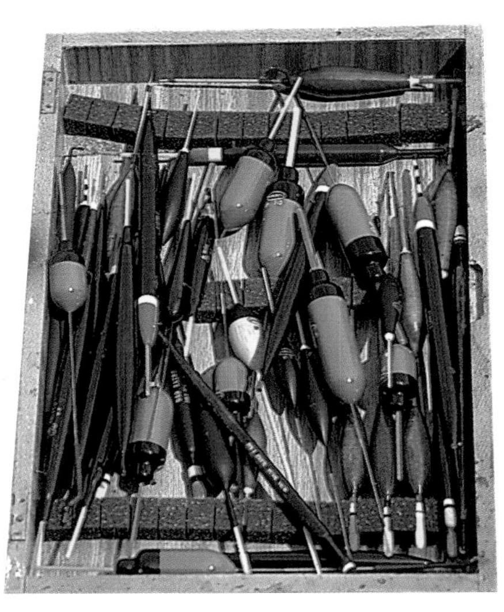

The reel, a light fixed-spool spinning reel, can be either open- or closed-face. The spool is loaded with 500 feet (150 m) of 0.12 to 0.14 mm nylon line. It is important to match the line with the style of fishing chosen. If a waggler is used, it is best to use a line that sinks easily, because the float is designed for fishing in deep water.

When fishing for roach or bream in mid-water or particularly near the surface, a floating nylon line is recommended.

■ *Bream fishing at Vichy Lake, Allier, France.*

Rigs

The float should match the circumstances. In calm, shallow water, a long, very sensitive fixed float is preferable. When there is a current, or if waves appear on still water, only a squat, quilled float will be stable enough. Weighting also varies according to the conditions. When fishing rapid or deep currents a large bunched array is needed. In the opposite case, in calm or over-fished waters, the weight should be evenly spread. The fine steel hook has a long shank. Its size varies according to the bait used – the range is quite extensive.

■ *There may be a long wait before the bream make their presence known on the groundbaited swim: clouds of bubbles break the surface, indicating they are feeding on the bottom, rooting about in the mud.*

Baits

Animal and vegetable baits are equally good: a maggot on a size 18 hook, a bunch of bloodworms on a size 18 to 20 hook, a brandling on a size 16 hook, wheat on a size 16 hook. All varieties are equally possible.

Groundbaiting

The standard groundbait is a mixture of breadcrumbs, oil cake, milled hempseed and maize semolina, to which should be added a variable proportion (up to half) of sieved clay, to weight the preparation if fishing in a lively current. In the river, firing just maggots into the swim with a catapult can sometimes be very productive. It is important to groundbait heavily at the start, using six balls about the size of an orange.

It should also be realized that in a current, the float rarely drifts parallel to the bank, especially if some enticing movements are carried out. It is necessary to allow for this so as to groundbait the precise path taken by the line. This could make quite a difference to the final catch.

Fishing method

Before doing anything else, plumb the swim so that the bait can be made to drag on the bottom. Then use the line to check the whole length of the run carefully, watching the float for any unusual behaviour. The cast is made straight opposite; the rig only begins to "fish" from the moment it is downstream from the angler. It is actually impossible to control the line when it is cast upstream. Small enticing movements made by holding and releasing the line may tempt a cautious fish to bite.

Legering with swing-tip and quiver-tip bite indicators

This technique is very effective when fishing at long distances in rivers where the current is slow, in lakes, and in ponds. With it a great variety of white fish can be caught (even carp!) on very light tackle.

This angler is fishing from the bank, English style, the rod held in both hands to cast the bait well into open water.

The tackle

A standard English rod is used, not longer than 13 feet (4 m), fairly soft, and generally in three sections. The tip ring is specially threaded to take the bite indicator.

A light fixed-spool spinning reel, open or closed face is chosen. It should be an excellent make, above all with a sensitive, very reliable drag. When the fish pulls, the line should run out smoothly and not be weakened by repeated sharp jerks.

Rigs

The spool of the reel is loaded with a line of 500 feet (150 m) in 0.14 mm nylon that should sink easily. The weight takes the form of a sliding lead (pear-shaped) fixed at the end of a short link protected by a soft plastic sheath. This precaution prevents the drifting rig from becoming tangled with the line during the cast or in the water. The link is attached to the line by a sliding link bead.

The pear lead weighs between 4 and 15 g according to the depth of the water and the distance to be cast.

The cast, in 0.12 mm nylon, is attached to the line by a small swivel. It is about 3 feet (1 m) long and ends with a size 14 or 18 hook according to the size of the bait. The significance of the bite indicators is that they allow bites to be detected at a great distance, bites that are impossible to detect with a standard float or just the rod tip. The most unobtrusive bites are immediately detectable, even at more than 130 feet (40 m) from the bank and at a depth of 16–32 feet (5–10 m). There are two types of indicator: the swing-tip and the quiver-tip. The swing-tip is very flexible and sensitive, and is used in calm waters. It consists of a short, bent rubber tube bearing a fine stem in light alloy. The rigidity of the joint will depend on the strength of the current and the presence or absence of waves. The quiver-tip can be used in calm water and in a fairly constant current. It consists of a simple fibreglass stem screwed into the rod tip that faithfully relays the bites.

Baits

Generally two maggots are used on a size 16 hook, or a maggot/barberry combination on a size 16 hook (highly effective!) and a whole assortment of different baits and colours combined.

Groundbaiting

The standard groundbait previously described is perfectly suitable. A catapult can be used to cast in some handfuls of maggots, balls seeded with larvae, and vegetable baits such as wheat and maize.

Setting the rods

When using a swing-tip, the rod is placed on the rest so that the end of the indicator just brushes the surface of the water. With a quiver-tip a single rest is used and the rod tip is kept in the air, at an angle of 45° to the water.

Fishing method

After casting, wait for the lead to reach the bottom. Put the rod on its rest after taking in any slack, keeping the line under slight tension, not too much. The bite, which is sometimes very unobtrusive, raises the swing-tip, or causes the quiver-tip to tremble.

This method of fishing calls for constant attention; the whole difficulty lies in detecting bites taking place 130 to 160 feet (40–50 m) away! Strike immediately at the very least abnormal sign from the indicator; make sure the strike is long enough to more than take up any slack. If there are no bites after ten or fifteen seconds, try letting a little line go a few times. This technique often produces fine fish (carp, for example) that are difficult to handle on such fine line.

Above all, finesse

line in 0.14 to 0.18 mm nylon

feeder

feeder

swan shot

swivel

size 12 to 20 hook

No.6 to 8 shot

size 10 to 20 hook

■ *Rig for fishing with a feeder.*

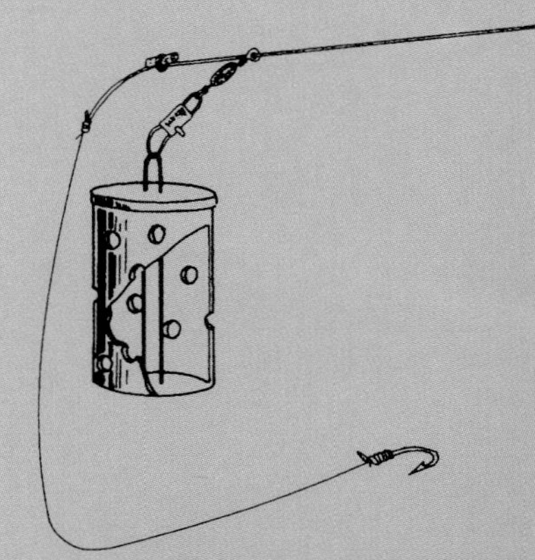

■ *The swim feeder, formerly the spiral feeder, allows accurate groundbaiting close to the bait on the hook.*

Bream swims

Bream like calm areas rich in vegetation. In rivers they are found on the bends and in back-waters, slow eddies and holes. In lakes they are found near weed beds, and close to banks of reeds or by a sluice gate.

■ *One can even fish for bream right in town, as here, on the Seine in Paris.*

Tench like warm still waters where they root about on the bottom in search of worms and vegetable debris. The canal is one of their favourite haunts. Unfortunately, pollution here can deplete their numbers.

The tench is a shy, wary fish whose debonair appearance conceals a certain strength not easily overcome when using a fine rig. It is often caught when fishing for roach, carp or bream. Its fine flesh, though somewhat oily, will be appreciated by the gourmet. The tench is generally fished for in calm water rich in vegetation.

FLOAT FISHING

Animal and vegetable baits

The tackle

The telescopic or sectional rods used are fairly long (16–30 feet/5–9 m), with a canal rod butt, and an internal elastic or a straight tip. For long distance casts (in the open water in lakes) an English rod is recommended. This has the advantage of being able to handle big fish such as carp that often gather in tench swims.

Rigs

The strength of line used depends on the size of fish present and the degree to which the water is cluttered.

A good compromise is to use 0.12 mm nylon for the line, with a 0.10 mm cast on the end, using a hook whose the right size for the bait. The spindle-shaped float, very sensitive because the fish is so cautious, is carefully balanced with small shot spread along the cast below an olivette.

Tench

Deeply elegant

Latin name: *Tinca tinca*
Family: Cyprinidae

■ ***The tench attracts many sporting anglers because it puts up a good fight.***

Groundbaiting

Tench are readily attracted to any bottom groundbait intended for roach or bream. They have a liking for groundbait rich in animal bait: chopped brandlings, maggots, and bloodworms. The groundbait is generally based on a mixture of maize semolina and cornflour, breadcrumbs, and peanut oil cake, to which sieved clay can be added for weight.

As the tench is a very timid and cautious fish, it is sensible to groundbait generously the night before, to avoid having to do it again while fishing.

Baits

These are either animal or vegetable, namely bloodworms (two worms on a size 16 hook or a larva on a size 20 hook), which are the most fetching, one or more maggots on a size 14 or 16 hook, or a grain of wheat on a size 16 hook. Vegetable baits are particularly effective in the summer.

Fishing method

Tench are essentially bottom feeders. Thus after the water has been plumbed, the float must be adjusted so the cast and the bait lie at that level. The bite is betrayed by a quivering of the float, which may sometimes rise a little. The cautious tench examines the bait with suspicion before sucking it in. It is worth giving it time to swallow it confidently, waiting for the float to make a definite dive before striking without too much violence. The tench puts up a powerful, stubborn defence. It sticks to the bottom and sometimes tries to shoot off toward the weeds. Close contact should be maintained, but without maltreating the fish and terrifying it. After going round and round on the spot until its strength is exhausted, the tench allows itself to be brought to the net without incident.

Enticing movements are sometimes needed to stimulate the fish's hunger. These consist of slow withdrawals and small movements on the spot. In the summer tench are frequently found at the surface among floating weed. They can be fished at sight, offering them a worm on fly the tackle. This highly entertaining roving technique calls for nylon line strong enough (0.16 to 0.18 mm) to handle the larger specimens which will invariably plunge deep into the weeds when hooked.

To keep the nervous tench in one spot, it is essential to groundbait thoroughly the night before.

Tench swims

Tench like calm, warm waters overgrown with vegetation. They are found near water lilies and banks of pondweed in water about 5 to 6 feet (1.50–2 m) deep. Their presence is suggested by clouds of bubbles breaking the surface, indicating they are busy digging in the mud.

■ ***The tench in its fine green-bronze livery.***

Speedy bleak fishing specialists use very short rods called "machine guns". These two champion anglers, members of a club in Epernay, France, are fishing the river Marne not far from the famous Champagne vineyards. The concentration on their faces and the intensity of their body language speaks volumes.

Fishing for bleak is often considered a pastime for children, beginners, or the occasional angler – in the same class as fishing for gudgeon or minnows. In fact it is nothing of the kind, and the magnificent catches regularly achieved by some anglers are the fruit of long experience and consummate skill. Apparently simple, bleak fishing conceals boundless ingenuity. It calls for the use of specific high-performance tackle and ultra-rapid reflexes. It is a competitive discipline mastered with extremely difficulty. Devoted anglers have perfected remarkable baits and techniques for catching bleak at record speed. Fishing for these magnificent little silver fish is not just a delight to the expert angler. Catching them on the surface can be very subtle and highly exciting. Those fishing by dapping or with an artificial fly will find it a wary fish, tempted with difficulty, whose capture calls for lively reflexes.

■ ***Some bleak specialists deploy a real arsenal of tackle, with great effect.***

FLOAT FISHING

The tackle

Depending on whether one is fishing in a small watercourse or on the banks of a reservoir, The tackle differs greatly. In lakes, the shoals of bleak circulate far away from the bank, so a telescopic or sectional rod 16–30 feet (5–9 m) long is needed. Carbon fibre is an excellent material that combines lightness and rigidity. These qualities ensure rapid, efficient strikes. The stiff rod tip, as used on canals, is fitted with an elastic shock absorber. The need to respond almost instantaneously to the bite makes a very short rod, or "machine gun" preferable whenever possible. This is telescopic and generally measures from 3 to 10 feet (1 to 3 m).

Bleak

Diminutive but discerning

Latin name: *Alburnus alburnus*
Family: Cyprinidae

Rigs

The way the line is rigged and the distribution of the weights vary according to the depth at which the shoals of bleak are swimming and the characteristics of the water (calm water or a rough current). Pick a small, very sensitive float, for the bleak is extremely cautious.

The elongated (drop-shaped) float is weighted so that it barely floats, with just the coloured tip of the antenna visible above the surface. The 0.08 mm line ends in an 8 inch (20 cm) cast in 0.06 or 0.07 mm nylon. The hook, a size 22 or 24 according to the size of the bait, can be attached directly to the line. The placing of the weights varies greatly. Whether partly spread out or in a mixed array, they must suit the circumstances. When the bleak are swimming at various depths and difficult to pin down, widely spread shot is best. The bait will sink more slowly and there may be bites as it does so. If the depth at which the shoal lies is already definitely known, it is preferable to use grouped shot (dust shot touching each other) or an olivette. In this way the bait will quickly reach the desired level.

The bleak is one of the rare cyprinids most active in the winter, promising good catches for anglers who are not afraid of cold weather.

Groundbaiting

An inexhaustible topic of conversation among specialists, good groundbait is the key to success when fishing for bleak. The real experts all have their infallible "kitchen recipes" whose secrets are jealously guarded. Above all, the aim of groundbaiting is get the bleak excited, not to fill them up! It is distributed frugally to a regular rhythm, in small pinches every two casts. All groundbait for bleak is light in weight and colour, and works quickly. Its consistency varies according to the depth fished. For fish on the surface, the groundbait is just moistened. It should explode and break up on contact with the surface. When a shoal is more than 3 feet below the surface, and especially if there is a rapid current, the groundbait should be given a particular texture (kneaded into pellets) so it can reach the desired depth before breaking up into thousands of particles. Regular groundbaiting should have the effect of maintaining a constant cloud in suspension that attracts and excites the fish.

There are dozens of recipes, each with its extra ingredient giving the effective personal touch, or not. Bleak groundbait generally comprises a mixture of cornflour, maize semolina, creamed rice, breadcrumbs and milled hempseed.

Fishing method

Bleak fishing needs very sharp reflexes because the fish is hooked as it bites, the instant there is anything the least unusual about the way the float drifts. It sometimes happens that the fish are unwilling to come back to the cloud of groundbait. When this happens, carry on fishing cautiously in the immediate vicinity.

The same thing can happen as regards the depth. The level at which the shoal is swimming must be pinpointed by adjusting the float to different depths until the result is satisfactory.

Fishing with maggots

This bait is really good for bleak and is fished on the surface or in mid-water, mainly in the spring and throughout the summer. When a good spot has been found, throw in a few pinches of groundbait along with some maggots before casting into the suspended cloud. The maggot is used on a size 22 hook.

Fishing with bloodworms

The bloodworm is readily taken by bleak. While groundbaiting exactly as above, some light bloodworm diggings can be added for completeness. The bait is put singly or in pairs on a long-shanked fine steel size 24 hook.

When fishing at speed in a well groundbaited swim, one catch follows another at a stupefying rate.

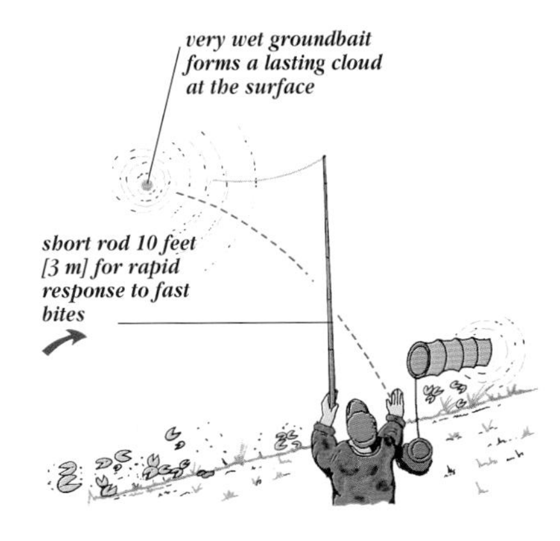

Fishing a bleak swim.

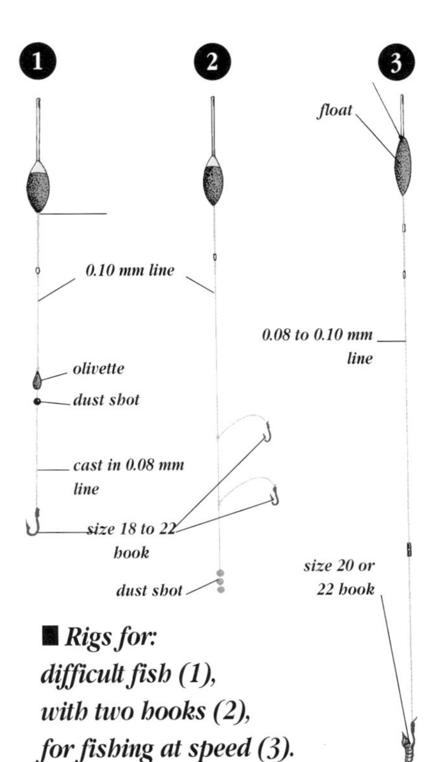

Rigs for: difficult fish (1), with two hooks (2), for fishing at speed (3).

■ *After groundbaiting, the long wait!*

Bleak swims

In running water, bleak particularly like places that are slightly coloured. They can be found in the proximity of drains, downstream from washing-places (increasingly rare!) where they swim amid the soap bubbles. They also like eddies close to the edge, downstream of obstacles such as rocks and bridge piers, and runs at the edge of the main current.
In the summer they often enter fairly rapid currents. In reservoirs their presence is revealed by their characteristic rises breaking the surface. The largest gatherings are generally to be found near the entrance of some large tributary.

Fishing with paste

A very simple recipe can be used: a pellet of soaked bread flake or a commercially available artificial paste will do nicely. The bite is very fleeting and calls for a faster response than with other bait.

Fishing with a pearl

The pearl, which is red, translucent and about 3 mm in diameter, is the kind used for necklaces or bracelets. It is threaded on the nylon, then slid down the shank of a size 22 hook until it stops at the curve. If one manages to round up a large enough shoal, impressive scores can be achieved by striking very fast at the slightest movement of the float.

The painstaking preparations of the bleak fisherman

Fishing with bacon

Tiny 2-mm cubes of bacon are fixed on a size 2 hook. Two further hooks can be added on droppers, and double or even triple catches can be reliably made. The subtle bite is often only perceptible as a tiny quiver of the rod tip or a sideways movement of the float. The strike in response must be immediate. Experts who fish with bacon use a very short line to be able to strike faster. By making enticing movements, holding and letting go, the number of bites can be increased significantly. A shoal of bleak may swim at different depths during the same fishing session, so the float must be adjusted when one notices the frequency of bites has diminished. Fishing with bacon is practised mostly in winter.

Fly fishing in a backwater of the middle Loire, France. The thick background of overhanging trees obliges the angler to use a rod not much more than 7 feet (2.3 m) long.

Fishing with blood

Another winter practice, fishing with blood calls for plentiful groundbaiting. An excellent groundbaiting method that will keep the bleak close is to fill a canvas or finely perforated plastic bag with blood and keep it upstream of the swim. Coagulated blood (mixed with cotton wool so that it stays on better) is cut into tiny cubes and fished on a size 24 hook.

■ *Emergent flies in duck tail.*

FLY-FISHING

Not displeasing to the trout or grayling purist, fly-fishing for bleak is one of the finest, most subtle disciplines there is. It requires ultra-rapid reflexes, for this devilish little fish that heartily swallows any prey coming its way also spits it out again with a speed that never ceases to astonish. A rapid strike does not mean a violent one; the bleak's very delicate mouth can be torn by the lightest sharp tug. It is a matter of touch and moderation. The tackle is essentially the same as that used for trout as far as the rod is concerned; this is about 10 feet (3 m) long, and is used with a fine fly line. The cast is very fine (from 0.07 to 0.08 mm) and will snap if the strike is too hard. The flies, mounted on size 18 or 20 hooks are generally small grey, red, black or tricolored palmers, imitations of winged ants or small ducktails. Some anglers, not content with hooking bleak on one fly, add three to eight flies on droppers. When cast to a shoal of bleak which are all biting together, it would be an exception if the strike did not happen to hook at least one of them. With a little bit of luck they can be caught in twos and threes!

Fly-fishing for bleak is reserved for fine days. It is deadly at the beginning of autumn when flying ants are hatching.

FLY-FISHING WITH NATURAL INSECTS

We cannot close this chapter on bleak without mentioning fishing with natural insects, which is particularly deadly on fine summer and autumn evenings when the fish excitedly gorge themselves on the hatches. With this method large bleak can be caught, especially on reservoirs. The stiff 10 to 16 foot (3–5 m) rod should have a flexible top section. A fine floating fly-line of about 15 feet (4.5 m) is attached to an 8 foot (2.5 m) nylon rat's tail cast thinning to a diameter of about 0.08 mm. The hook size depends on the bait used. The technique consists of casting upstream of the rises, smoothly, to prevent tearing the bait (and avoiding false casts, which damage it). The most effective baits are a housefly, a winged ant (awesome), a greased maggot or an ant's egg. The bite is usually signalled by a rise followed by a tiny tug. Wait a second before striking. When the bait has sunk, the bite may be no more than a slight sideways twitch of the cast, or it may dive suddenly, hence the advantage of greasing the nylon well.

Several droppers can be added to the cast. In this case, when casting to a rise, the baits are retrieved in jerks. With this system a few fish can be caught at the same time.

■ *Three sedges in duck tail.*

A vast swim on the river Allier, France, where float fishing can produce medium-sized carp as well as hotu. However, more suited to fishing in the current are the English and Bolognese styles.

Barbel

A formidable bearded adversary

Latin name: *Barbus barbus*
Family: Cyprinidae

The barbel offers fascinating possibilities to the angler who wishes to tackle a powerful, fighting adversary. When using light tackle in great backwaters littered with obstacles, its capture is both risky and spectacular. Weight for weight, the barbel is one of the most difficult freshwater fish to handle. Its defence generally consists of sticking obstinately to the bottom until it is completely exhausted. The angler must therefore show patience and above all avoid restraining it too much. In its panic, this fearsome opponent can dash into a fast current and in a matter of seconds drag dozens of yards of line off the screaming reel.
Playing a fish that can weigh as much as 18 lb (8 kg) on a 0.16 mm line can only be described as great sport. Float fishing or legering are used to catch barbel. As far as catching large specimens is concerned, the second of these methods seems to give the most consistent results.

FISHING WITH NATURAL BAITS

Float fishing

The tackle

The extreme fighting nature of the barbel fully justifies the use of a powerful rod, especially when dealing with large specimens. A length of 15 to 16 feet (4.5–5 m) allows the current to be properly exploited and permits long runs to be fished. Either a telescopic or sectional type can be chosen.

To be able to allow the bait to drift a long way down a run, a light fixed-spool spinning reel is recommended. (It is not unusual to take a fish after drifting for 100 feet/30 m). The drag should be reliable and with a low setting can be used to handle large fish.

Rig

The frequent presence of eddies and counter-currents characteristic of barbel haunts justifies the use of a very stable, stubby (Toulouse style) float weighted with mixed or bunched shot. Generally, an olivette rests on the knot attaching the cast, which is weighted with a few judiciously spread dust shot.

Since the barbel is a cautious fish, a long cast of about 20 inches (50 cm) in 0.14 to 0.16 mm nylon is recommended.

The line is in 0.18 to 0.20 mm nylon according to how cluttered the water is and how large the fish to be dealt with are. The float is always adjusted so that the bait drags on the bottom.

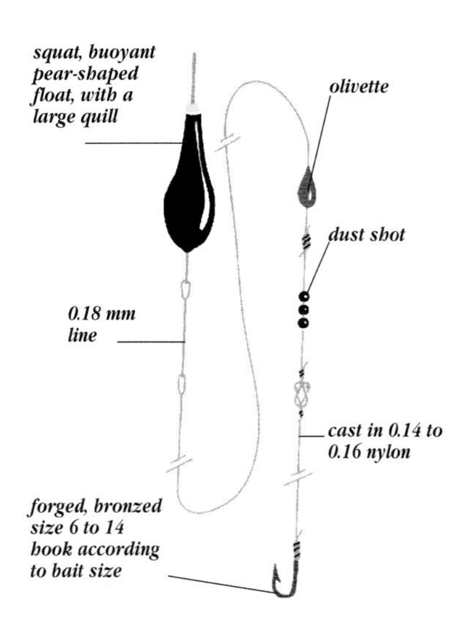

■ ***Basic rig for barbel fishing with a float.***

Barbel swims

Barbel like lively water. According to the season, they favour fast, wide, runs over a pebbly bottom, deep holes upstream or downstream of rapids, big eddies, below bridge piers, and fast stretches full of obstacles.

They are mainly found downstream of dams, close to places where the water is in rapid movement, even where there is white foam. In the summer they seek out oxygen and are likely to be found in very turbulent water, generally in places you might expect to be inhabited by trout.

Good spots for barbel can also be recognised by the characteristic sound they make turning over pebbles in search of food.

Baits

As an omnivore, the barbel appreciates animal and vegetable baits equally well. It's all a question of the season, the conditions, and the state of the water.

The maggot is an excellent bait suitable for all seasons. Two or three are generally fixed on a size 12 to 14 hook.

Bloodworms are irreplaceable when the water is coloured, for example after a storm. Two frisky specimens can be presented on a size 12 hook.

The caddis is a prey much sought by the barbel, especially in lively waters, in rapid currents and the disturbed water typical for trout or grayling. It is best to offer one larva on a size 14 hook. With this bait, it is not unusual to hook a dace, a chub or ... a fine trout!

Mayfly larvae are sometimes used under the same conditions as one would use a caddis larva. Their small size means using fine line and a small hook. This can be a disadvantage when contact is made with a large specimen, which will exploit the strength of the current to escape. In addition, its frailty means frequently re-baiting the hook.

Fishing method

It is very difficult to set up a barbel swim because the current is often very strong. Groundbaiting is very useful but the groundbait needs to be sticky and heavy to remain in place long enough. It can consist of pellets of sieved clay the size of a pigeon's egg, with added brandlings or maggots, thrown upstream of the run. When float fishing for barbel one should generally be positioned above a suitable run, allowing the line to drift in the current and occasionally braking as it runs out. This produces pulling and

■ ***Fishing Bologna style "with wet feet"; a pleasant and amusing way to pass a fine summer's day in a bit of sport.***

releasing actions that often lead to a bite. The drift can be allowed to continue for a good distance; bites can sometimes occur as far as 100 feet (30 m) away from the angler! The bites differ according to the size of the barbel. Small ones have quite a lively bite, causing the float to dive suddenly. Sometimes the float simply stops and sinks under the pressure of the current. There is no way of distinguishing a bite from being snagged on the bottom. If there is the least doubt, strike sharply and keep the line taut, for sometimes barbel sit tight on the bottom for a few seconds before making off. Given the fineness of the line and the combative nature of the fish, it is essential to set the drag very light. The fish generally stays where it is, stubbornly diving until completely exhausted. Sometimes, especially when played too hard at the beginning (a mistake to be avoided), it leaves its hole and dashes into the fast current, tearing off line at astonishing speed to a high-pitched scream from the reel. The outcome of the contest is now at risk because in addition to the strength of the fish backed by the force of the current, it will deliberately try to reach a snag (a rock or a log) to break the line.

■ *With currents going in opposite directions and the divisions between still and moving water clearly visible, waters like this lend themselves to fixed Bolognese style or English style barbel fishing.*

Fishing in summer

Throughout the summer barbel lying in holes and deep in the current may be tempted with the tail of an American crayfish, a cricket or a grasshopper. During this period the fish gather in shoals that hang listlessly in mid-water refusing most of the traditional baits. Drowsy, they move very little, but their desire may just be aroused by a line baited with a cricket and presented at their level.

■ *Fishing English style on Vichy Lake, France. Here long-distance groundbaiting is essential.*

Legering

The tackle

Most anglers fishing with a sinker use a standard trout spinning rod. However, the power of the fish, and above all, the strength of the current, which require the use of heavy weights (from 30 to 40 g) dictate the use of longer, more powerful rods. Choose a powerful rod about 10 feet (3 m) long with a stiff top section, of the type used for pike.

The reel should be of excellent make and provided with a trustworthy adjustable drag. Nowadays light or medium fixed-spool spinning reels are used. The wide spool is loaded with 500 feet (150 m) of 0.20 to 0.26 mm nylon line, depending on the anticipated size of the fish and how cluttered the site is.

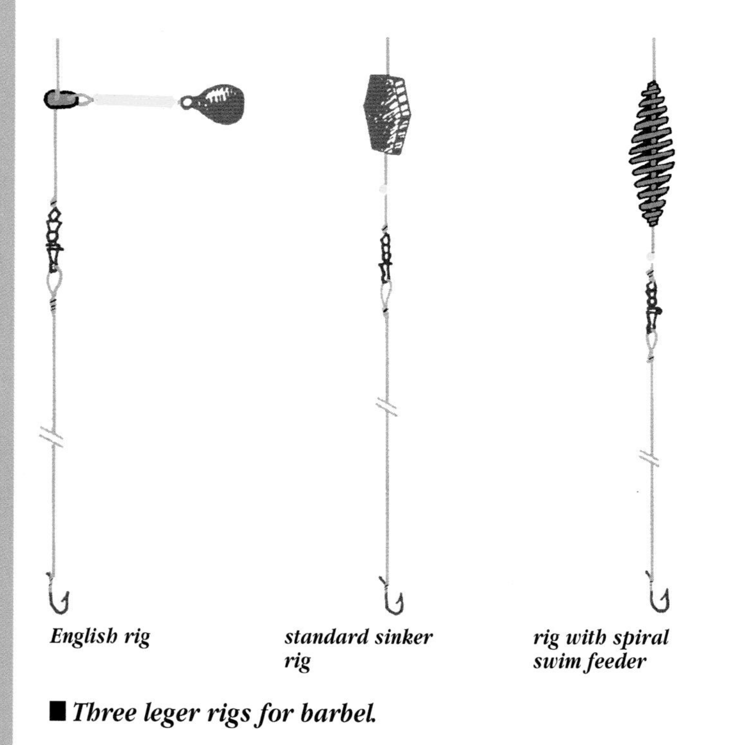

■ *Three leger rigs for barbel.*

Rig

A 20–40 g olive (depending on the strength of the current) rests on a single dust shot immediately above a swivel clip. Some anglers use a spiral swim feeder. This is hollow and filled with maggots. Its virtue is that from the moment of immersion the escaping maggots provide an accurate supply of groundbait to the swim being fished. The cast, in 0.16 to 0.18 mm nylon, is about 2 feet (60 cm) long so that a weight too close to the bait does not arouse the interested barbel's suspicions.

Baits

Five or six maggots can be threaded on a size 6 or 8 hook. The same bait can be offered in a bunch on a size 12 or 14 treble. Clay pellets containing maggots (see the chapter on carp) are used for groundbait. Because of the strength of the current, it is very difficult to "stabilize" a barbel swim unless using sticky materials. If worms are used, a brandling or a large earthworm can be fixed on a size 2 hook. These baits are mainly used in coloured water. The earthworm is very effective bait for large barbel during the first autumn spates, particularly when fishing in eddies or deep currents close to the bank.

■ *Caught in Spain, these barbel belong to a different sub-species.*

The crayfish is another bait highly prized by big barbel, and is especially productive early in the summer.

Only American crayfish may be used; since they are fairly small, they should be used live and whole.

With larger shellfish the tail is cut off the thorax and used on the hook by itself.

Barbel are also very keen on cheese. They particularly like soft cheeses, best of all cream of Gruyère offered in small cubes. The well-known Apéricubes do well, leading one to think the barbel a great gourmet! The cubes are threaded onto a size 12 treble hook by means of a baiting needle so as to hide the bends inside the cheese. The cast, in 0.18 mm nylon is secured by a loop to a swivel clip. The standard weight (a sliding olive of 20–40 g rests on a small stop weight so that repeated shocks to the swivel do not fatigue the attachment knot. In view of the size of the fish that take this bait, the line is in 0.22 mm nylon.

Some anglers knead the cheese with cotton wool to make it stay on the hook better.

A formidable bearded adversary

■ *Playing a big Mediterranean barbel in the clear waters of Lake Caspe, Spain.*

■ *Barbel often dig around on the bottom in this large river backwater; a good reason to offer them an appetizing mouthful lying motionless on the mud just ready for the taking.*

Groundbaiting

This is indispensable; scatter morsels of cheese upstream of the swim. Unfortunately much of it will be ineffective because the current will carry it away. To counter this drawback, the cheese can be inserted into the holes in a porous stone or a block of cinder. This will slowly release the groundbait in the place fished. (The use of cheese as a bait is forbidden in some first category rivers. When seeking barbel in such places, it is just as well to check the local regulations.)

Fishing with pellets

Barbel take pellets very well; these are similar to those used for carp, but smaller in size. The standard tackle consists of an English carp rod about 12 feet (3.5 m) long (nothing is safe from this fish when fishing with pellets) fitted with a light spinning reel loaded with about 300 feet (100 m) of 0.24 to 0.26 mm nylon line depending on the size of the fish and the extent to which the water is obstructed. The rig is identical to that specified for carp: a fixed olive of 20 gm held on the line by two dust shot; a swivel clip leading to an 8 inch (20 cm) cast in 0.18 to 0.20 mm nylon, ending in a single size 5 hook baited with maggots. Groundbaiting should be generous, and is based on sticky clay mixed with maggots or possibly peanut oil cake or crushed potato. Balls the size of pellets are thrown into the swim. The weight can be replaced by a swim-feeder, which has the advantage of distributing groundbait accurately in the strongest current. Fishing with pellets is particularly effective in the summer. Look for the places that are best during this season, namely wherever there is turbulent, well-oxygenated water, for example, just below a dam.

Fish close to the bank so that the pellet does not get damaged by casting.

The bite is signalled by a quivering of the rod tip, followed almost immediately by a slow, powerful departure.

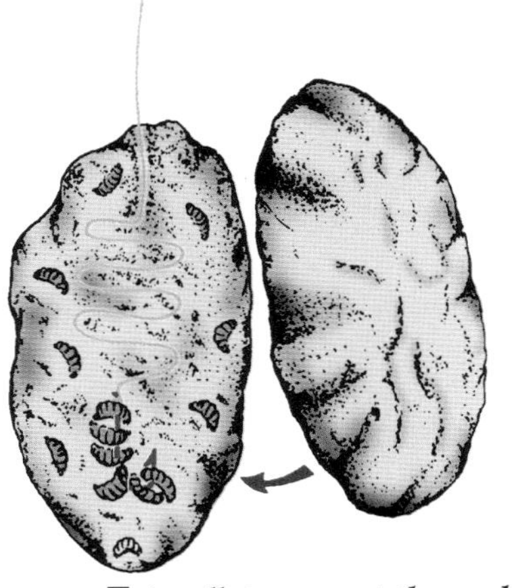

■ *A pellet seen cut through*

■ *The barbel only gives in after a tough fight.*

Hotu

A much maligned capricious cyprinid

Latin name: *Chondrostoma nasus*
Family: Cyprinidae

Though the hotu may sometimes bite at a spoon or a very light lure, it is basically fished for with a baited hook. It is not a greatly sought-after quarry; its capricious nature puts many anglers off. It has the appalling habit of persistently refusing the best presented baits then, without anyone knowing why, and unfortunately only on occasion, suddenly starting to behave wildly and swallowing any bait on sight. Its flesh, which is insipid and full of bones, rounds off its bad reputation. Trout fishermen also revile the hotu. On approaching a promising spot, they see the swim spoilt by a shoal of hotu in frantic flight from between their boots, spreading panic in the whole area.

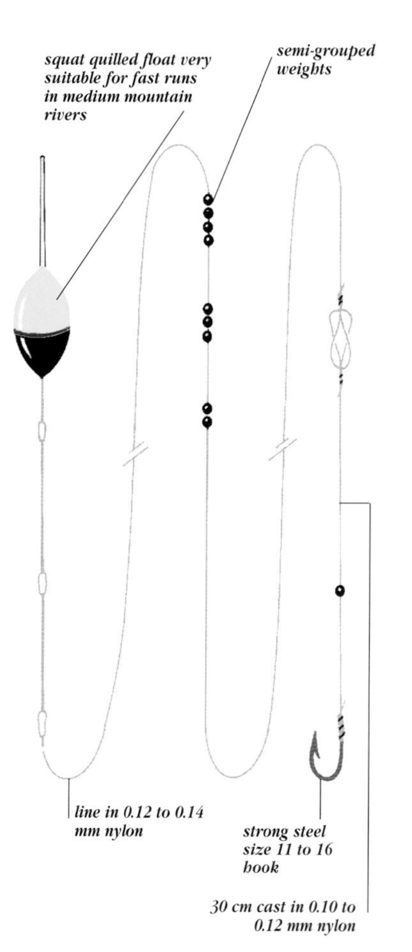

■ ***Float fishing rig recommended for hotu.***

FISHING WITH LIVE NATURAL BAITS AND WITH MOSS

The tackle

The hotu is a mistrustful fish, whose pursuit requires the use of a long telescopic rod of between 20 and 23 feet (6 and 7 m) with or without rings. A small centre-pin reel is usually perfectly adequate.

The line is .12 to .14 mm nylon with a small spindle-shaped float (stubby if fishing in a strong current) balanced with an olivette or closely-grouped shot. The cast in .10 to .12 mm nylon ends in a size 14 to 16 hook.

Baits

For the most part hotu eat small animals living among the pebbles on the river bed. Thus mayfly and caddis larvae are indicated. Maggots are equally effective, as are small brandlings or a bunch of bloodworms when the water is coloured. In the summer, and especially during a heatwave, moss is the most effective bait.

Fishing method

Shoals of hotu are easily visible in the current because their sides flash silver as they turn while feeding. Fishing on sight is thus possible as long as one is careful to be unobtrusive. The most effective method consists of groundbaiting a deep, slow run (using mixed clay and maggots) where there are thought to be hotu. Let the float drift down the run, taking care to adjust its height so that the bait skims along the bottom. The hotu is a fish that rakes and burrows, and only rarely feeds in mid-water or on the surface. The rises hotu make may indicate playful behaviour rather than the capture of drifting insects. Enticing movements, holding and releasing, are essential to stir this strangely behaved fish. The bite is indicated by an abrupt stop followed by a slow descent of the float, which can be mistaken for snagging on the bottom. The angler should let the fish bite, then strike without undue violence.

■ ***A magnificent hotu taken by the Bolognese method is landed in a most unorthodox manner.***

Hotu often put up a feeble defence. Nonetheless, because fine tackle is used and since they are used to fighting the current, they can cause problems when they reach a good size.

During spates, hotu sometimes gather in bends sheltered from the force of the main current. A fat earthworm or a slug positioned on the bottom may stimulate their appetite!

Fishing on holiday with family and friends...

For the whole of the summer the feeding activity of predatory fish slows somewhat, except of course for black bass. But there are other fish that bite. It's time to get one's feet wet, and have fun with methods such as dapping, fly-fishing, fishing while wading and so on.

The chub is the most omnivorous of our cyprinids, and the one that can be fished for in the most ways! Dapping is one method which many anglers enjoy.

Scorned by many fishermen, the chub is considered a last resort or a "face saver" not even worth touching with a fork, so insipid and packed with bones is its flesh. This is wrong, for the chub is an extremely wary fish, often harder to lure than a trout. It also mounts an energetic defence if only during the first stages of the fight. Its diet is undoubtedly the most varied among all the cyprinids, and this offers numerous possibilities for its capture. Some traditional methods (dapping, for example) are fun in summertime. At the height of the heatwave when trout refuse to bite, the fly-fisherman will find this fish a pleasing diversion. And the white fish angler can carry on with his sport in winter, when most other fish are less active.

■ ***Dapping, a traditional method on the banks of the river Allier, France.***

FISHING WITH INSECTS

Dapping

This ancient method is very productive, and in former times was a favourite with the anglers on the banks of the Seine. Akin to fly-fishing, it allows an insect to be projected a good distance without the suspicious chub becoming aware of the angler. The difficulty lies in casting the very delicate bait, which will tear if the movement is too violent.

■ ***Don't go by the size... chub can reach a weight of several kilos.***

Chub

Greedy and cunning

Latin name: *Leuciscus cephalus*
Family : Cyprinidae

The tackle

A very soft bamboo rod not longer than 15 feet (4.5 m) is recommended.

The line should be a little longer than the rod. It consists of a parallel fly-line of about 16 feet (5 m) long continuing with a 5 foot (1.5 m) rat's tail cast tapered to 0.16 mm at the point, where it is attached to a size 8 to 10 hook, depending on the size of the bait. The cast is greased to within 8 inches (20 cm) of the hook.

Some anglers use a ringed rod and a fly-reel so as to be able to vary the length of the cast.

Baits

Many insects are suitable for dapping. The best are grasshoppers, crickets, small maybugs, Colorado beetles, houseflies or flying ants. The larvae of aquatic insects (mayfly, caddis) can also be used, as can moths or maggots.

Fishing method

The actions are akin to those of fly-fishing, but are wider and slower to avoid cracking the line and snapping off the insect. False casts should be avoided for the same reason, and the lift should be slow and careful. In small rivers and streams, fish three-quarters upstream as with the fly, trying all the likely places for chub, particularly under overhanging foliage.

In wider rivers one can fish from a boat or wade, casting perpendicular to the bank under the foliage opposite.

■ ***Catching grasshoppers can be a tedious business. The best time to collect them is at dawn when they are still drowsy.***

When the bait touches the water, to some extent "dumped in" by the line, it is allowed to drift along an inch or so under the surface. In small rivers often the angler may see the fish leave its position and throw itself on the insect. The greased cast may suddenly go under, or there may be a rise to the floating bait. When this happens, leave it to bite for a second, then strike smoothly. Watch out for big chub that often rush away and inevitably break the line, and above all, approach the fish and cast very carefully or it will certainly refuse the bait.

A variant of dapping consists of casting by catapulting the line; on an overgrown river this makes it easier to place an insect under the foliage than with a big rod. With the rod handle in the right hand, hold the cast in the left about 8 inches (20 cm) from the hook, pulling it so that the rod tip comes up and back. Let go of the cast and flick the rod to send the bait in the desired direction. With this method one needs to wade down the riverbed.

"Surprise" fishing

"Surprise" chub fishing is very similar to trout fishing with natural baits, and requires at least the same degree of care to escape the vigilance of this suspicious and wily fish. It consists of placing the insect close to the chub, surprising it, and stimulating its curiosity and hunger. This fascinating process is something like hunting. The victim is located in advanced and must be approached without the smallest sound, the angler's silhouette blending with the surrounding plants, taking particular care not to cast shadows on the water. If the fish detects nothing suspicious, it will take the bait without hesitation.

The tackle

A telescopic rod 16 to 20 feet (5–6 m) long, with internal rings to make it easier to manoeuvre the line amongst foliage.

A simple centre-pin reel wound with 165 feet (50 m) of 0.14 to 0.16 mm nylon line is adequate.

Some anglers use even simpler tackle: a 20 to 23 foot (6–7 m) rod to which is attached 3–6 feet (1–2 m) of line ending in a size 8 to 16 hook depending on the bait used. Varnished or brightly coloured rods that can flash in the sunlight must always be avoided. A matt finish is suitably inconspicuous.

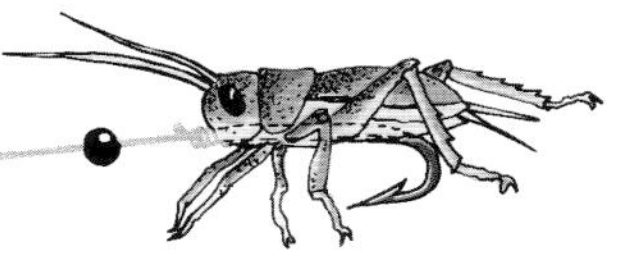

■ ***When the chub are deep, it sometimes pays to weight the insect with a small lead shot.***

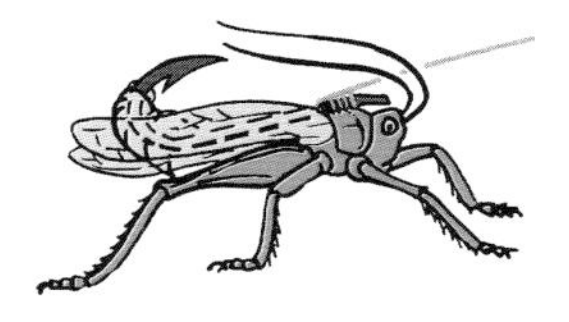

■ ***A grasshopper hooked through the back for fishing on the surface.***

■ ***A live cricket hooked under the wing case to avoid damage.***

■ ***Drifting a grasshopper among the weeds where unwary chub are likely to lie in ambush.***

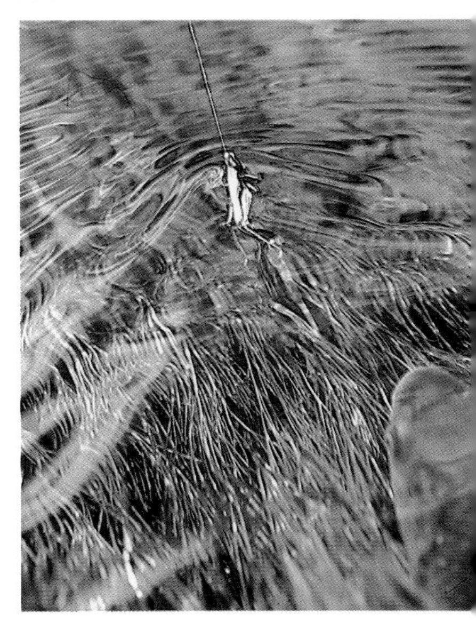

Yielding after a few rushes, this chub was finally taken on a grasshopper.

■ *An educated gourmet, the chub will not ignore a drifting grape. During the grape harvest, this is the bait to use.*

Fishing method

Look for the chub in all their standard haunts (eddies, slow currents passing under foliage, below waterfalls).
When a fish has been located, approach cautiously, then drop the insect near its tail (never just in front of it, which would arouse its suspicions). Again, take care not to panic the chub by allowing the rod or your body to cast a shadow on the water.

FISHING WITH VEGETABLE BAITS

Fishing with fruit

Some fruit are excellent bait for big chub. They should only be used at times when the fish would naturally come across them in the river.

The tackle

Depending on the width of the river and how cluttered it is, a spinning rod of 5 feet (1.5 m) can be used with a light fixed-spool spinning reel, loaded with about 300 feet (100 m) of 0.18 mm nylon line. Otherwise, a ringed bank rod 16–20 feet (5–6 m) in length (fitted with a small centre-pin reel) or an English-type rod with a light spinning reel, for fishing under foliage on banks a good distance away.

The line can be of 0.2 mm nylon, and the float squat, highly visible and weighted with an olive. The cast is in 0.18 mm nylon and ends in a size 12 treble hook. When using a spinning rod, the float can be replaced by a bubble float, to which is attached a 0.16 mm nylon cast 50 cm long, ending in a size 12 treble.

Baits

Choose cherries, blackberries or grapes, according to the season.

Fishing method

Only very ripe but unspoiled fruit should be used for groundbaiting. With cherries, do not forget to stone them, then use a baiting needle to put them on the hook, embedding the bends in the flesh. Groundbaiting is not necessary when the fruit trees or brambles border the river and the berries fall into the stretches to be fished. If this is not so, the angler should scatter the fruit over likely looking runs. Groundbaiting for some days in advance will often have more effect. The most likely places are slow, deep runs and holes. The bite is definite and sometimes even violent, and calls for an immediate strike because the bait does not stay on the hook very well.

Fishing with bread

Equally effective in the winter, fishing with bread requires the same The tackle as fishing with blood, namely an English-type rod with a light fixed-spool spinning reel. The spool is wound with 330 feet (100 m) of 0.16 mm nylon line.

Because of the distances at which one fishes, the float should be highly visible. It is weighted with bunched shot. The cast is in 0.14 mm nylon and ends in a size 8 hook.

Fishing method

When fishing at long distances like this, it is best to try in slow, deep currents. Once the float has been adjusted to make sure the bait passes close to the bottom, cast the line, baited with a pellet of fresh bread flake, into the current three-quarters upstream. Leave the pick-up open and let the line run out naturally. The further away the float is, the harder the strike should be.

■ *Long river runs are just right for chub fishing.*

FISHING WITH ANIMAL BAITS

Fishing with blood

Most of the fishing methods intended for chub can only be used in the summer. However, this fish is just as active in the winter, a fact that cannot fail to interest the white fish angler.

Fishing with blood is undoubtedly one of the most effective methods of catching big chub in wintertime.

The tackle

A telescopic or sectional rod of 16 to 20 feet (5–6 m), or an English rod will be suitable.

In the first case, a simple centre-pin reel is enough. For the English rod, use a light spinning reel.

The line 0.18 mm in diameter takes a spindle-shaped float weighted with grouped shot. The cast is in 0.16 mm nylon and ends in a single size 8 hook or a small treble.

Fishing method

First, it is just as well to choose a suitable spot, namely a slow, deep current, a hole, or somewhere there are eddies. Groundbaiting with molehill earth and fresh blood is essential. The hook is baited with clotted blood. When the blood clots, it forms a durable mass that can be cut into little cubes. Since this substance does not stick to the hook at all well, fix a tiny piece of sponge or cotton wool soaked in fresh blood on the barb. A small cube of bloody liver is also effective.

In the winter the fish often stay close to the bottom. The float should be adjusted accordingly. When there is a bite, usually quite definite, strike immediately because the bait does not stick to the hook very well. Often several chub can be taken in the same swim. If the fish are large, the bites soon become less frequent after two or three have been caught, because they become suspicious. Then is the time to move on.

Preserving blood

The angler can obtain plenty of blood from the slaughterhouse, chicken blood being by far the best.

The first thing to do is to allow about 3½ pints of blood to clot in a bucket. The clot to be used for fishing is then put between two flat pieces of wood with a weight (a stone) on top to squeeze out the serum. Cotton wool is added. This is the only way to obtain the consistency needed for good adhesion to the hook. The blood can be preserved in the refrigerator for the following 12 to 24 hours only.

Fishing with small livebait

■ *An omnivore, the chub can be caught by most methods used for trout or white fish.*

Fishing with small livebait is certainly one of the most effective ways of catching big specimens. If you are moving about while fishing, there is also a chance of catching other fish such as zander, perch or trout. Were it not so hard to get, Planer's lamprey would be an even better bait.

The tackle

A ringed telescopic trout rod about 16 feet (5 m) long is sufficient.

A light or very light fixed-spool spinning reel loaded with 330 feet (100 m) of 0.18 mm nylon completes the outfit.

The line carries a stubby, fairly buoyant float weighted with an olive. The cast in 0.16 mm nylon ends in a single size 6 hook (for a lamprey), or a size 8 or 10 for a small minnow.

Fishing method

Look for suitable spots for chub, above all in large eddies, big troughs and deep runs with plenty of obstructions. Adjust the float to make the livebait swim in mid-water or close to the bottom, and let the line drift.

The bite is savage; leave it a few moments, then strike vigorously.

Float fishing with maggots and grubs

The tackle and methods are the same as those used when bank fishing for bleak, though a stronger rig (a cast in 0.14 mm nylon) is needed.

main line in 0.18 mm nylon

spindle-shaped float

decreasing weights

cast in 0.16 mm nylon

size 8 or 10 hook

■ *Livebaiting rig.*

■ *Chub readily take dry flies, but beware! This is a wily fish and inevitably spots anything unusual in their appearance or the way they are presented.*

FLY-FISHING

Dry fly

Unfairly despised by the fly purist, the chub is one of the hardest fish to deceive by this means. As such, it provides excellent schooling for the beginner, and since it is much more numerous than members of the salmon family, it is caught more frequently.

The tackle

A standard 9½ to 10 foot (2.8–3 m) trout fly rod with a simple or automatic reel and a floating line will be fine. The cast tapers to 0.12 or 0.14 mm. All types of fly are good for chub, but they seem to prefer palmers or sedges.

Fishing method

In major rivers, chub occupy more or less the same places as trout, though they also seem to prefer calm areas, big pools and slow currents.

In such places, fishing for them becomes quite an art, for anything unusual detected by the fish (the line too obvious, the fly wrong, the angler visible) leads to obstinate refusal, all the more vexing since the fish often takes its time rising to the fly, following it slowly until the inevitable wake of the cast puts it to flight.

■ *During the summer chub are found close to the bank, in the shade of the trees, waiting for insects to fall.*

ULTRA-LIGHT CASTING

Insects and metal lures

This prize adversary will even take a spoon!

Trout fishermen often catch big chub on dead minnows or metal lures, but only ultra-light casting is really suitable for chub fishing and can overcome their natural caution.

The tackle

Identical to that used for trout fishing. Ultra-light casting permits the use of insects such as the grasshopper which can be accurately cast to places where the fish lie.

Chub will not refuse streamers or large lightly wound palmers. Small fly spoons and flies weighted at the head are also effective.

Fishing method

Identical to that used for trout, requiring as least as much caution and precision in casting. When an insect is fished, it should be lightly weighted. Cast it three-quarters upstream, then allow it to drift with the line taut, held in the left hand.

The bite is felt as a series of small tugs at the rod point or seen as a slight movement of the line. Let it bite for a few moments, then strike, allowing for the amount of slack let out.

Dace

Fly-fisher's challenge

Latin name: *Leuciscus leuciscus*
Family: Cyprinidae

This charming little fish is most appealing in the fine season. When the trout stubbornly refuse all lures and baits, however well they are presented, it becomes a favourite target for the fly-fisherman, for it bites heartily, particularly during the evening rise at the end of a heavy, stormy day. It is on dace that the fly-fishing beginner tries out his first armament and makes his first decent catches. This cyprinid can live in the upper reaches of rivers and occupies the same positions as trout, offering young anglers a "dry run", as it were, with an opportunity to sharpen their reflexes. Their lively rises call for lightning reactions, but missing doesn't matter. Dace are well-behaved fish, and when they rise in shoals covering the surface in rings, the angler looking for his next victim is spoilt for choice.

■ ***Fly fishing for dace on a big river can be really exciting for amateur and expert alike!***

Gnat in duck-tail feathers

FLY-FISHING

The flies most used for dace are the dry flies suitable for bleak or rudd, dressed on size 16 or 18 hooks. The best artificial flies are palmers, spiders or ants. The tip of the cast should be fine (from 0.12 to 0.14 mm), because although dace sometimes bite heartily, they show a certain mistrust if the nylon is too thick or the flies are badly presented.

Gnat

OTHER METHODS

All surface fishing methods used for chub, rudd or bleak are suitable for dace. They can also be caught using a float. The best baits are those found at the bottom of the river. Mayfly larvae, or caddis larvae with their cases removed are also first-class bait.

Gnat

Gudgeon and

With its cute moustache, the gudgeon somewhat resembles a miniature barbel.
It is making a remarkable comeback in our rivers.

■ *Fried freshly-caught gudgeon are delicious!*

Gudgeon and minnows are not just delicious fried. They also make excellent livebait for pike, perch and zander. Minnow fishing is just made for children. Requiring only the simplest tackle, it gives plenty of excitement because bites are bold and plentiful, and young anglers are encouraged when their catch pleases their elders, who can use them for catching trout. Catching minnows means acquiring the reflexes that will turn a beginner into a confirmed practitioner. If a child takes to it, he or she will always hope to catch bigger fish. In short, such an introduction to fishing will mark the starting of a new vocation and a great adventure. This is the worst we can wish them!

FISHING WITH NATURAL BAIT

Fishing with rod and line is not the sole preserve of the lonely amateur by some wild river, or the dry fly purist, nor yet the bleak or salmon champion. For many of us it is a convivial activity, a welcome diversion at the traditional picnic by the water, on outings with family or friends. And if there is one fish that lends itself to this form of amusement, it is the gudgeon. In earlier times this appealing moustachioed character delighted our elders, providing them with an excuse for getting the family together on the banks of the Marne, or elsewhere. A happy age when flourishing open-air cafés reserved a special place on the menu for "fried gudgeon at all hours". A blessed time when neat shoals of these little fish teemed in the current. Over the years, pollution and poor water management have decimated their ranks. Despite this, the gudgeon is making a timid return, and perhaps it will once more be possible to witness those marvellous times when, feet in the water, a smiling group devotes itself to this amusing activity. Gudgeon fishing is not particularly difficult. Doubtless this is one reason it is so popular; the other is the delicacy of its flesh when popped into the frying pan.

Float fishing

The tackle

Rudimentary, it comprises a telescopic or sectional rod 10 to 16 feet (3–5 m) long. The line should be no thicker than and shorter than the rod by 20 to 30 inches (50–80 cm), to facilitate unhooking the fish.

minnows

The fishing school

Gudgeon Latin name: *Gobio gobio*
Family: Cyprinidae

Minnow Latin name: *Phoxinus phoxinus*
Family: Cyprinidae

■ ***Unlike most cyprinids and despite its tiny size, the minnow is carnivorous.***

A short, fat, float that drifts freely and will not be sucked under by an eddy is recommended. The single weight can be an olivette. The cast ends in a size 18 to 20 hook according to the bait used.

Baits

The gudgeon is carnivorous, and prefers bloodworms. Brandlings, maggots, caddis or sections of earthworm are also effective.

Fishing method

Having located a place where gudgeon gather (they particularly like runs with sandy or fine gravel bottoms) the first thing to do is groundbait. The groundbait should be based on sieved clay or molehill earth, to which bloodworms or sections of earthworm are added. Groundbait based on flour (peanut or maize) will do just as well if powdered blood is added.

Some anglers are content with passing a rake across the swim at regular intervals. Groundbaiting with pellets the size of a walnut should be repeated as soon as the bites begin to lessen. Try to avoid groundbaiting too often to avoid overfeeding the fish. Gudgeon rarely feed in midwater. It will pay to plumb the water so that the bait can drag along the bottom. As it drifts, keep the line over the

■ ***A gudgeon taken on a bloodworm.***

line in 0.1 mm nylon
small quilled stubby float suitable for rough water
dust shot, spread out or bunched, depending on the strength of the current
10–11 in. (27 cm) cast in 0.08 mm nylon
size 18 hook
line in 0.1 mm nylon
sensitive float
cast in 0.08 mm nylon
sliding weights
size 18 to 20 hook

■ *Two standard gudgeon rigs.*

groundbaited area, and make enticing movements to excite the fish. The bite is usually bold: the strike should be slightly delayed.

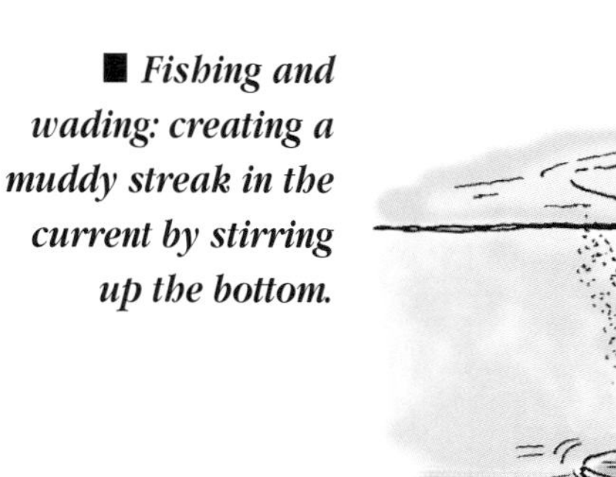

■ *Fishing and wading: creating a muddy streak in the current by stirring up the bottom.*

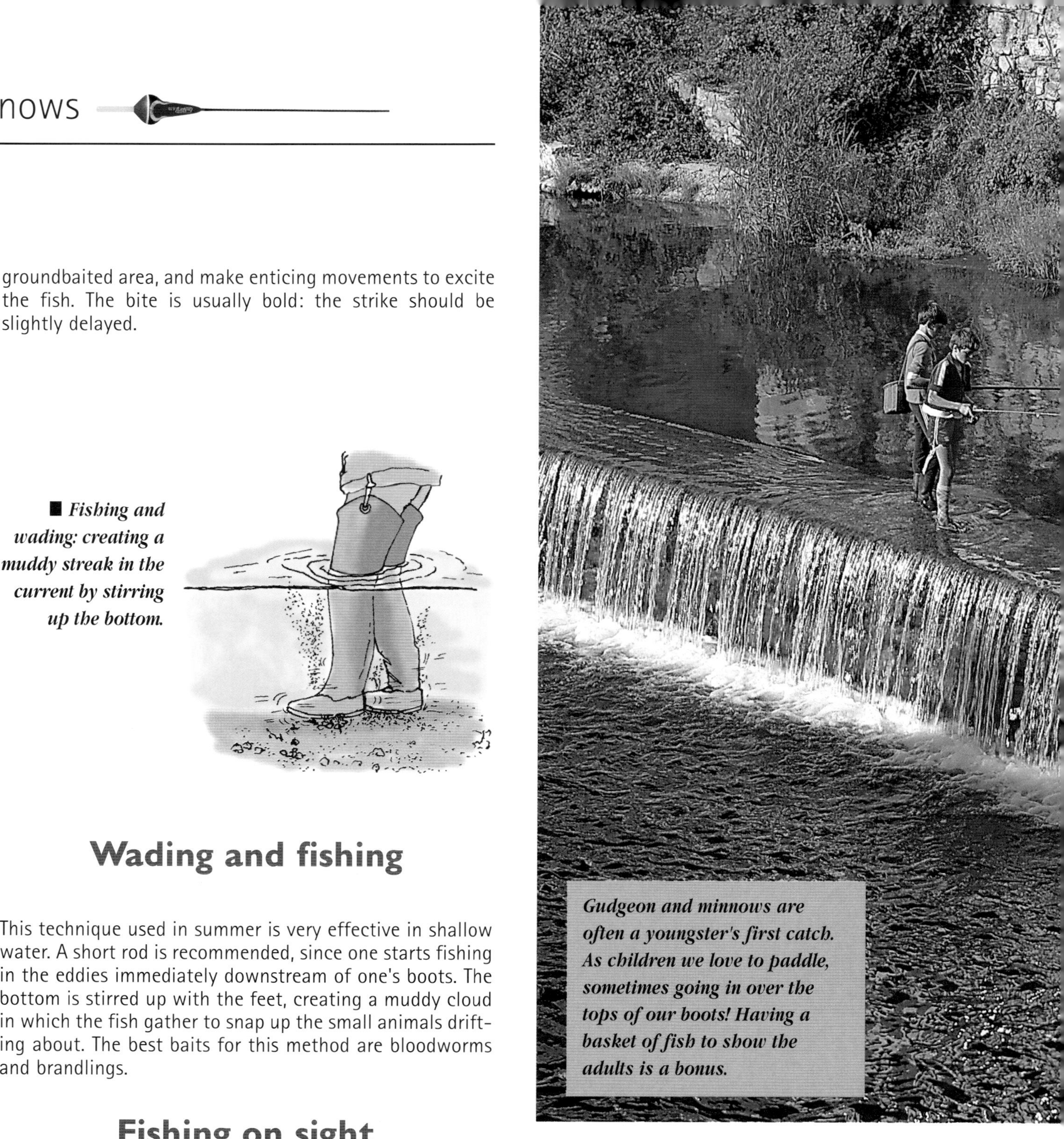

Gudgeon and minnows are often a youngster's first catch. As children we love to paddle, sometimes going in over the tops of our boots! Having a basket of fish to show the adults is a bonus.

■ *Wading and fishing for gudgeon is a pleasant way to pass the time.*

Wading and fishing

This technique used in summer is very effective in shallow water. A short rod is recommended, since one starts fishing in the eddies immediately downstream of one's boots. The bottom is stirred up with the feet, creating a muddy cloud in which the fish gather to snap up the small animals drifting about. The best baits for this method are bloodworms and brandlings.

Fishing on sight

This method catches big gudgeon that live among the pebbles and in flat stretches on large rivers with clean water. These fish are clearly visible during the heat of the day, and they may be caught easily on a worm or a caddis larva. If the gudgeon sometimes appear indifferent to the bait, some skilful enticing movements may help. The bait should sink rapidly and is weighted with a single clump of shot. Use a size 18 hook on a 0.1 mm nylon line. These large gudgeon make excellent livebait for pike and zander.

Float fishing for minnows

The tackle

Any old stick will do at a pinch, but a small telescopic rod of 10 to 13 feet (3–4 m) serves well. The line, in 0.1 mm nylon ends in a 0.08 mm cast to which is attached a single barbless hook (always best when the fish are to be kept alive), size 18 to 24, depending on the size of the bait. The running water where minnows swim justifies the addition of a group of shot that will take the bait rapidly to the bottom.

Baits

The minnow is omnivorous and likes many different baits. If the bloodworm is one of the best, small brandlings or sections of earthworm are also appreciated, as are maggots. (Check the regulations in force on major waters!) The minnow may also take artificial paste, natural paste (based on flour soaked in sugared water) or bread flake.

■ *Minnows are basically gregarious fish that live in large shoals. This is one of the cyprinids that reaches highest in our rivers, spreading mainly in trout territory.*

Fishing method

Having found a promising spot (a small eddy, the end of a run) use groundbait to gather the fish at the swim. The angler must remember that minnows are voracious and quickly satisfied.

The groundbait, based on sieved earth mixed with sections of worm or bloodworms, should be distributed economically: it is merely intended to keep the shoals of fish in place. Minnows mostly feed on the bottom, so the float should be adjusted so that the bait trails on the sand or pebbles. If adjustment does not give good results, progressively reduce the depth. Enticing movements can be important in exciting sulking fish to bite.

Some trout fishermen catch the livebait they want with an old wine bottle with the bottom knocked out. Baited with sections of worm, this is put in the river and can be taken out at any time. A good number of minnows can be caught in this way.

■ *A home-made minnow trap: an old wine bottle with the bottom knocked out.*

Eel

■ *To get round an obstacle, the eel readily takes to the land and slips through the wet grass before regaining the water further upstream.*

Description

The eel's shape is so characteristic it would be difficult to mistake it for another fish. The serpentine scaleless body is covered in thick mucus. The small poorly defined head has a deeply cut mouth. The powerful jaws are armed with numerous small sharp teeth. The diminutive gill openings are positioned next to the pectoral fins. Adults possess a single, unequally dorso-ventral fin supported by 500 rays, and two fan-shaped pectoral fins with 18 rays each. There are no pelvic fins.

Coloration

The adult has a dark back, yellowish sides and a creamy-white belly. During migration downstream the females turn silvery.

Size

The adult hardly ever exceeds about 9–10 feet (2.80 m), with a maximum weight of 6 lb (2.5–3 kg). On hatching, the larvae are 6 mm long. The elvers measure about 2½ inches (6 cm).

Biology

Diet

This changes with age and environment. The adult is a voracious omnivore and feeds on fry, dead fish, insect larvae and various invertebrates. The larva, or leptocephalus, feeds on plankton but fasts during metamorphosis. The adults do not feed during their river descent.

Reproduction

Having reached maturity at 8–15 years, the eel descends to the sea to breed. Unlike the salmon it is a catadromous migrant. It travels some 1,800 to 3,000 miles (3,000 to 5,000 km) across the Atlantic ocean to the Sargasso Sea. Its extra-ordinary sense of direction has not yet really been explained. The adult is almost certainly guided by an astonishing ability to detect the smell of substances dissolved in the water. It also possesses an advanced faculty for analysing water and sensing variations in salinity and temperature with great precision.

Behavior

The eel begins its voyage in the autumn and continues throughout the winter. When it reaches its destination each female lays about a million eggs at a depth of some 1,300 feet (400 m). The eggs have an incubation period of about four weeks. On hatching, the leptocephalus larvae (tiny translucent fish) are carried away by the current. Drifting in the Gulf Stream, they reach the coasts of Europe. Arriving at their destination after a journey of two or three years, the larvae undergo metamorphosis and turn into elvers, the miniature eels so actively netted along our coasts. The first of them, the males, remain on the coast or in coastal lakes for ten years. The overwhelming majority of females ascend the rivers, often right to the source, and stay there for up to 15 years. Few obstacles are impassable to eels. They travel overland to circumvent dams, taking advantage of rain or dew, and are able to breathe through their skins. The factor that induces them to set off for the sea seems to be controlled by the thyroid gland, which stimulates the development of the sexual organs and causes the digestive tract to regress. The thyroid is also responsible for the external signs that announce the eel's descent: dark colouring on the back, the development of pectoral fins and an increase in the size of the eyes. If prevented from migrating, eels can continue to live in fresh water up to the age of about 50.

Habitat

Eels live in most aquatic environments, from the estuaries right up to the river sources. They can be found in small ponds and the smallest of streams.

■ *Massacres like this account for the shrinking eel population and thus less food for large fish.*

■ *The eel is catadromous unlike most other migrant fish, which are anadromous. It reproduces in the Sargasso sea, but grows up in fresh water.*

The snake in slow waters

Latin name: *Anguilla anguilla*
Family: Anguilidae

With the sun's first rays the eel, which tends to shun the light, returns to its lair.

The eel is a fine fish; the excellence of its flesh needs no proof, especially when stewed in a wine sauce. Because the eel's habits are nocturnal, catching it can unfortunately be unpredictable. However it is possible to make a good bag when the conditions are right; when the water is high, in a sudden spate after a storm, at dawn or dusk, and in estuaries, where eels are active during the day. In former times most catches were made on a string left in at night and recovered at dawn. This method is equally effective in clear or coloured waters.

FISHING WITH NATURAL BAITS

Fishing with a sliding leger

The tackle

A powerful ringed pike rod 12 to 13 feet (3.5–4 m) long will do the job. A light or medium fixed-spool spinning reel is used, with about 300 feet (100 m) of 0.3 to 0.35 mm nylon line (don't be afraid to use thick line, the eel is not very cautious), on which slides a 15–30 g olivette stopped by a swivel clip. The cast, about 20 inches (50 cm) long in 0.28 to 0.3 nylon, ends in a size 2 to 5 hook, depending on the size of the bait.

Baits

The eel is a carnivore and only takes animal baits, among which are large earthworms, small live- or dead bait fish, a section of fish (excellent for big eels), a crayfish tail, a slug (deadly in coloured water) and, best of all, Planer's lamprey.

Fishing method

Put the line in at a likely spot for eels: large eddies, deep holes, close to a bridge pier, where the bank is caving in and cluttered with obstacles under the water. When the weight reaches the bottom, tighten the line slightly and place the rod on its rest. The bite is announced by violent shaking of the rod tip, at which the rod should be lowered so the fish feels no resistance from the line. Allow it to bite a few moments, (the larger the bait, the longer the wait), then strike vigorously and haul it to the surface as quickly as possible.

The eel has an annoying habit of winding itself about the first snag it can find as soon as it feels itself hooked. Its body, covered in mucus is not easy to handle especially when, as often happens, the eel swallows the bait right down. The best way of holding it is to grab it in some newspaper. To kill it, there is one solution: hit it hard on the tail, where all the vital organs are.

Eels from the St Lawrence river are sometimes enormous!

A magnificent female eel caught, it must be said, on tackle that was scarcely likely to break! All the same, we offer congratulations to this young angler. Well done!

Worm fishing

This traditional method is most effective after nightfall. It is therefore advisable to check with the local authorities before using it.

The tackle

The rod is about 13 feet (4 m) long and very stiff. If need be, a long stick will do instead. The very simple line consists of about 7½ feet (2.5 m) of string. Weighted with a lead of 40 g, it ends in the worm-ball, a large bunch of worms fixed to the string.

The worm-ball

Using a baiting needle, thread 15 to 20 earthworms on a length of wool, then arrange the string to form a ball.

Fishing method

Look for a good place for eels, where the banks have plenty of vegetation and clutter, and make sure the water is no more than 3 feet (1 m) deep. Put the worm ball in and wait for the smell of the worms to attract a fish. A characteristic jerking marks the bite. Wait a good while so the eel can seize the whole ball of worms, gripping it tightly in its sharp teeth. Then pull it out slowly in a single continuous movement, speeding up as the surface is reached. Put the eel on an upside-down open umbrella; when unhooked it will entangle itself in the spokes and not be able to escape.

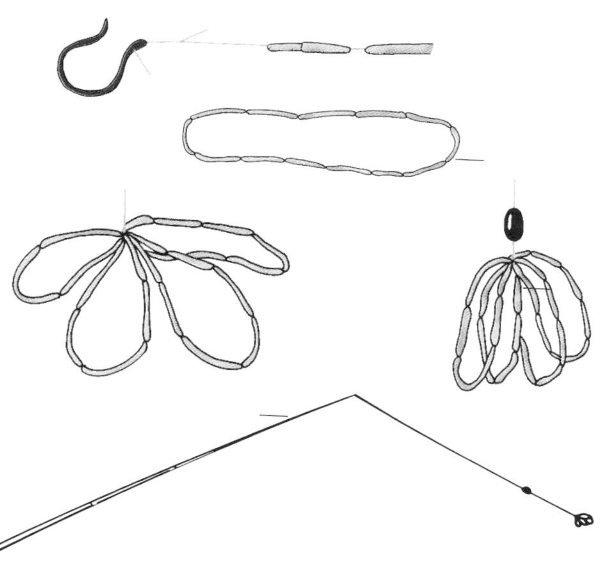

■ *A worm-ball: large earthworms are threaded on a length of wool or cotton. Altogether they should form a bunch on which the eel will bite greedily.*

Burbot

Latin name: ***Lota lota***
Family: Gadidae

What a pity for gourmets the burbot is a fish with nocturnal habits! The delicacy of its flesh owes nothing to the much sought-after sea fish (actually an angler fish) found on the fishmonger's slab and incorrectly given the same name.

This is why in former times it was so widely fished for, with nightlines.

Nowadays the burbot can only be caught in periods of high water (autumn and spring) or after a spate following a storm. It is best to fish from late afternoon until dark or at dawn. One can roam about trying all the likely looking spots (eddies, steep banks with deep runs full of obstacles) using a float. When the water is very high, a running leger can be used.

Float fishing

The tackle

A ringed telescopic rod of 13 to 16 feet (4–5 m) or an English-type rod can be recommended.

The light fixed-spool reel is loaded with about 165 to 330 feet (50–100 m) of 0.2 mm nylon line.

The line is fitted with a squat float balanced with grouped shot. The cast, in 0.16 mm or 0.18 mm nylon line, ends in a size 8 to 10 hook.

Bait

An earthworm or a bunch of brandlings is effective, but cannot replace small livebait for large burbot. Planer's lamprey is particularly deadly.

Fishing method

The burbot feeds near the bottom, so the float should be adjusted accordingly. The bite is signalled by an abrupt departure, on which line should be let out, especially when livebaiting. Wait a few moments, then strike vigorously.

If the burbot does not put up much of a fight, that does not mean it should be needlessly played and allowed to find the nearest refuge. just as with the eel, it is best to land the burbot as soon as possible before it becomes caught on some snag or other.

Fishing with the running leger

The takle

Choose a 13 foot (4 m) ringed telescopic rod, or a fairly powerful spinning rod about 6 to 8 feet (2.20 -2.5 m) long.

For the real, choose a light spinning type loaded with about 300 feet (100 m) of 0.2 mm nylon line.

The line carries an olive 8-15g in weight, stopped by a swivel to which is attached a cast in 0.18 mm nylon ending in a size 6 to 8 hook.

Fishing method

Cast into promising spot (a deep hole or an eddy) and wait for the lead to reach the bottom. Put the rod on its rest with the line slightly taut.

The bite is announced by a trembling of the road tip.

Leave the fish to bite for a few moments, then strike. The more line is out, the harder the strike should be.

■ *A fine display of burbot; by all appearances already well fed! So much for being greedy.*

■ *Float rig for burbot.*

■ *A small burbot from the river Besbre, Allier, France. It took the bait in daylight, but note the river, coloured by the rain from a violent storm.*

Useful addresses

A. I. D. S. A.
Association internationale
de défense du saumon atlantique
Institut océanographique
195, rue Saint-Jacques
75005 Paris
Tel: +33 - (0)2 31 62 21 63

National Federation of Anglers
Halliday House
Egginton Junction
Derby DE65 6GU
Tel: +44 - (0)1283-734 735
Fax: +44 - (0)1283-734 795
E-mail:
office@nfahq.freeserve.co.uk

Scottish Anglers National Association
Caledonia House
South Gyle,
Edinburgh EH12 9DQ
Tel: +44 - (0)131-339 8808
Fax: +44 - (0)131-317 7202

National Federation of Sea Anglers (NFSA)
Head Office
51a Queen Street
Newton Abbot
Devon TQ12 TQJ
Tel: +44 (0)1626-331 330

Through NFSA:
- The Confédération Internationale de la Pêche Sportive
- The European Anglers Alliance

Fédération française des pêcheurs sportifs à la mouche
Tel. +33 (0)4 66 34 01 01
Fax: +33 (0)4 66 34 05 00

UK Department of the Environment, Transport and the Regions
Eland House
Bressenden Place
London SW1E 5DU
Tel: +44 (0)20-7944 3000

Maison nationale Pêche et Eau
36, rue Saint-Laurent
25290 Ornans
Tel: +33 (0)3 81 57 14 49
Fax: +33 (0)3 81 57 19 81

Union nationale des fédérations départementales des Associations Pêche et Pisciculture de France
17, rue Bergère
75009 Paris
Tel: +33 (0)1 48 24 96 00
Fax: +33 (0)1 42 46 36 08

T. O. S. (Truite Saumon Ombre)
Association nationale
pour la protection des eaux
et des rivières
13, rue Saint-Michel
78150 Le Chesnay
Tel: +33 (0)1 39 55 29 52

Eaux et rivières de Bretagne
Association régionale
de protection
de l'environnement
Venelle de la caverne
22200 Guingamp
Tel: +33 (0)2 96 21 38 77
Fax: +33 (0)2 96 44 33 97

Index

Further Reading

Among the most popular angling magazines

Angler's Mail
Angling Times
Coarse Fisherman
Improve Your Coarse Fishing
Salmon, Trout and Sea Trout
Sea Angler
Trout and Salmon
Trout Fisherman

A few books on the art of angling

Ball, Ian. *Begin Fishing the Right Way.* Elliot Right Way Books, 1996.
Ball, Ian. *Secrets of Fly-fishing for Trout.* Elliot Right Way Books, 1998.
Ball, Ian. *Sea Fishing Properly Explained.* Elliot Right Way Books, 1998.
Bigon, Mario, and Guido Regazzoni. *The Complete Guide to Knots.* Vermilion, 1992.
Church, Bob. *Bob Church's Guide to Trout Flies.* The Crowood Press, 1997.
Dawes, Mike. *The Fly Tier's Manual.* Collins Willow, 1995.
Falkus, Hugh, and Malcolm Greenhalgh. *The Salmon & Sea Trout Fisher's Handbook.* Excellent Press, 1997.
Falkus, Hugh. *Salmon Fishing.* Orion, 1984.
Fling, Paul N., and Donald Puterbaugh. *Basic Manual of Fly-tying.* Ward Lock, 1993.
Gierach, John. *Standing in a River Waving a Stick.* Simon & Schuster Books, 1999.
Gustafson, Paul. *How to Catch a Bigger Pike.* Collins Willow, 1997.
Hughes, Rob, and Simon Crow. *Strategic Carp Fishing.* The Crowood Press, 1997.
Jardine, Charles. *The Sotherby's Guide to Fly Fishing for Trout.* Dorling Kindersley, 1991.
Kaminsky, Peter. *Fly Fishing for Dummies.* IDG Books Worldwide Inc., 1998.
Kreh, Lefty. *Fly Fishing in Salt Water.* Lyon and Burford Publishers, 1997.
Leeson, Ted, and Jim Schollmeyer. *The Fly Tier's Benchside Reference.* Frank Amato Publications, 1998.
Maddocks, Kevin. *The Beekay Guide to 2000 British and European Carp Waters.* Beekay International, 1997
Mansfield, Kenneth, and Chris Clifford. *Coarse Fishing for Beginners.* Foulsham, 1997.
McNally, Tom. *The Complete Book of Fly Fishing.* Ragged Mountain Press, 1997.
Miles, Tony, and Trefor West. *Quest for Barbel.* The Crowood Press, 1999.
Morgan, Paul. *Saltwater Flyfishing: Britain and Northern Europe.* Coch-y-Bonddu Books, 1998.
Nudd, Bob. *Bob Nudd's Illustrated Guide to Pole Fishing.* Emap Pursuit Publishing Ltd., 1998.
Owen, Peter. *Pocket Guide to Fishing Knots.* Merlin Unwin Books, 1998.
Paxman, Jeremy. *Fish, Fishing and the Meaning of Life.* Penguin Books, 1995.
Russ, Mel. *The Sea Angler's Step-by-step Guide to Baits and Rigs.* Emap Pursuit Publishing Ltd., 1999.
Yates, Chris. *The Secret Carp.* Merlin Unwin Books, 1997.

Photographic Credits

Berthoule/Nature: 4 mbl, 5 m, 21 b, 22 bl, 34 t, 35 b, 35 tl, 37 t, 38 br, 38 t, 41 t, 43 t, 71 br, 79, 113 br, 119 m, 120 bl, 125 r, 125 l, 126 bl, 126 tl, 127 br, 131 b, 131 t, 134-135, 137 br, 138, 139 br, 139 tr, 144 t, 151 t, 157 b, 157 m - **B.M.I.-Photothèque C.S.P.:** 47 tr - **Buttin/Nature:** 69 bl, 70, 72, 74 t, 75 t, 75 m, 105 b, 156 b - **Carmié:** 47 br, 48-49 t, 51 br, 51 t - **Chaumeton/Nature:** 32, 50 t, 51 ml, 68, 88, 94, 104 tl, 107 b, 124 t, 150 t, 153 b, 153 tr, 154 br - **Cortay:** 111 bl, 113 tr, 114 l, 115 bl, 115 r, 116 b, 117 b - **Courdot:** 46-47, 48 mr, 49 tr, 50 b, 54 bl, 54 tr, 57 b, 58 t, 60-61 t, 62 b, 64, 65 t, 65 mr - **Durantel:** 61 br, 62 t, 63 b, 63 t, 148-149 t - **Durantel/Nature:** 4 bl, 4 mbm, 4 mtl, 5 b, 5 t, 6, 10-11, 12-13 t, 12 tl, 14 b, 15 tm, 16 bl, 16 tl, 17 br, 18-19 t, 18 b, 20, 21 t, 22-23 t, 22 tl, 24-25 t, 25 b, 26 l, 27 b, 28, 29, 30, 31 b, 31 t, 35 tr, 36 tr, 36 tl, 39 b, 39 m, 40 t, 41 b, 42-43 b, 42 tl, 42 ml, 43 mr, 44-45, 52 b, 53 t, 55 t, 55 mr, 56 m, 59, 61 tr, 69 t, 74 bl, 76 bl, 78, 82 t, 84 br, 86 l, 87 t, 89 l, 90-91 t, 90 b, 90 tl, 91 tr, 91 mr, 93 t, 93 m, 96 ml, 98 b, 98 t, 99 br, 102 t, 104 bl, 104 tr, 106 bl, 111 tr, 112-113 t, 117 t, 118-119, 119 br, 123 b, 123 t, 126-127 b, 128 m, 129 br, 130 t, 133 t, 136-137, 136 bl, 140, 142-143, 144 br, 144 bl, 145 br, 145 bl, 146 t, 148 br, 149 tr, 150 b, 151 b, 155, 156 t - **Gohier/Nature:** 146 b, 154 bl - **Grebot:** 37 mr - **Houdou/Nature:** 23 bl, 24 l, 56-57 t, 71 t, 73 b, 77, 82 b, 82 m, 96 tl, 97 tm, 99 bl, 102 b, 108-109, 120 ml, 124 b, 129 bl, 130 b, 132 b, 132 t, 154 t - **Lanceau/Nature:** 141 , 147 - **Lemaître:** 60 b, 110-111 - **Losange:** 4 t, 15 r, 17 tr, 18 tl, 33 tr, 36 r, 37 br, 39 t, 40 b, 55 ml, 56 l, 65 bl, 84 bl, 91 br, 92 br, 92 bl, 92 tl, 92 mr, 93 bl, 133 b, 133 m, 149 br - **Magnan/Nature:** 4 br, 8-9, 11 r, 12 bl, 15 tl, 16-17 t, 18 ml, 26-27 t, 33 br, 33 bl, 34 b, 66-67, 69 br, 71 bl, 73 t, 76 tr, 80, 81, 83, 84-85 t, 84 tl, 86-87 t, 89 r, 90 tm, 95 r, 95 l, 96-97, 99 t, 100-101 t, 100 l, 101 b, 106-107 t, 106 tl, 114-115 t, 120-121 b, 120 t, 121 mr, 122 b, 122 t, 128 t, 129 tr, 148 tl - **Nature:** 139 tl, 152-153 t - **Prevot/Nature:** 69 m.